To the –
Love from
Jude
xxx

SHAKESPEARE GOES TO PARIS

SHAKESPEARE

TRADUIT

DE L'ANGLOIS,

DÉDIÉ

AU ROI.

Homo ſum : Humani nihil à me alienum puto. Tér.

TOME PREMIER.

A PARIS,

Chez
{
La Veuve DUCHESNE, Libraire, rue Saint-Jacques.
MUSIER, Fils, rue du Foin-Saint-Jacques.
NYON, rue Saint-Jean-de-Beauvais.
LA COMBE, rue Chriſtine.
RUAULT, rue de la Harpe.
LE JAY, rue Saint-Jacques.
CLOUSIER, rue Saint-Jacques.
}

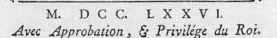

M. DCC. LXXVI.
Avec Approbation, & Privilége du Roi.

The title page of Le Tourneur's Shakespeare.

Shakespeare Goes to Paris

How the Bard Conquered France

John Pemble

The French, advis'd by good intelligence
Of this most dreadful preparation,
Shake in their fear, and with pale policy
Seek to divert the English purposes.

Henry V

Hambledon and London

London and New York

Hambledon and London
102 Gloucester Avenue, London NW1 8HX

175 Fifth Avenue
New York, NY 10010

First Published 2005

ISBN 1 85285 452 9

A description of this book is available from the
British Library and from the Library of Congress.

Typeset by Carnegie Publishing, Lancaster,
And printed in Great Britain by Cambridge University Press.

Distributed in the United States and Canada
exclusively by Palgrave Macmillan,
A division of St Martin's Press.

Contents

Illustrations

Preface

This curious story has hitherto been told in fragments – mostly in French, in widely scattered and esoteric publications. It seemed worth retelling as a whole, in English, because it is loaded with historical and cultural interest. Shakespeare is now a dominating presence in the artistic economy of France. His plays are constantly performed, his name is always in the press, and the time seems unreachably remote when it was commonly thought impossible that he should ever be at home there. Far from being difficult to imagine the literary and theatrical French living with Shakespeare, it has become difficult to think of them living without him.

For this reason the controversy that once surrounded his work in France now seems strange. Yet it also seems familiar, because although Shakespeare is now removed from its turbulence, the polemic by which he was once engulfed continues unabated. It is fraught with all the ideological contradictions, all the emotional tension between fascination and fear, that are generated when a highly organised and sophisticated society confronts the exotic. The terminology has changed. The word 'classique', which was carried by the Shakespeare debate to the centre of public rhetoric in France, has been displaced, in response to Islamic pressures, by the word 'laïque'. But the complexes and concerns are the same. 'Laïque' resonates with all the anxieties about national identity and cultural survival that began to obsess the educated French when they first encountered Shakespeare.

I have been motivated, therefore, by the gravitational pull of a weighty topic. But my reasons for taking the story up are partly sentimental. Shakespeare and France first came together in my experience more than forty years ago, when as a stagestruck schoolboy I went with the Youth Theatre (it was not yet 'National') to Paris. Following the extraordinary privilege of performing *Hamlet* at the Queen's Theatre in

London's Shaftesbury Avenue, had come the even more extraordinary one of performing it at the théâtre Sarah Bernhardt in the place du Châtelet, as part of the prestigious Théâtre des Nations festival. The Queen's was newly and splendidly refurbished. It was filled with the smell of fresh paint and pristine upholstery. The Sarah Bernhardt was huge and shabby. Its crimson and gold had been dimmed with years, and a faint but prevailing odour backstage was that of gaslight and faded roses. (The latter, we were assured, was the spirit of Mme Bernhardt herself, whose theatre this had been). The building was already doomed. Soon it would be gutted, internally rebuilt, and rebaptised as the théâtre de la Ville. But for the time being it was intact, a mansion of thespian spectres and reminiscences, and we set up our Elsinore on the very same stage where, sixty years before, the legendary actress had set up hers. Quite possibly there were, in our smart and even glittering audiences, a few who remembered it.

The sixties had then barely begun. Ten years later, when I was living in Paris as a student, the Sarah Bernhardt had gone and the city was noticeably changed. The Shakespearean associations, however, were stronger than ever. They were renewed vividly for me by *Richard II* at the Odéon. This production, directed by the youthful Patrice Chéreau, made me fully aware of the universality of Shakespeare. I now knew how seriously he was taken in France; that translation (in this instance by Pierre Leyris) was not all loss; that French actors and the French language could compensate for what they obscured with what they revealed of a Shakespearean text.

Memories of these two experiences kept alive, during many years of involvement in other projects, my determination to write one day about what I was more and more convinced had been a cardinal event in the secular traffic of European culture. That I have finally been able to do so is owing in great measure to labour not my own. I have reaped where others have sown, and if I have been able to see a whole, it is because so many fragments have been retrieved by a multitude of dedicated historians, biographers, critics, and editors. The notes at the end of the volume indicate the extent of my indebtedness. But this is a work of interpretation as well as of synthesis and survey, and for errors of judgement I am alone responsible. Translation throughout is my own, except where otherwise indicated.

It would be impossible to mention, or even to recollect, all the people and institutions in Britain, France, and the United States entitled to my gratitude for having assisted my interest in Shakespeare and his reputation abroad. I can however thank those in the University of Bristol Library and Theatre Collection, in the Bodleian Library, and in the British Library who helped me during the later stages of research and writing. I am grateful, too, to Neil Curtis and Mike Craig at the Queen Mother Library, University of Aberdeen, to Martin Durrant at the Victoria and Albert Museum, to David Rhodes at the British Museum, and to the staff of the Arts Faculty Photographic Unit at the University of Bristol, for their co-operation in the preparation of the illustrations. Special thanks are due, and rendered, to my publishers, Martin Sheppard and Tony Morris, for encouragement, advice, and support; to Annie Burnside for her book-hunting in France and her expert checking of the proofs; to Lucy Steeds for helpful questions and acute suggestions; and to Anne Merriman for first-class secretarial assistance. I recall with affectionate gratitude all those friends in the National Youth Theatre in whose company I discovered and acted Shakespeare. I dedicate this book to them or, where the fell sergeant has been swift in his arrest, to their memory.

Bristol   Summer 2004

Introduction

There is no evidence that Shakespeare ever went to France, though his imagination often dwelt in its 'vasty fields' and visited the 'mistress-court of mighty Europe'. He had a fair knowledge of the French language, but it seems that he reached France – as he reached Italy, Sicily, Illyria, Bohemia, Syracuse, Athens, Egypt, and all the other exotic locations in the stories and chronicles that were his stock-in-trade – via the routes that we are bidden to follow by the Chorus in *Henry V*. He played with his fancies, worked his thoughts, and eked out performance with his mind.

There is no evidence, either, that during his lifetime and a long period after his death he was any better known to France than France was known to him. Somehow, sometime when Louis XIV was reigning, a copy of his works found its way into the royal library in Paris; but for many years it remained apparently unnoticed. In the France of the Sun King it seems never to have occurred to anyone that it could be important. Only a few scattered references testify to a knowledge even of Shakespeare's existence. One is in a copy of the catalogue of the royal collection, printed in 1684. Nicolas Clément, the king's librarian, commented in a jotted note that Shakespeare was a fluent, imaginative poet, but that his merits were obscured by garbage ('ordures'). It seems unlikely that Clément had actually opened the bulky folio. Probably he was repeating what he had read about Shakespeare in the Jesuit *Journal de Trévoux*, in April 1704; and the journal was itself merely repeating an opinion that was current among educated people in London.[1] To men and women of Clément's time and nationality, little was significant that was not written in Hebrew, Greek, Latin, or French.

The royal copy of Shakespeare was one of only three recorded in France, and Shakespeare was not alone in his exclusion. Few English works were listed in the catalogues of French libraries and booksellers, either in English or in translation. Translations were plentiful, but they were mostly of theological treatises, printed abroad and read by French Protestant exiles. England featured only dimly in the consciousness of metropolitan France. In learned circles the islanders had acquired a certain renown for moralistic wisdom and experimental science. Works by Bacon, Hobbes, and Joseph Hall enjoyed a measure of prestige, and English researches in medicine, mathematics, astronomy, and the esoteric humanities were reported in the French reviews. Yet no one imagined that the finer flowers of civilisation could flourish in that chilly archipelago. Connoisseurs of literary curiosities knew of Philip Sidney's *Arcadia*. George Buckingham's Latin tragedies were still remembered by amateurs of the drama. To accomplished French society, however, Britain was beyond Europe. It was *Ultima Thule*: remote, unvisited, and all but uncharted.

During the earlier part of the eighteenth century this view completely changed. The sea-girt outpost of the Continent, the afterthought of the muses, became a commanding presence in sophisticated France. Britain made her entry into cultural and intellectual Europe, disturbing hallowed systems of thought and canons of art. New constellations formed; the climate changed; old almanachs and calendars became obsolete. Strange English and Scottish names, and even the unwieldy English language, made ever more pressing claims on the attention of educated minds. The Swiss writer Béat de Muralt wrote in 1725 that a knowledge of English was becoming indispensable. It should be learnt, he said, 'in preference to other modern languages'. Meanwhile the work first of Newton and Locke; then of Pope, Milton, and Swift; and then of Shakespeare appeared in France in French.

Shakespeare's arrival was all the more portentous for having been so long delayed. The dramatist had been dead for more than a century when he became known across the Channel, and his sudden appearance in France was associated with revaluations and reversals immeasurably more significant than any quirk of fashion or capricious change of mind. It triggered one of the most sustained and vertiginous flights of posthumous fame in the history of art and literature, and it resurrected a past that had been pronounced dead and superseded. French recognition transformed Shakespeare from an obscure, insular curiosity into a cosmic celebrity. It launched his reputation in Germany, in Italy, in Central Europe, in Russia, and throughout the wide francophone diaspora. It heralded the return of a banished music – too powerful to be ignored, yet too terrible to be heard. It may be that Shakespeare went to Paris because the world was changing. It may be that the world changed because Shakespeare went to Paris. Either way, his arrival coincided with some fundamental process of disintegration, some alchemy of enrichment that was also a malediction. Shakespeare exemplified both the new French word 'civilisation', and the old French word 'barbarisme'. He was the epitome of Europe's achievement, and antidote to its anarchy – a triumph of the humanity that transcended race. But he was also a threat to refinement and coherence: as deeply implicated in the collapse of the European order as the Enlightenment that reclaimed him and at the same time disowned him. When Shakespeare went to France, history resumed; the poets re-entered the Platonic republic. Reason was shaken by passion, and the monoliths that had fortified Europe's repose dissolved in relativity and flux. Beauty, Time, Taste, and Truth itself were no longer always and everywhere the same. Problems deemed settled, debates presumed extinct, revived and became imperious. As Shakespeare moved across frontiers and between languages, hallowed dogmas abdicated and an era of provisional dispensations began.

The sense of flux and insecurity that came with Shakespeare was compounded for the élites of France by the emergence of a new world order – an order not of their own making and detrimental to the hegemony of their language and their culture. In the trauma of readjustment their vocation was inverted. Their ecumenical ideals were checked and reversed by national anxieties and the discovery of a racial identity. The ambassadors of mankind, the architects of a Cartesian, homogeneous universe, became theorists of disparity and relativity: crusaders for difference and diversity.

This preoccupation with ethnic integrity worked against Shakespeare. It made him seem foreign and intrusive. Viewed in the context of the new world order, he represented the menace of Anglo-Saxon domination. He was a threat to the cultural heterogeneity that would safeguard Frenchness. Nevertheless, these anxieties could not cancel the debt of deference that was owed to genius. Shakespeare was among the 'prodigies' – those defined by the *Encyclopédie*, voice of the French Enlightenment, as 'people who, more favoured than others by heaven, open up new roads unaided, and tread them without guides'; and prodigies, belonging only to themselves, spoke not of human races but of a Human Race.

For 150 years Shakespeare would figure in French consciousness as both a genius and a stranger. Yet it remained axiomatic that genius was a stranger nowhere. It knew no bounds, as readers of the *Année Littéraire* had been told in 1754, 'save the limits of the world'.[2]

How, then, should Shakespeare be regarded? As a gifted vagrant from a remote barbaric place? Or as a paladin of the human spirit? As an Anglo-Saxon alien, or as a leading citizen of the world? Understanding was deferred as French debate moved endlessly back and forth between these preemptive questions. Polemical push equalled polemical pull, and Shakespeare remained on a threshold, never fully present in France, and never wholly absent. He was familiar, yet unknown; desired, yet denied. To no other people did his reputation owe so much, and at the same time so little. The French discovered Shakespeare. They brought him, as the journalist and salon satirist Antoine Rivarol said in 1783, out from the depths of his island.[3] But then they abdicated any real critical or artistic engagement with their discovery. Unable or unwilling to confront the threat that Shakespearean drama – Shakespearean tragedy especially – posed to familiar and reassuring assumptions about history, about providence, about moral values and social order, they resorted to drastic reconstructions and sham dialectic. These banished authentic Shakespeare from the stage, and foreclosed any meaningful discussion, by intercepting the painful challenges and subversive implications that issued from his work. French theatres made do with barely recognisable adaptations and 'imitations'. French comment either deployed a web of qualifications and exclusions that restricted Shakespeare's relevance and intelligibility to his own time and country – that reduced him, in effect, to an historical and local curiosity; or proclaimed his genius in mythopoeic terms that reduced him to a force of nature. 'It's as though you are transported to a tropical landscape', wrote one nineteenth-century critic of the encounter with Shakespeare,

> everything swells and runs riot under the action of a splendid sun. The flowers smoke like censers, the insects unfold dragons' wings, the rocks emit

the fires of carbuncles, panthers swim among the creepers, pythons wrap
their knotted scales around trees glittering with hummingbirds.[4]

'The river', wrote another, 'carries on its current tall ships, refuse, wisps
of straw; it turns the wheels of mills that will nourish people, and it
broadens from an estuary into the infinite sea.'[5]

This style of writing dehumanised Shakespeare and turned him into
an ontological riddle, above and beyond contingency and explanation.
In a public lecture of 1856, Desiré Nisard, a literary historian and professor at the Sorbonne, described Shakespeare, typically, as 'hover[ing]
in a mysterious and peaceful distance, evading the curiosity of erudition
which exhausts itself in searching for a man where there is only one of
the greatest sources of creative poetry'.[6] When the poet and journalist
André Suarès published a long essay on Shakespeare in 1921, he sancti-
fied the subject by having his text printed like a missal, with coloured
inks, lavish margins, and triangular patterns of type. Shakespeare he
identified with Prospero, the archetype of the tragic poet who 'saves life
and the world through poetry – that is to say, through creation, a heroic
act of the spirit'. Suarès scorned historians, biographers, and psycholo-
gists. They worked, he declared, on the corpse of a writer. 'The mystery
is indeed great, and erudition will never explain it.' But the secret that
erudition cannot penetrate proved equally impervious to passionate
empathy. There is no revelation at the heart of Suarès' book. There is
merely a vacuum enveloped in eucharistic rhapsody:

> The flash of one or two words rends the thick veils of common mediocrity,
> and one is alone on the summits of thought. One breathes the air of moun-
> tain peaks. He is light; he alone nourishes. The beauty of Shakespeare is
> majesty. He is common man and prince. He is king. He is everything he
> wishes to be. All things considered, when one knows what it is to live, to will,
> and to create, it is difficult not to feel the presence of God.[7]

To authors like André Gide, who cherished their Frenchness, this sort
of mystical extemporising portended fanaticism and intellectual night.
Gide deplored the 'false sublimity' of Suarès, his amorphous rhetoric
reeking of solitude and megalomania.[8] And since these were habitual
when French admirers wrote of Shakespeare as genius, they seemed to
demonstrate the fragility of conquests painfully won and anxiously
guarded. Clarity, rationality, rigour, and restraint were put at risk by the

excesses of *shakespearomanie*. This sense of risk explains the need felt by many French intellectuals to invalidate the enthusiasm: to proscribe it as eccentric, unFrench.

The circumstances of Shakespeare's arrival could only reinforce this compulsion. He had appeared at a turning point in French intellectual and political fortunes, and the shifts and disruptions associated with his name enhanced regret for a vanishing world. Pre-Shakespearean came to mean prelapsarian. It signified a time of calmness and beatitude, bathed in a golden, classical light. In Voltaire's view the age of Louis XIV had been one of the summits of human history, and France's interlude of greatest happiness and perfect beauty:

> Between the last years of Cardinal Richelieu and those which followed the death of Louis XIV, there occurred in our arts, our minds, and our manners, as in our government, a general revolution which must serve as an eternal witness to the true glory of our country ... It seemed that nature then took delight in producing in France the greatest men in all the arts, and in assembling at the court the finest specimens of men and women that had ever existed.[9]

This vision, made ever more alluring as conflict and revolution became recurring features of French public life, developed into an abiding myth. It was periodically expressed as a recall to classicism, Latinity, and political order, and as a nostalgic evocation of the time when history had ceased to fulminate and stood chastened in the enchanted precincts of Versailles. One notable appearance was in a book by Suarès' contemporary, the popular cultural historian and academician Paul Hazard. *La Crise de la conscience européenne*, published in 1939, depicts the European consciousness as engaged in a perpetual labour of Penelope, weaving, unravelling, and reweaving the fabric of its thought and art. The later years of the Sun King's reign figure in this scenario as a delectable respite. They were an exquisite moment of equipoise and repose – an intermission of fretful effort and a reprieve from tormenting awareness of the provisional. In retelling the myth, Hazard again demonstrated its power to captivate. 'Could she', he asked of the weary weaver,

> create forms more beautiful and more enduring? So beautiful, and so enduring, that we still admire them today, and they will deserve to be proposed as

models to our children and our grandchildren's children. But this beauty itself presupposes a confidence in the minds that produced it. Classicism found the means to practise Christian wisdom without abandoning the wisdom of the ancients; to balance the faculties of the soul; to found order on happiness and on admiration; to achieve a hundred other miracles and – to sum it all up in a single word – to make humanly possible a state akin to serenity.[10]

Hindered by such preoccupations and longings, the real entry of Shakespeare into France was delayed well beyond the century of neglect that followed his death. As late as 1949 a French scholar commented on the 'incredible lack of boldness' that had characterised French responses to Shakespeare during the previous fifty years.[11] The French habitually either automatically prostrated themselves before Shakespeare, or automatically recoiled. But in the second half of the twentieth century they became fully involved in the interpretation and interrogation of his work. For by then history had clearly identified him as their contemporary, and a radical change in critical thinking was finally demolishing the cult of genius and the fiction of race.

1

Farewell the Tranquil Mind

The French did not discover Shakespeare until they discovered England; and they did not discover England until Voltaire, the abbé Prévost, and the baron de Montesquieu crossed the Channel at various times in the 1720s. These were the men who made the English familiar in France, and in doing so they made Britain great. Hitherto the English had been known to the French only as free-ranging denizens of the wider world.[1] 'The English', wrote Prévost, 'are commonly regarded as a hardy and proud people, suited only to warfare and navigation.'[2] They were explorers, colonists, traders, soldiers, tourists, travellers, exiles, and *loups de mer*. No one knew of the English as domestic people, because England was an undiscovered country from whose bourne travellers either did not return, or returned with no tale to tell. The French Protestant refugees who went there in their tens of thousands to escape persecution by the zealous Louis XIV did not come back. More favoured visitors – diplomats, aristocratic exiles, and the artists, musicians, and literary men attracted by the bounty of Charles II – circulated around the court and hardly ever ventured beyond the limits of fashionable London. Their memoirs and narratives owed less to direct observation than to gazetteers, old foreign guidebooks, and the common fund of myths and stereotypes. When he went to England, Prévost soon perceived that the French view of the English was essentially uninformed. 'The English', he explained,

> are separated from the Continent by a dangerous sea. Few people ever visit them, so they are widely misunderstood. The old prejudice concerning them still prevails, and misleading appearances have produced an inaccurate portrait. You have to go to England before you can claim the right to judge the English.[3]

Voltaire, especially, could claim that right. Although he went to England involuntarily, in 1726, under sentence of official displeasure and banishment, he made the most of his two-year exile. He learnt to read and to write English, and managed to speak it with fair fluency. He investigated avidly British intellectual, religious, and social life – something he was well able to do, because he was already sufficiently well known as a writer and polemicist to arouse the curiosity and interest of élite circles in London. Soon he knew everybody worth knowing – whether Whig or Tory, literary or scientific, fashionable or commercial. He was introduced to the Duke of Newcastle and the Duchess of Marlborough; he was on familiar terms with Lord Bathurst and Lord Peterborough; he was patronised by Queen Caroline and George I. His friends included Swift, Congreve, Thomson, Young, Cibber, and Sir Hans Sloane, President of the Royal Society. He lodged with Sir Everard Fawkener, a wealthy merchant, at Wandsworth, and frequently visited Pope at Twickenham and Bolingbroke at Dawley. He stocked his mind with remarkable facts and lasting impressions, and throughout his long and brilliant career as dramatist, historian, philanthropist, scourge of the Church, and sage and counsellor to the mighty of Europe, always regarded himself, and was regarded, as an authority on England and things English.

It was the English at home that Voltaire, Prévost, and Montesquieu undertook to reveal to their compatriots. When these travellers returned to France they did have a tale to tell, and their accounts of their experiences gave the islanders a new identity and a new prestige. They told of an Eldorado: a land that was free, wisely governed, politically stable, and intellectually dazzling. 'Public spirit', wrote Prévost, 'a taste for practical knowledge, a horror of slavery and flattery, come almost naturally to this happy people.' Voltaire agreed. 'The English', he wrote,

> are the only nation on earth who have managed to control the power of kings by resisting them, and who, through unremitting effort, have finally established that wise system of government in which the sovereign is all-powerful for good purposes but has his hands tied for bad ones; in which a lord is great without insolence and without vassals; and in which the people participate without confusion.[4]

Montesquieu, likewise, was deeply impressed. In his monumental *De l'Esprit des lois*, published in 1748, he reserved for the English constitution some of his highest praise.

Following the lead of these three anglophiles, ignorant and indifferent France became interested and admiring. Fashionable Paris, in the middle years of the eighteenth century, succumbed to *anglomanie*. It took English lessons, devoured English novels, copied English fashions, mimicked English recreations. It even experimented with English cuisine, testing its digestion on *rosbif* and *plomb pouding*.

The paragon was not without blemishes, however. Prévost found the common people 'grossier' and 'féroce', and he was repelled by the strain of coarseness and brutality in English sports and pastimes.[5] Even Voltaire, on parole from the Bastille and predisposed to favour England by the humiliation he had suffered in France, realised that there were drawbacks to life across the Channel. The climate he judged detestable, the people generally misanthropic and uncouth. He abhorred English Sundays – a legacy of Cromwell the regicide, the mere thought of whom made him shudder – and he missed the French theatre.

For the theatre was Voltaire's passion. While in London he spent many evenings at Drury Lane, as the guest of Colley Cibber the poet. Night after night his small trim figure could be seen in the pit, closely following the play in a text supplied by courtesy of Mr Chetwood, the prompter.[6] The experience greatly improved his knowledge of the English language, but it diminished his opinion of the English stage. In philosophy and mathematical science the islanders, he decided, were sophisticated and supreme. In the drama they were backward and inferior. There were no Lockes, no Newtons, of the English theatre. The best native dramatist was Addison, whose compositions were refined but frigid. The most popular was William Shakespeare, who had come too soon into a world too young. Since he had died as long ago as 1616, Shakespeare had, inevitably, been uncivilised, so their addiction to his work had retarded the English in their appreciation of the stage. 'Their theatre', Voltaire told his French readers, 'has remained in a grossly infantile state.' To Lord Lytton he wrote (in English): 'The taste of your politest countrymen in point of tragedy differs not much from the taste of the mob at Bear-Garden.' He was shocked and even disgusted by what he saw in the plays of Shakespeare – a Moor strangling his wife; mad royalty; a prince, his mother, and his stepfather drinking together; gravediggers digging a grave while quaffing and singing rude vaudeville songs; a crowd of Roman plebeians haranguing patricians; Roman conspirators washing their hands in the blood of a murdered dictator. Every now and then, unexpectedly refulgent amid these revolting barbarisms, there was a passage of great dramatic force or striking beauty – of sublimity even. Voltaire translated one such passage – freely, not literally, as he was at pains to explain – for the benefit of the French public:

> Demeure; il faut choisir, et passer à l'instant
> De la vie à la mort, ou de l'être au néant.
> Dieux cruels! s'il en est, éclairez mon courage.
> Faut-il vieillir courbé sous la main qui m'outrage,
> Supporter ou finir mon malheur et mon sort? ...

But Shakespeare was not redeemed by isolated morsels such as this monologue of Prince Hamlet. His work was incorrigibly 'bizarre' and 'gigantesque' – and quite superseded in the age of sensibility and reason. That was why it had never crossed the Channel. Shakespeare was an insular writer whose work, unlike that of the great French dramatists, could never have an international appeal. 'French masterpieces', Voltaire told the Académie Française in 1777,

> have been performed before every court and in every academy of Italy. They are played everywhere from the borders of the Arctic Sea to the sea which separates Europe from Africa. It will be time to argue when the same honour has been done to a single piece by Shakespeare.[7]

Yet the unthinkable was already happening. Even before Voltaire's first remarks about the English stage had appeared in French (his *Lettres philosophiques* were published first in English), Prévost had made a much more favourable assessment. He declared that he knew of nothing, either in Greek or in French, which had more tragic power and emotional appeal, or which demonstrated better dramatic skill, than *Hamlet* and certain plays by Dryden, Otway, and Congreve. In his weekly review *Le Pour et Contre*, which appeared between 1733 and 1740, he reported the news and views of Shakespeare current in England, and repeated his own eulogistic verdict.[8] From this time Shakespeare was written about and talked about in polite Parisian circles, and when David Garrick came to Paris, in 1751 and then again in 1765, he enthralled the fashionable salons with impromptu recitals of famous bits from the plays.[9] The massive *Encyclopédie* edited by Denis Diderot and

Jean d'Alembert (1751–72) did not contain an entry for Shakespeare, but there were articles on 'Stratford' and 'Tragédie' which ratified uncritically the verdict of Pope, that Shakespeare was the greatest genius known to dramatic literature.[10] The note of approval amplified, and Diderot wrote to Voltaire's Genevan friend, François Tronchin: 'Ah, Monsieur, this Shakespeare was a terrible mortal ... a colossos who was gothic, but between whose legs we would all pass without our heads even touching his testicles.'[11]

Voltaire learnt with incredulity, and with growing rancour, of the advance of the barbarian into France. In 1746 the first, selective, translation of Shakespeare's works appeared. Thirty years later the whole dramatic canon was published in French – under royal patronage, what is more. When he read the preface by Pierre Le Tourneur, the chief translator, Voltaire was outraged. Le Tourneur claimed that Aristotle would have rewritten his *Poetics* if he had lived to know of Shakespeare's work, which was greater than that of Sophocles or Euripides. 'If our water-carriers wrote for the theatre,' retorted Voltaire, 'they'd make a better job of it.' The English demeaned themselves by remaining attached to this clod-hopping primitive. 'I still can't understand', he wrote to d'Alembert, 'how a nation which has produced geniuses of taste and even delicacy, as well as *philosophes* worthy of you, can carry on priding itself on that abominable Shakespeare, who, if the truth were told, is nothing but a provincial clown.' The growing infatuation with Shakespeare in France was an insult to Corneille and Racine, the monarchs of the French theatre, and it was an insult to himself, their acknowledged successor. Chafed vanity fed the bile of old age, and he gnashed his toothless gums. 'I've seen the end of the reign of reason and taste', he cried; 'I shall die leaving France barbaric!' When he remembered that he was himself responsible for this deplorable state of affairs, he beat his breast and tore his hair:

> What makes the whole thing even more calamitous and horrible is the fact that I am the one who first mentioned this Shakespeare; It was I who first revealed to the French the few pearls that I had discovered in his enormous dungheap. Never did I expect that one day I'd be helping to trample underfoot the crowns of Racine and Corneille so that they could be set on the head of a barbaric barnstormer![12]

He made amends by adopting the posture of an old warrior defending the national honour. From his retreat at Ferney, deep in the French countryside near the Swiss border, he schemed, he plotted, he stormed, he expostulated, and he deployed all his considerable battery of sarcasm and invective in an effort to rally his *confrères* of the Académie Française behind his campaign to stop Shakespeare. His acquaintance with the culprit was slight. The only plays he knew well were the three he had seen in London – *Hamlet, Julius Caesar,* and *Othello.* Four others (*Macbeth, King Lear, Henry V,* and *Richard III*) he had dipped into. Further than that his knowledge did not go. Nevertheless he undertook to reveal 'this divine Shakespeare in all his horror and all his unbelievable baseness'. Assembled on a hot August afternoon of 1776 for the annual commemoration of the death of Louis IX, the academicians sweltered under court dress and powdered *perruques* while his old articles of impeachment, recycled into an interminable peroration, were read aloud by d'Alembert, the secretary.[13] People in high places began to find him embarrassing. Was he not making France look foolish in foreign eyes, and damaging the new-found friendship with Britain?[14] And Voltaire himself, in his heart of hearts, faltered in his indictment. Certainly, Shakespeare was a 'drunken savage'. How otherwise could one describe a dramatist who began a tragedy with a common soldier saying that his guard had not been disturbed by a mouse?[15] And yet – those beauties! That sublimity! Often, when he was reading Shakespeare, his desiccated eye would moisten; his prickly carapace would soften.

> For who would bear the whips and scorns of time,
> The oppressor's wrong, the proud man's contumely,
> The pangs of dispriz'd love, the law's delay,
> The insolence of office, and the spurns
> That patient merit of the unworthy takes ...

How such poetry spoke directly of his own experience! How it stirred his deepest feelings! In 1761, he had made a second, more literal translation of the *Hamlet* soliloquy, and found himself admiring, almost envying, the remarkable strength and versatility of Shakespeare's idiosyncratic periods. 'Penetrating the obscurity of this scrupulous translation', he admitted, 'you will discover a truth, a profundity, a *je ne sais quoi* that grips you and stirs you much more than mere eloquence would.'[16] He could not deny, furthermore, that Shakespeare was pastmaster in the craft of drama. 'I've seen Shakespeare's *Caesar* performed, and I confess that right from the first scene I began to be interested, to be moved ...'[17]

In continental Europe, during the last years of Voltaire's life and the half-century following his death, Shakespeare swept from complete obscurity to illustrious fame. 'They affect for Shakespeare an admiration so partial and so outlandish', wrote the marquis de Pompignan of the literary French of the 1780s, 'that not even his compatriots could forbear from laughing at it.' In literary Germany he was idolised. His works were fully translated first by Wieland and Eschenburg (1762–77), and then again, to loud acclaim, by Schlegel and Tieck (1796–1833). Wieland called Shakespeare the greatest dramatic poet the world had ever known. Gerstenberg, in his *Schleswiger Briefe* (1766), defined him as W*eltschöpfer*, or demiurge. He was revered by Herder, Goethe, and the other young exponents of *Sturm and Drang*. 'When I first read Shakespeare,' wrote Goethe, 'I was like one who, having been born blind, by a miracle is suddenly granted sight.'[18] The inspired but clumsy artisan was now unapproachably superhuman, and exempt from the jurisdiction of aesthetics. His works were no longer read as literature but as transcriptions of cosmic reality: prodigies of creative perception that required not to be judged, but to be worshipped. Academic criticism, with its talk of 'beauties' and 'faults', was irrelevant; Shakespeare could be discussed only in the language of the numinous. This youthful *Shakespearomanie* soon became an embarrassment to Goethe. In his Weimar years he rediscovered the attractions of classicism, and preferred his Shakespeare manicured and domesticated. Schlegel, too, dissented from Romantic antirationalism by stressing the evidence of contrivance and discipline in Shakespeare's work. Nevertheless the Shakespeare of *Sturm und Drang* continued to levy an extravagant tribute, especially in France. It was as *der grosse Wilde*, the consecrated savage of German Romanticism, that Shakespeare was most widely traded and promoted in early nineteenth-century Paris.

This, the second phase of his career in France, had all the triumphalism of an apotheosis. To the young literary generation of the Restoration years (1815–48) the name 'Shakespeare' was an incantation, and the performance of several of his plays by an English company in Paris during the two seasons of 1827 and 1828 featured as a cardinal event in the annals of the *Ecole Romantique*. The performances were not particularly distinguished. They were hastily put together by an *ad hoc* troupe with a few star names and décor from the scenery-stores of the Odéon and the Salle Richelieu. Charles Kemble, at fifty-two, was obviously too old as Hamlet and Romeo, and his Othello was judged by an English critic the worst he had ever seen. Edmund Kean, who played Richard III and Othello, was tired, half-drunk, and visibly past his best. An actor called Terry, who specialised in comic roles, was ludicrous as Lear. The only noteworthy appearances were by William Macready as Othello, and the unknown Harriet Smithson, whose Ophelia and Juliet made her the toast of Paris. Yet this was theatre such as Paris had never seen before. Shakespeare's plays (followed with the aid of specially published bilingual texts) exposed whole new areas of human psychology and human experience. The English actors astounded, shocked, and in some cases disgusted Parisian critics and audiences with their 'Shakespearean' style of performance. The French tragic stage was changing. It was no longer as ritualistic and ceremonious as it had been when David Garrick came to Paris. Heroes and heroines in *perruques*, gloves, *panniers*, and powder, declaiming their lines in dignified immobility before a classical temple or palace, were a thing of the past. Costumes and scenery had become more authentic; performances less constrained. Players now 'acted' in the modern sense of the word, by moving around, inflecting their voices, and addressing each other rather than the audience. Nevertheless, the English company suddenly made them all seem inadequate and old-fashioned. The foreign actors were remarkable because they were 'natural'. They spoke as one did in life, in a room. Moreover they made use of what was called 'pantomime' to an extent that French actors never did. They registered emotion and sensation by means of gesture, facial expression, convulsion, physical contact, and vocal extemporising – sobs, shrieks, groans, laughter. Thespian, literary, and artistic Paris was overwhelmed. Actors and actresses of the Comédie-Française practised before their mirrors in order to reinvent their craft. A critic, writing in *Le Corsaire* in 1828, commented caustically on influential members of the Comédie who, 'swearing by Shakespeare and completely spellbound by the English actors, require[d] an agony of a good five minutes after a stabbing, and retching after a poisoning'.[19]

Leading figures of the Romantic school, including Alexandre Dumas, Victor Hugo, Alfred de Musset, Théophile Gautier, and Hector Berlioz, remembered these scrappy Shakespearean evenings as a rite of passage, an initiation into an expanded sense of possibility and vocation. 'From that time,' wrote Dumas,

> I had an idea of what theatre was ... It was the first time I had seen real passion in the theatre, animating men and women of flesh and blood ... The English actors ended their series of performances leaving my heart breathless with unknown impressions, my mind dazzled by new lights.[20]

Berlioz recalled the first performance of *Hamlet*, in September 1827, as his moment of epiphany: 'Shakespeare suddenly fell upon me like a thunderbolt ... I recognised true greatness, true dramatic beauty and dramatic merit. At the same time I became aware of the fatuity of the ideas about Shakespeare broadcast in France by Voltaire.'[21] Obsessed with Harriet Smithson – whom he had never met – he embarked on a pursuit of Shakespeare in her and of her in Shakespeare which summarises all the destructive addiction to hyperbole, all the torturing of life by art, that followed from the French Romantic encounter with the great Elizabethan. Like the player in *Hamlet* who 'forces his soul so to his conceit' that he weeps for Queen Hecuba, for 'a fiction ... a dream of passion', Berlioz acted out an inflated scenario of torrents, tempests, and whirlwinds of passion; of pangs of disprized love; of gothic anguish amidst graves and worms and epitaphs. In 1830 he proclaimed himself 'a very unhappy man, a creature almost isolated in the world, an animal afflicted with an imagination he cannot carry, devoured by a limitless love which is repaid only with indifference and scorn'. When, after ignoring or rejecting for five years the pleas and declarations of this alarming young French composer, Harriet finally – and apprehensively – accepted him, his illusions ran rapidly aground on the reality of two lives not converging but moving inexorably apart.

They could hardly communicate. His English was rudimentary, her French limited to a few words and phrases. Her theatrical ventures had collapsed; she was losing her looks; her inability to master the language left her with no prospects as an actress in France. During the next ten years his career burgeoned and flourished while hers withered and died. Frustration and despair were compounded by postnatal depression, and she started to drink heavily. Berlioz watched horrified as Ophelia became middle-aged, slovenly, and overweight; as a poem of exquisite love became the sordid platitude of a disastrous marriage. He fled from the squalor and confusion of their *ménage* into illicit liaisons and long concert tours abroad, thereby increasing her loneliness and bitterness, and burdening himself with a heavy sense of guilt. Her health was wrecked, she suffered a series of strokes, and for the last five and a half years of her life, while all Europe was thrilling to music inspired by her charisma and youthful beauty, she was a semi-paralysed invalid, pathologically obese and hardly able to speak. She died in 1854, aged fifty-three, and a decade later there was an aptly Shakespearean epilogue to her pitiful story. The old cemetery of Montmartre was being cleared for redevelopment, and in his memoirs Berlioz described how, like Hamlet, he watched as workmen broke open a grave – not Yorick's in this performance of the play, but that of 'the fair Ophelia', whose decayed remains were being disinterred for transfer and reburial. Theatre was life, all the world was a stage, and a poet was God:

> Shakespeare! Shakespeare! It is thou who art our father, thou who art in heaven, if there be a heaven. God is stupid and atrocious in his infinite indifference; thou alone art the God worthy of the souls of artists; receive us on thy breast, oh father; put thy arms around us! [22]

When Shakespeare touched their lives, famous Frenchmen took to playing theatrical roles. They made themselves too stagy for the light of common day; too clamorous for the public peace. Voltaire became the betrayed patriarch, supplanted by the upstart he had patronised. Berlioz became the suffering artist, martyred by misfortune and malignant envy. And Victor Hugo became the hierophant, striking transcendental postures and speaking with the voice of destiny.

Hugo, like Voltaire, spent time as a political refugee in Britain. For nearly twenty years, from 1851 until 1870, he was an exile first in Jersey and then in Guernsey. But unlike Voltaire he never learnt English and he made no contact with English people – except with one, that is. Seven times, during the spiritualist séances that were regularly held around a turning table in Marine Terrace, St Helier, and Hauteville House, St Peter Port, Shakespeare himself responded to the ectoplasmic summons. Once he told Hugo (speaking, obligingly, in French) that since he

(Shakespeare) was now permanently in the presence of the Almighty, he had had to abandon writing and concentrate on adoration. On another occasion he improvised a gratifying tribute to his eminent interlocutor:

> Aujourd'hui Phidias et demain Prométhée,
> Aujourd'hui moi, Shakespeare, et demain toi, Hugo![23]

No doubt he had been flattered by the glowing homage that Hugo had paid him in the preface to his drama *Cromwell*, published in 1827; and Hugo, now grateful in his turn, repaid the compliment with another, vastly inflated eulogy. This was the essay *William Shakespeare*, which appeared in 1865.

The preface to *Cromwell* overflows with the language of the numinous. Shakespeare is expounded as a divinity ('ce dieu du théâtre') and as a trinity (combining the genius of Corneille, Racine, and Molière). His province was not art, but nature, and the gospel of his votaries was 'la Nature donc! La Nature et la Vérité!' Shakespeare's work, said Hugo, was one of the three supreme achievements of the poetic muse. As the primitive age had culminated in the Bible – whose language was lyrical and dealt with what was eternal, ideal, colossal, and naive; and as the antique age had culminated in Homer – whose instrument was the epic recounting history, the grandiose, the gigantic, and the simple; so the modern age had produced Shakespeare – whose medium was the drama and whose notes were those of life, reality, humanity, and truth. In the essay of 1865, which was written to commemorate the publication of his son's translation of Shakespeare's complete works, Hugo restated at enormous length and full volume the fundamental article of the Romantic creed. He set up a delirious verbal vortex around the idea of Shakespeare as a god. It was an essay in which the light was feeble, but the heat tremendous. The matter was banal, the critical perception insignificant; but the tone was dithyrambic as only Hugo could make it. Visionary utterances are swept along on torrents of hyperbole. Weighty words like 'infini', 'immense', 'abîme', 'insondable' swirl around in the cataract. In order to enhance his subject's cosmic, timeless magnitude, he invoked all the mighty names of world literature and art – Homer, Aeschylus, Lucretius, Juvenal, Tacitus, Job, Isaiah, Ezekiel, Dante, Rabelais, Cervantes, Michelangelo, Rembrandt, Beethoven, the Vedas, the *Ramayana*, the *Mahabharata*, the *Niebelungen*, and (modestly forbearing to mention his own name) 'a few others besides' ('quelques autres encore'). Within this constellation six figures were paramount, superlative among superlatives: Homer, Aeschylus, Job, Isaiah, Dante – and Shakespeare. In the preface to *Cromwell* Hugo had compared Shakespeare to an oak tree, with its 'bizarre habit, knotty branches, sombre foliage, rough and rude bark'. In the essay of 1865 Shakespeare became the ocean, the earth, existence, the whole of nature ('toute la nature'), a mountain summit, and 'fertility, strength, exuberance, the swollen udder, the foaming cup, the brimming vat, superabundant sap, torrents of lava, swarming germs, the vast rain of life ... vegetation, germination, light, flame'.

These were the tactics not of persuasion, but of attrition. Hugo the evangelist did not argue. He laid siege to resistance and set about haranguing it to death. And he failed. Never was the name of Shakespeare so ostentatiously emblazoned; and never was misgiving so stubborn and resistance so prolonged. Despite all the language of apotheosis and apocalypse, Shakespeare's second entry into France was no less controversial than the first. There was doubt, hesitation, perplexity. French opinion, having brought Shakespeare to the world's attention, prevaricated, and distanced itself from the world's approval.

When Hugo wrote about Shakespeare, he was working to transform the act of writing from a social function to a sacerdotal mission. He was also working to reactivate the Revolution and liberate literature from privilege, politeness, and academic aesthetics. 'There is today', he wrote in the *Cromwell* preface, 'a literary as well as a political *ancien régime*. The last century still weighs on the new almost at every point.' Its legacy was the bland, monotonous elegance of the sort of writing favoured by Voltaire, in which reality was presented selectively, according to the rules of taste and propriety. Voltaire's own tragedies Hugo dismissed as 'sententious talk' ('des sentences qui parlent'). Shakespeare abetted the rebellion against this artificiality because he demonstrated the artistic possibilities of the grotesque. By invoking deformity and ugliness, he pointed the way to a literature which embraced the whole of creation and offered infinite scope for variation and renewal. In his *Postscriptum à ma vie*, Hugo scorned Voltaire's denigration of Shakespeare. 'Shakespeare's a drunken savage? Yes, he's savage! He lives in the virgin forest. Yes, he's drunk! He's the drinker of the Ideal.' But Voltaire continued to haunt large tracts of French opinion. His description of Shakespeare's *œuvre* as a promiscuous jumble of jewels and refuse was still a critical commonplace long after Voltaire himself was dead and his reputation as a dramatist was following him to the grave. It was frequently heard in 1827 and 1828, when the English company was acting in Paris and everybody was discussing Shakespeare. The press talked about 'traces de sauvagerie', 'génie inculte', 'l'art à son enfance', 'monstrueuse tragédie ... où brillent di si grandes beautés', 'puerilités et ... bizarreries [avec] beautés de détail', and so on.[24] Voltaire might well have written the article in the *Courrier des Théâtres* which expatiated on 'the bizarre beauties, the extravagant boldness of a literature set apart and confined to an island, as though destiny had wanted to keep it separate from all the others'.[25]

During Voltaire's lifetime it was smart and enlightened to know about the wider world and to be tolerant of foreign oddities. Fashionable and intellectual Paris prided itself on being *cosmopolite* a word that came into general use in the middle years of the eighteenth century.[26] However, cosmopolitanism had its adversaries too. By substituting the cold abstraction of humanity for the vital loyalties of citizenship and nationality, it seemed to be subverting a whole rubric of civility: surrendering virtues that were rooted in local attachments for vices that knew no frontiers. So, in the wake of 'cosmopolite', the word 'patrie' returned to favour; and patriotism was increasingly prescribed as an antidote to pernicious universalism. This reaction was especially apparent in the first years of the Revolution. Cosmopolitanism featured in much early republican propaganda as an article of impeachment again the *philosophes* and their aristocratic patrons.[27]

Voltaire was incriminated with the rest; and his reputation was further damaged during the aftermath of the Revolution, when intellectual and political Paris, traumatised by the memory of the Terror, was looking for explanations and culprits. Why had civilisation collapsed precisely where it had seemed most secure? Who, what, was to blame? The scepticism and irreverence of the *philosophes* came readily to mind; and so too did the corruption of public manners and public taste by a degenerate theatre. For this corruption Voltaire was held mainly responsible. According to Julien-Louis Geoffroy, undisputed prince of theatre critics during the Napoleonic era (1799–1814), Voltaire, by launching

Shakespeare into France, had denationalised French drama and vitiated the French character. He had indeed left France barbaric. He and his disciples had scavenged in the Shakespearean 'dungheap' and poisoned theatrical and literary life with 'English atrocity'. This had stimulated an appetite for bloodshed and violence; unleashed a destructive tide of emotion. 'I have seen', wrote Geoffroy in 1805, 'the greatest partisans of theatrical terror and pity, the men who had most wept and shuddered at the tragic novels of Voltaire, show themselves to be the cruellest enemies of humanity.' The lesson was clear. 'We should leave to the English their scaffolds, their executions, their monstrous horrors.'[28]

But Voltaire had been ambivalent about Shakespeare, and in the longer term it was as Shakespeare's enemy that he was remembered. In this role he featured not as the corrupter of Frenchness, but as its epitome. His acerbic objections to the English dramatist had set him apart from philosophical opinion, and these objections proved to be the embryo of notions of 'difference' and 'exception' that would persist and flourish in French political and intellectual circles for the next 250 years. Throughout the nineteenth century and well beyond, the belief never went away that in his obsessive and half-baked complaints against Shakespeare Voltaire was defending something that was supremely worth preserving and whose survival seemed less and less assured. The values he had defended as universal truths came more and more, in a world of relative standards and conflicting cultures, to seem quintessentially and vulnerably French. Voltaire's way of thinking and writing became subsumed into a model of French identity, an archetype of Frenchness, to which the intellectual and political élites committed themselves as the ambit of French power and the French language contracted. Even Victor Hugo, for all the gulf that divided him from the age of Reason, was linked by a flux of sympathy to its supreme pontiff. His very antirationalism, his resort to occultism and spiritualism, revealed a community of temperament. When Hugo charted his soul's pedigree, he discovered several Classical ancestors.[29] It transpired that during the various stages of metempsychosis, he had been Isaiah, Aeschylus, Judas Maccabeus, Juvenal, several painters, and two kings of Greece whose names he could never remember. There was no sign of Shakespeare among these previous incarnations, and the reason for this was revealed when Hugo remarked that Shakespeare was 'very English – too English' ('très anglais – trop anglais'). He knew that according to modern think-ing the great poet was not just a natural phenomenon, but a Teutonic phenomenon as well. This ethnic classification made him an alien and even a hostile presence in France.[30]

Shakespeare had arrived in Germany as a discovery of the Enlight-enment. His admirers had spoken the cosmopolitan language of its aesthetics. They talked of what was 'sublime'; of 'Genius', 'Freedom', 'Nature', and 'Truth'. But in Germany, too, there had followed a strong reaction against the cosmopolitan spirit. Inspired by Herder and Lenz, the Romantic *Stürmer* had hitched their evangelism not to the univer-sal categories of the *philosophes*, but to the German *Volksgeist* and its legacies – folklore, folksong, national history, vernacular literature, Gothic art and architecture. They recognised in cosmopolitanism the vehicle of French vices and French hegemony, and they enlisted Shake-speare for their campaign against it. They proclaimed Shakespearean drama to be the prototype of a national theatre; they identified in Shakespeare himself a Nordic poet. This germanisation of Shakespeare, which would culminate in the Valhalla of a resurgent Reich, set a new agenda for the debate about Shakespeare in France. It persuaded the French that they were addressing not just a tension between what was barbaric and what was civilised, but a conflict between what was Gal-lic, or Latin, and what was Teutonic, or Anglo-Saxon, as well. It therefore made Shakespeare crucial to the long and painful adjustment of French consciousness to a world in which France and the French language were no longer paramount.

2

A Genius in the Kingdom of Taste

In 1783 Antoine Rivarol, in a prize-winning essay called *De l'Universalité de la langue française*, wrote of a France that was visited by everybody and a French language that was spoken everywhere. The Frenchman had no need to travel, because the world came to him; no need to speak foreign tongues, because his own had global currency. Yet Rivarol's was the generation that thought of itself as coming after the feast and before the deluge. It was haunted by the question that the Academy of Berlin had asked and Rivarol had answered: Would the French language retain its universality? France was supremely rich in human and natural resources. Her language and her literature were paramount in Europe. Yet the future did not seem to be hers. Her glory had not survived 'le Grand Siècle' of Louis XIV, celebrated by Voltaire in his best-known historical work. As it receded ever farther into the past, the age of the Sun King figured more and more as the last great epoch in French history. The humiliating convulsions that France endured after 1789 increased awareness of unsustainable recovery and inexorable loss. After the Second Empire had ended disastrously, in 1870, the historian Hippolyte Taine investigated the origins of contemporary France and discovered a catalogue of disaster: 'The *ancien régime* was a fiasco; the Revolution was a fiasco; the Empire was a fiasco. That is why we are sinking into the mire.' In France in the 1870s a flood of works appeared dealing with national decline and catastrophe. And as France waned, Britain waxed. By subjecting the French to military defeat in Europe, by supplanting them in India and North America, by dominating the oceans and monopolising the world's trade, the British became the new universal presence. 'Since 1688', wrote the novelist and *bas-bleu* Germaine de Staël in 1817, 'no people of Europe have been comparable to the English.' The nineteenth century was the British century. The world now spoke English, and came to England.[1]

When the French compared themselves with this ascendant rival, two differences became especially apparent. They had had no Reformation, and they had had no Shakespeare.

No Reformation – no official break with Rome, that is, no doctrinal and liturgical overhaul of the national church following the summons of Luther and Calvin. Plenty of French people had become Protestants, or 'Huguenots'; but orthodoxy in France had been defended by agencies too powerful and too ruthless for even monarchs to defy: by the Sorbonne, by the *parlement* of Paris, by the Jesuits. The reformers, who had many supporters among the *noblesse* as well as among the people, had not been easily thwarted, and for most of the sixteenth century France had been a battleground of rival religious forces. Protestantism had survived proscription, persecution, burnings, massacres, and civil war. But it had never achieved more than a precarious toleration, and when that, too, was withdrawn, many Huguenots chose exile rather than further resistance. After Louis XIV had revoked the Edict of Nantes, in 1685, hundreds of thousands fled to Holland or to Britain, taking with them valuable industrial and entrepreneurial skills. It seemed that France, culturally and spiritually divided between the North and the South, between the Atlantic and the Mediterranean, had chosen at this critical moment of history to link her destiny not with the new Protestant world of the Dutch, the British, and the Germans, but with the old Catholic world of declining Spain and fragmented Italy.

No Shakespeare – that is to say, no literary genius who had nurtured a national memory and set hearts beating faster with a sense of purpose, possibility, and destiny. This absence was lamented in 1827 by Abel-François Villemain, a young professor at the Sorbonne and a future minister of public instruction. 'Let as figure to ourselves', wrote Villemain,

> that a man of genius had sprung up at the first cultivation of our language and our arts; that expressing himself with wild energy he had produced upon the stage ... the revengeful deeds of Louis XI, the crimes of the palace of Charles IX, the audacity of the Guises, and the furious atrocities of the League. Would not such plays, were they still performed, maintain an immortal authority in our literature and an all-powerful effect in our theatre? And yet we have not, like the English, any taste for our manners, nor, above all, any portion of the enthusiasm of national patriotism.

Genius, according to Diderot's *Encyclopédie*, was difficult to define but easy to recognise. In the presence of genius you experienced an unmistakable *frisson*, a quickening of the pulse, a delirium of the soul. You were excited by a rush of vitality and renewal; shocked by daring and *enthousiasme*; uplifted by sudden, apocalyptic insight; overwhelmed by a sense of the sublime. This complex reaction was often provoked by reading English authors, and especially by reading Shakespeare. 'Sublimity and genius', said the *Encyclopédie*, 'flash in Shakespeare like lightning in a long night.' But it seldom came from reading anything written in French. French literature was not daring and apocalyptic. It carried the burden of an Antiquity in which everything had already been said. We have come, said La Bruyère in his *Caractères* (1688), seven thousand years too late to say anything new. Belatedness precluded discovery. It was the pleasure of recognition that French literature provided: the pleasure in old truths revisited and old form perfected. But too often what was familiar was also tedious and predictable. 'Our literature', complained the marquise du Deffand to Horace Walpole in 1768, 'is as abundant in production as it is sterile in imagination.' Pierre Le Tourneur, translator of Shakespeare and of Edward Young, wrote of the well-made French literary work: 'You know it by heart before you have even read it. You find there none of those ideas which arrest the reader, give a jolt to the soul, and alert the mind. Nothing that surprises you, that suddenly floods your soul with light.' There was no evidence of genius – the visionary, creative impetus which, as the *Encyclopédie* put it, 'seems to change the nature of things'. French literature was lit by a steady, focused light, whereas the lights of genius 'project beyond the past and the present, and illuminate the future'.[2]

It was impossible to believe that France was naturally deficient in genius. Alexis de Tocqueville, the nineteenth-century historian, reckoned that the French had more genius than good sense. However it did seem – both to outsiders like Goethe and to many French observers – that genius in France was thwarted by ritual and routine. Cultural stagnation and sterility, the absence of a Shakespeare, were apparently the price that France had to pay for having rejected the Reformation.

The philosophical offensive of the Age of Reason put an end to Christianity as the dominating influence on French intellectual life and as the official faith of the French state. But it did not end the dominance of Catholicism. In the post-Christian era, Catholicism survived as a secular religion. It forsook the Gospels and the Saints, but it still governed French habits and thought with a papal apparatus of dogma, ritual, and authority. In the region of art, the real attack against the *ancien régime* did not come until the Romantics (called by their adversaries 'the Protestants of literature') tried, with little success, to work their own revolution. This long survival is not surprising, because the dissident intellectuals of the eighteenth century – like those of the nineteenth and the twentieth – wanted not to destroy but to inherit the Catholic universe. The *philosophes* aspired to replace the theological world order with a mathematical one. They dreamt of an order of Cartesian absolutes and invariables, with themselves as its sacerdotal caste. They denied the rationality of belief; but they preached belief in rationality, and they were inquisitorial in their intolerance of opposition.

Nothing better illustrates this stubborn endurance of Catholicism than the fate of Shakespeare's works in France. For a long time they were treated by intellectuals much as scripture was treated by priests. They were 'divine' texts, essential to salvation, but at the same time esoteric: inscrutable and even perilous to the laity. Montaigne had said of the Bible, 'ce n'est pas l'étude de tout le monde' ('it's not to be studied by everybody'), and like the Bible Shakespeare's works were reserved to the instructed few, for use in the privacy of the *cabinet de travail*. Before they could be exposed on the public stage they had to be adapted to liturgical custom, made inoffensive to pious minds. Small wonder that the eminent critic Sainte-Beuve would one day remark: 'In France we shall remain Catholic long after we have ceased to be Christian.'[3]

When Pierre Le Tourneur published his translation of Edward Young's works in 1769, he wrote at length in his *discours préliminaire* about Young's *Conjectures on Original Composition*. In this treatise Young had rejected the idea of belatedness. He said that the great achievements of Bacon, Bayle, Newton, Shakespeare, and Milton, proved that there were harvests still to be gathered. He also said, however, that these were the inheritance of Protestant virtues. The case of Alexander Pope proved the stifling influence of Catholicism. Pope's mediocrity made it clear that true poetry, like true religion, abhorred idolatry. Le Tourneur implied that the example of French literature did likewise. French writers were timid and deferential: 'The French smother their talent with taste and conformity ... No one dares for an instant to write freely and alone.' Young's own poetry delivered the message that English literature reverberated still with the Shakespearean charisma. *Night Thoughts* (translated into French as *Les Nuits*) abounded in 'new ideas ... daring images ... ardent expressions loaded with feeling'.

This Protestant initiative seemed to operate in all areas of life. Protestant science cancelled immemorial systems and shaped an intellectual landscape in which the old maps were useless. Modernity was born with Newton and came of age with Darwin. In his monumental *Histoire de France* (1833–67), and in his lectures at the Collège de France, Jules Michelet harped on the theme of a nation retarded by the incubus of institutional Catholicism. Its spirit was crushed by 'the gloomy education which conquers minds before they come of age, and doses them with chloroform from the start'. George Sand made this the subject of her novel *Mademoiselle La Quintinie* (1863), and looked for regeneration to liberal Protestantism. Leading intellectuals of Michelet's and Sand's generation, which witnessed the creation of a huge new Protestant empire in Europe and its military defeat of Catholic France, were convinced that the failure of the Reformation in France had been a national calamity. 'France', said the philosopher Charles Renouvier, 'missed the boat, as they say, in the sixteenth century.' Then the scandals and disorders of the Third Republic – syndicalism, the Dreyfus affair, Boulangism, *Décadence* – reinforced the view that recurring revolution in France was not a healthy, regenerative reflex, but a symptom of chronic distemper. It was not the Protestantism of Geneva that the intellectuals admired – Calvinism was too obviously popery minus the incense – but that of the Anglo-Saxons. The New World seemed to be flourishing on the virtues that France lacked – endeavour, fortitude, tolerance, fearless empiricism, self-confidence. America's phenomenal display first of political idealism and material success, then of literary vitality, has fascinated – obsessed almost – intellectual France since the era of the War of Independence. Awareness of the New World then coincided with awareness of Shakespeare to reshuffle the priorities of many among the educated classes. This was the moment when, in the words of a modern French historian, 'the weight of tradition was felt as a brake and not as a stimulant'.[4]

Evaluations of genius now emphasised, as never before, originality.

The Promethean genius of Renaissance literature, the bearer of a gift stolen from the gods, gave way to the demiurge, the source of creative potency. Genius now spoke not with a borrowed voice, but with an inner voice equally divine. 'This term "genius"', wrote Voltaire in 1771, 'ought it seems to designate not just great talent, but that talent which includes invention ... An artist, however perfect he may be in his genre, is not reputed a genius if he is not inventive, is not original.'[5] Few could be original in this superhuman sense, but all could learn to cherish originality. In order to open French minds to its achievements, English works were translated on a scale never before known and the twenty-eight volumes of the *Encyclopédie* garnered into French a *résumé* of the world's best enterprise. The eighteenth-century translators and *encyclopédistes* turned the French language into a vast *jardin d'acclimatation*, stocked with everything from the global heritage that was superlative, rare, and curious. Their activity was not, as Revolutionary propaganda was to claim, anti-patriotic. It was an effort to revitalise an ailing organism by a transfusion of new blood. This was made clear by the translators of Shakespeare. They stressed the benefits that would accrue to French literature from a knowledge of this exotic genius. Pierre-Antoine de La Place, the first translator of Shakespeare into French (1745) claimed that study of the English dramatist's work would broaden the French intellect and help to perfect French literature. 'It matters little', he wrote,

> that Shakespeare worked in a style different from our own, our curiosity must be redoubled for that very reason ... Such study can only favour the perfection of art ... The French frame of mind is not necessarily that of all nations, and in reading Shakespeare we do not merely perceive the difference between the English spirit and the French spirit, we also discover feats of strength, new and original beauties.[6]

Thirty years later, the successive volumes of Pierre Le Tourneur's version of Shakespeare were welcomed as a national benefit even by orthodox critics. In 1778 the *Année Littéraire*, a journal founded and edited by the Catholic polemicist Elie-Cathérine Fréron, hailed the translation as a valuable antidote to the sense of belatedness that was paralysing the French theatre. It would help to combat the 'sterility and dearth' that had been afflicting the national stage for a long time.[7] The *Journal des Savants*, a long-established and officially favoured review of international literature, predicted that general improvement would result from comparing and contrasting the literatures of different nations.[8] Shakespeare was never proposed as a model to be imitated. Imitation was precisely what he was recruited to discourage. He was offered, rather, as an example to be emulated. He demonstrated the enormous promise in an alternative approach to literary composition. His admirers praised his work in terms that revealed their envy of the Protestant beatitudes. To eighteenth-century critics and dramatists like Diderot, Mercier, Marmontel, and Lemercier, Shakespeare was 'fougueux' and 'sublime'. What they revered in him was his 'originalité', 'écarts', 'ardeur', 'mouvement', 'fierté', 'audace', 'force', 'chaleur', and 'hardiesse'.

French opinion accepted that genius was essential to the chemistry of artistic creation. Without it there could be no great eras of civilisation. French opinion also accepted, however, that genius alone was not sufficient. Since genius was a whim of nature, it was ephemeral and untutored. Jean-François Marmontel, secretary of the Académie Française and prominent *encylopédiste*, called it 'une sorte d'inspiration fréquente, mais passagère [et] souvent inculte'. It therefore required a supplement, an additive, that would give it sustenance and soften its asperities. Genius could initiate art, but it could not perfect it, and in educated circles in France the aesthetic quality of perfection was habitually esteemed above all others. 'We respect the geniuses who have rough-hewn the arts', wrote Voltaire, 'but the minds which have perfected them are more our sort.' The essential supplement was taste (*goût*). *Goût*, said Marmontel, was judge, counsel, and guide. Jean-François de La Harpe, who lectured to fashionable society at the Lycée in Paris in the 1780s, defined the ages of great literature as 'les siècles de génie et de goût' – centuries that had already been identified by La Harpe's master, Voltaire, as those of Pericles, Augustus, Leo X, and Louis XIV. Without taste, genius was errant and grotesque. 'Genius led by taste', declared Voltaire, 'will never commit gross errors ... Genius without taste will commit enormous ones.' François-René de Chateaubriand later summarised a consensus when he wrote that 'if it is genius that conceives, it is taste that conserves. Taste is the good sense of genius; without it, genius is but sublime madness.'[9]

Taste was the first article in the aesthetic creed of both Christian and secular France. Until well into the twentieth century it was impossible to read or hear of art or literature without encountering the word *goût*. It came to the mind, to the lips, to the pen with greater frequency than any other in the lexicon of criticism. The French regarded their country as the habitat of taste, its kingdom. It was taste, said Rivarol, that had made France the cultural centre of Europe. Taste tamed the conflicting currents from Europe's extremities, and blended them into a common heritage of delight. It was only in France, wrote Chateaubriand, that taste had fused with genius to produce a perfect literature: a literature marred neither by excess nor by lack. Voltaire talked about taste much as theologians talked about grace. 'Almost the whole universe is barbaric', he said; 'taste belongs to a very small number of favoured souls.' And like grace, *goût* engendered hubris in those who thought they possessed it. 'Those who reckon they have taste', observed Germaine de Staël in 1809, 'think as highly of themselves as those who reckon they have genius ... It is regarded as a proof of wealth, of birth – or at least of the habits pertaining to them both.'[10]

It was from these two concepts – genius and taste – that the French constructed their first and most persistent verdict on Shakespeare. Shakespeare had the one – in abundance – but he had not the other. 'Shakespeare', wrote Voltaire in 1729, 'was a genius full of strength and fecundity, of naturalness and sublimity, without the tiniest particle of good taste.' This judgement became proverbial, and it was repeated as common wisdom throughout the next 150 years. It served to explain why Shakespeare was much less than perfect ('not one of his plays', said the abbé Le Blanc, 'is readable from beginning to end') and to justify his exclusion from the French stage.[11]

But what, exactly, was *goût*? Did it denote absolute or relative value? Was it a Cartesian norm or a cultural variable? Was it, like genius, a spontaneous and random gift of nature, or could it be acquired through habit and study? Were men and women of taste born, or made? Eminent literary minds endlessly pondered these questions, only to become aware, like Rousseau, that the wider they cast their inquiries, the less certain were their conclusions. The debate belonged half to the age of Reason, and half to the age of theology, and it changed direction as the world order changed. The leaders of French opinion were Cartesians when they needed to vindicate the French hegemony. They became relativists when they needed to protect the French exception. Until the Romantic era the apostles of taste were defending preferences they believed to be universal. Thereafter, they were defending preferences they believed to be French. Taste and its discontents thus became merged into racialist ideology.

Intellectually the French had been at home with relativity since the time of La Bruyère. That famous and rather jaundiced observer of high society had pointed out in his *Caractères* (1688) that the criteria of civilisation were not everywhere identical. 'With such pure language', he wrote, 'such elegant dress, such cultivated habits and such fine laws, we, with our white faces, are barbarians in the eyes of some peoples.' Later, the historicising, comparative method of inquiry adopted by Montesquieu, Voltaire, Turgot, and Condorcet favoured the idea of disparate tastes, rather than of universal Taste. It was often asserted that taste had no absolute validity; that it was a social convention, varying according to time and place. Geoffroy, for example, argued that the art of one age or society should not be judged by the taste of another: 'If you want to read the Classical authors, imagine yourself in the century in which they lived ... Can we claim that our taste and our conventions are the rule of beauty?' Yet belief in a transcendent, permanent scale of values, rooted in a human nature that was always and everywhere the same, remained strong and stubbornly persistent. Voltaire distinguished between what he called 'beautés locales' in literature – details of speech and turns of phrase – and the beauties admired by 'l'homme de goût, le connaisseur'. The development of taste seemed to depend on accidents of history, on the wealth and leisure that facilitated study, comparison, and selection; but ultimately it was a matter of instinct and feeling, and the things it valued never varied. They were 'beauties of all ages and all countries'. French opinion clung to this unverifiable hypothesis, and made a fetish of the celebrated rules (*règles*) that had been drawn up by French academic theorists in the middle years of the seventeenth century. In these prescriptions, devised as a *rappel à l'ordre* at a time of political, religious, and cultural turmoil, it discovered the deductions of unimpeachable Taste.[12]

In theory the rules were not inflexible or peremptory. They were an aid to the understanding and appreciation of literature and art, rather than a rubric governing their creation. No one ever denied that genius

made its own rules, and that the final criterion of worth was not correctness, but survival and the awakening of pleasure. The 'legislators of
Parnassus' were often satirised and flouted. In practice, however, the
highest approval was reserved for art and architecture that were regular
– for Greek architecture and French seventeenth-century dramatic literature especially. A contributor to the Correspondance Littéraire referred
in 1776 to 'un culte excessif et superstitieux' for the classical models. This,
he said, was in no way different from theological intolerance.[13] French
connoisseurs of the seventeenth and eighteenth centuries arbitrated
against the joys of discovery in favour of the joy of recognition. They
steered public preference away from the bizarre, the restless, and the
rough, towards restraint, stasis, smoothness; away from the complex,
turbulent gestures of the Baroque towards the gentler language of
Rococo, and thence to the austere, unbroken contours of Neo-classicism.
The German rediscovery of Greece (of Doric architecture especially) was
crucial in the history both of taste and of the theory of taste in France.
Greece became the final authority in aesthetics. Johann Winckelmann's
famous message ('good taste was born under the sky of Greece') lodged
itself in the substratum of all French thinking about art and literature.
'Taste' meant Greek taste. It was to Hellenic Classicism that aesthetic instinct reverted when free from local and contingent pressures. Classicism
was set up as the style in office, the orthodoxy of art and literature, and
not all the efforts of Romanticism could dislodge it.

Victor Hugo protested against its wearisome reiteration of the 'beauté
universelle'. 'Sublimity piled on sublimity', he wrote in the preface to
Cromwell, 'hardly admits of contrast, and one gets tired of everything,
even of the Beautiful.' Romantic youth agreed – and then lapsed into
classical middle age. In 1845, when he reviewed the Romantic achievement, the poet Gérard de Nerval could find no evidence of victory.
What he called 'le vieil esprit français' had never been completely overcome. It had proved 'a force that cannot be conquered by genius itself,
nor by time or necessity'. He attributed its strength to the hieratic rigour
of French education: 'The University, like the Church, is a dogmatic
power, jealously devoted to form and regulation, which dominates us by
authority when we are young, and by habit when we are old.'[14]

Relapse was personified in the painter Eugène Delacroix. In the 1830s
Delacroix outraged conventional Paris with his Romantic extremism.

'Delacroix', recalled Théophile Gautier, 'felt more vividly than anyone the fever of the age. He was full of its restless, tumultuous, lyrical, disordered, paroxysmal spirit.' He was Romantic not least because he was inspired by Shakespeare. His pictures on Shakespearean subjects long determined French visualisation of the famous characters – of Hamlet in particular. He was regarded as the Shakespeare of modern painting, and he was attacked in terms similar to those reserved for Shakespeare. Gautier remembered how his work was constantly refused by the Institut, and how he was vilified by the 'fogeys' ('grisâtres') as 'un sauvage, un barbare, un maniaque, un enragé, un fou'. He was obsessed, they said, with 'the ugly, the ignoble, and the monstrous'. He painted with 'a drunken broom' ('un balai ivre').[15] Yet the journals of Delacroix reveal a man deeply at odds with his own reputation. They proclaim 'the independence of the artist *vis-à-vis* tradition'; but they also disclose devout allegiance to 'the eternal laws of taste and logic'. Delacroix, the one-time Romantic *enfant terrible*, privately deplored Romanticism. Its obsessive pursuit of novelty, its iconoclasm, its 'turgid and incorrect manner', he reckoned were symptoms of a new barbarism. He judged the music of Berlioz, of Meyerbeer, and of Beethoven infinitely inferior to that of Mozart, Cimarosa, and Rossini. The Romantic drama he never liked. He conceded that the unblemished beauty of Racine's tragedies was a dramatic defect, since 'a perfectly beautiful object ... does not arouse the emotion that one feels in the presence of gigantic things'; but that made the theatre culpable, not Racine. Racine, by virtue of his exquisite taste, was as far above Shakespeare and the Romantics as he was above Corneille and Michelangelo.[16]

During these years of artistic ferment and feverish debate, two notable critics tried to calm the anxiety and misgiving aroused in France by the Shakespearean Baroque. They severed Shakespeare from Romanticism, and argued that there was no real incompatibility between his work and the values that the French had made it their mission to cherish and defend. One of these critics was François Guizot, the eminent scholar and statesman whose revision of Le Tourneur's translation of Shakespeare was published in 1821. Influenced by Schlegel's lectures on drama (published in French 1809–14), Guizot rejected accusations of conflict and disorder in Shakespearean tragedy. He argued that it was symphonic, a confluence producing synthesis and resolution. Shakespeare's writing was, no doubt, blemished by verbal excess, indiscriminate inclusion, and a straining after recondite links and affinities. It was 'the restless and fantastic reverie of a mind astonished at its own discoveries ... heaping ideas, images, and expressions one upon another'. Shakespeare 'had contracted the habit of that learned subtlety which perceives and assimilates everything, and leaves no point of resemblance unnoticed'. In common with all authors of his age, he 'frequently ... connect[ed] ideas and expressions by their most distant relations'. But in Shakespeare's case euphuistic exuberance had been absorbed into a pervading symmetry and homogeneity. There was a 'unity of impression' that made the distinction between tragic and comic meaningless and reference to other unities invalid. What mattered was not the means but the result. Shakespeare had had his own art. So much was attested by the sense of aesthetic enrichment given by his work, for everything perceived as beautiful is, said Guizot, logical in its way. 'Nothing is beautiful in the eyes of man which does not derive its effects from certain combinations.'[17]

Guizot's vindication of Shakespeare was endorsed by Philarète Chasles, a well known and influential professor at the Collège de France. Chasles insisted that Shakespeare was generally misunderstood in France, and that none misunderstood him more crassly than the French Romantics. One needed only to look at their own drama to realise that. Because they had failed to grasp the true nature of Shakespeare's art, their attempt to emulate it had been disastrous. They had cultivated 'fruits bizarres et monstrueux', fatiguing in their dissonance and monotonous crudity. The wild iconoclast that they had worshipped was a figment of their own disordered imaginations. Shakespeare had broken no moulds and proclaimed no manifesto. He had taken the drama as he found it, used whatever materials came readily to hand. He had tamed life and literature and yoked them to his purpose. His plays were not the effusions of a 'monstrous genius', of 'a clumsy peasant ... sublime by accident'. They were controlled by the synergising power that is the gift of true genius, because Shakespeare was an artist in command of his material, not a reckless adventurer riding the stormy tides of frenzy and desperation. Sounding very much like Winckelmann talking about the Laocoön, Chasles said that what, in Shakespeare, at first seemed violent and incoherent, was merely the troubled surface of a metaphysical calm.

Shakespeare's theatre was governed by 'that hidden soul which animates the world, keeps it eternally young, and sustains its immense harmony'.[18]

This interpretation explained why it was possible to be deeply moved by Shakespeare and at the same time desire the serenity of the Cartesian vision. It persuaded Delacroix that he had been wrong about Shakespeare – that he had overlooked 'a secret logic, an order unperceived in that piling-up of details which it would seem must be a misshapen mountain'.[19] Others, too, were momentarily convinced. 'There is', wrote Léon Daudet in 1917, 'no author more deliberate, less random, whose intentions are more covertly interwoven, than the author of *Hamlet.*' He referred to 'the Platonic wisdom that is in Shakespeare ... his thirst for repose and harmony in the midst of the worst tempests of the heart'.[20] André Gide once said that the most striking thing about Shakespeare's work was its order – 'that quality of intelligence which maintains equilibrium in such a diverse world'.[21] But these responses were uncharacteristic both of the men who made them and of the general state of French opinion. As late as 1914 Shakespeare was still being expounded in French academic circles as tasteless and chaotic. In *Shakespeare et la superstition shakespearienne* Georges Pellissier, a university savant with some reputation as an authority on the theatre, argued that Shakespearean drama was 'an enormous mess in which a handful of first-class scenes shine here and there'. It was 'un art rudimentaire' made intolerable to the modern audience by incoherence, unintelligibility, and a bizarre implausibility 'which the least *vaudevilliste* would disdain'. Shakespearean tragedy was 'un musée d'horreurs'; Shakespearean comedy was 'obscène, ordurière, ou, du moins, indécente'. To prove his point, Pellissier compiled a detailed inventory of Shakespeare's 'faults'. 'Is this a joke?' asked the critic René Doumic, bemused. On reflection, he decided that it was deadly serious, and he was almost certainly right – though Pellissier was clearly determined to be provocative.[22]

For the greater part of two centuries, Shakespeare was by common consent kept waiting below the summit of Parnassus. Endowed with extraordinary genius yet deprived of elementary taste, he was a candidate for apotheosis whom it was impossible to accept and at the same time impossible to reject. He was stupendous, but fatally flawed: a tortured, hallucinating demiurge, a barbarian transfigured by lightning flashes of inspiration. His work was 'monstrueux', 'barbare', 'lugubre', 'dégoûtant', 'convulsif '. His magnificence was blighted by 'délire', 'indé-cence', 'extravagance', 'désordre', 'folie'. Equally impelled by the urge to praise and the need to censure, the jury delivered again and again a divided verdict. The essayist Louis-Simon Auger, addressing the *séance annuelle* of the four French academies in 1824, trod the circular path of critical perplexity that had been followed many times already and would be followed many times again:

> Sublime and uncultivated genius, ignorant of the rules of the theatre and relying on the artifice suggested by a happy instinct, [Shakespeare] in his monstrous dramas extended time and space indefinitely, included places and years without number, jumbled together people of various ranks and styles of speech, misunderstood or flouted the distinctive customs of different eras and regions; but, close observer and faithful portrayer of nature, he diffused throughout his disordered and gigantic compositions a mass of those naïve, profound, and energetic strokes which depict a whole century, reveal a whole character, betray a whole passion.[23]

Sensitive souls grieved to think of what might have been. If only, lamented Alfred Mézières, professor at the Sorbonne during the Second Empire, if only Shakespeare had known, or had heeded, the example of the Greeks. What a theatre humanity had lost because this genius had not learnt his trade from Aristotle![24]

Critical ambiguity ensured that although he was accorded the full honours of translation, Shakespeare was denied the privilege of per-formance. For more than a century and a half he was in effect banned from the French stage. It was as a poet, a thinker, an observer of the human condition that he qualified as a cosmic genius. As a dramatist he was base metal. In 1760 the *Journal Encyclopédique* recognised in Shake-speare the 'great poetic genius' that Corneille was not, and in Corneille the 'excellent dramatic poet' that Shakespeare was not. In the view of Germaine de Staël his 'connaissance du cœur humain' was far superior to his 'connaissance du théâtre'. Delacroix reckoned that Shakespeare in performance would be intolerable. His plays, with their 'eternal entrances and exits ... changes of scene ... host of secondary characters' seemed no more than collections of fragments. Like Michelangelo, Shakespeare was a fatigued and hasty genius who was forever beginning what he found it impossible to finish. Without ever having been seen in performance, the original texts became 'known' as intractable anti-drama. They were mythologised as poetic improvisations that the theatre could not contain. Immense, crowded, unstructured, they registered less as drama than as direct, documentary transcriptions of the multiplicity and continuity of life. The essence of art, said Rivarol, is selection. Shakespeare was inartistic because he was inclusive. Anyone, asserted Chateaubriand, could write a 'Shakespearean' drama, simply by observing life and writing it down. The result would not, perhaps, contain much in the way of genius, 'but if Shakespeare the writer would be missing, Shakespeare the dramatist would not'. Shakespeare took no pains. There was no evidence of craftsmanship, of difficulty mastered – not even in his language. He used blank verse, and blank verse, said Voltaire, was easy to write. You just recorded everyday speech and chopped it up into lines. Only rhyme bespoke the discipline and skill that a sophisticated audience demanded:

> Blank verse costs only the trouble of dictating it. It's no more difficult than writing a letter. If we start using blank verse for our tragedies, and perform them on our stage, then tragedy is done for. As soon as you remove the difficulty, you remove the merit.[25]

And when he was not too incoherent, too chaotic for the modern stage, he was too subtle and too prolix. His obfuscation offended the 'homme raisonnable'. Germaine de Staël thought that the density of much of Shakespeare's dialogue resisted the dynamics of actual performance. The spectator wanted constantly to pause and reflect, and was left bewildered and floundering when the actors moved relentlessly on. A theatre audience required the sort of direct, uncluttered writing that characterised Greek and French classical tragedy. This was like the broad brushstrokes of painting intended to be seen from a distance. Emile Montégut, author of a highly regarded translation of the dramatic works of Shakespeare (1867–70), maintained that these could be fully appreciated only in the study:

> When you read Shakespeare, he is the greatest of poets; when you see him performed, he is only the first among melodramatists. [When you read the text] you are present at a psychological and moral spectacle of the most elevated kind; the theatre brings you down to the physiological spectacle of hallucination and delirium.

Shakespeare subjected his audiences to emotional assault. They were left

reeling from 'the rush of the action and the players' delivery'. Consequently they were not relieved by awareness of illusion. 'The shocking
action, the scandalous words, have gone before reflection has had time
to make it clear that it is wrong to be shocked and scandalised.' Furthermore on the stage Shakespeare's finest touches were lost amid bustle
and business – 'the noise of hurrying feet, the clink of arms, the tolling
of bells'.[26]

His distressing effect on the modern audience proved that Shakespeare had been crippled as a dramatist by his want of taste. It was
therefore impossible to grant him access to the French theatre. The theatre was under siege from clerics and moralists. Actors and actresses
were degraded by the state until the Revolution, and excommunicated
by the Church until the 1880s. In order to justify and protect its privi-
leges and subsidies, the Comédie-Française had had to transform itself
into the citadel of taste. Even Corneille and Racine had been rebuked for
breaching its code. 'The poet', said Diderot, 'must not surrender to the
full impetus of his imagination; there are limits set for him.'[27] But what
were those limits? Aristotle's edicts were notoriously cryptic, and everyone hesitated to curtail the prerogative of genius.

The debate was especially concerned with tragedy, because its tragic
repertoire was reckoned to be the French theatre's best asset, the guar-
antee of its reputation. The theatre was defended as the domain, above
all others, of Racine. His tragedies, written between 1664 and 1691, were
eulogised as a precious quintessence, distilled from the legacies of
Aeschylus, Sophocles, Euripides, and Seneca. They were more classical
than the Classics, creations of genius refined by the spirit of perfection.
Jealous regard for the standards of Racine meant that the production
and consumption of tragedy was hedged around with an elaborate protocol. Until 1791 only the Comédie-Française was permitted to perform
this class of drama, and for a long time thereafter tragic authors and
actors were subject to restrictions and requirements that supplemented
official censorship.[28]

There was no rigid etiquette, but there was a culture of surveillance
and self-regulation operating in the name of taste. The watchwords were
vraisemblance, convenance, and *bienséance. Vraisemblance* meant truth
perceived by reason and moral sense, rather than truth to everyday life.
It therefore required that vice should be punished, and virtue rewarded.

Convenance meant authenticity, historical accuracy; but it must not contravene *bienséance*, or propriety. This ruled out unseemly language, violence, bloodshed, and carnal behaviour – even eating and drinking. Strict adherence to Aristotle's unities of time and place (whereby the story occupied no more than twenty-four hours and spanned no distance greater than could be travelled in that time) was not demanded; but adherence to the unity of subject (no subplots and no intermixture of comedy) was.

From the days of Racine and Molière it had been a function of the audience to enforce these conventions. It did so with an armoury of vocal responses – mocking laughter, jeering, whistling, cat-calls. The reticence and decorum required on the stage were oddly absent beyond the footlights. The *parterre*, or pit, of the Comédie-Française, which offered standing room only until the company moved to the Salle Luxembourg in 1782, was notorious for its rowdy, derisive interjections. In the theatre, the Parisian aristocracy and bourgeoisie were a police exempt from the laws they enforced. Nowhere was the lot of the delinquent playwright or actor more miserable than in the city of *délicatesse* and *politesse*. 'Oh waggish and frivolous people', cried Diderot, addressing the Paris theatrical public, 'how you cripple art! What constraints you subject your artists to! And what pleasures your delicacy deprives you of! You are always ready to hoot off the stage the very things which would delight you, which would touch you, in painting.'[29] 'With us', wrote Stendhal in 1823, 'everything that is *strong* is called *indecent*. We jeer Molière's *L'Avare* ... because a son is disrespectful to his father.'[30]

The theatre audience as a magistrate of manners and taste had a long life in Paris. It was still in evidence in the later years of the nineteenth century, when the city lived by its reputation for naughtiness and illicit love. Parisians avid for lurid melodrama and titillating eroticism poured into the boulevard playhouses and the music halls; but when they went to the serious theatre they whistled and booed off the stage anything deemed improper or subversive. 'The very same Parisians', wrote the novelist and critic Paul Bourget,

> who swoon with grinning delight at the smuttiness of certain operetta songs, wouldn't have whistles enough for an author who dared to ridicule the *grands sentiments* on the stage ... The Parisian wants to be entertained, so he must not be left with too bitter an impression. The Parisian wants the *grands*

sentiments to be respected, so guilty heroes and heroines must not triumph too completely.[31]

In practice, the protocol of taste ensured that French tragedy was compact, claustrophobic, and static. The plot or *intrigue* would begin at a point close to the *dénouement* and proceed on an elevated note until evil had been punished and good apotheosised. There were no mundane allusions, and no comic relief. A solemn stillness prevailed. Scene changes, exits, entrances, and physical movement were all kept to an absolute minimum. The number of characters was very small, and no more than three or four would occupy the stage at the same time. At least one of the cast was always a *confidant* or *confidante* who played no part in the story and whose sole function was to listen and comment while the hero or heroine disclosed private thoughts and momentous passion. These supernumeraries were remnants of the old Greek chorus. They were more or less indispensable, since soliloquies were avoided as unnatural and obstructive. Violent and vile action was hidden from view, and the audience learnt of great crimes and catastrophes from narration. The dramatist therefore had no resource save language; but language was strictly governed by *bienséance*. Brutal and indecent speech was as taboo as brutal and indecent deeds. The language of tragedy was defined by René Rapin, a seventeenth-century Jesuit critic, as 'words without lowness and vulgarity, diction that is noble and magnificent'. It was still being defined in those terms in 1833, when Alexandre Duval, playwright and French Academician, wrote an open letter to Victor Hugo. Duval, whose work included the one-act comedy *Shakespeare amoureux* ('Shakespeare in Love'), called Hugo and the recalcitrant Romantic writers to order by reminding them of what had made French tragedy legendary and enabled every respectable man to take his wife and daughters to the Comédie-Française. The list included 'a moral lesson'; heroes and heroines 'above the vulgar'; 'a clear yet varied plot'; language which was 'natural, energetic, and always elegant'; an ending that was either 'a catastrophe that [was] not too horrifying' or 'a dénouement which offend[ed] neither reason nor decency'.[32]

French playwrights were conscientious and prolific. Nearly 200 tragedies were premièred at the Comédie-Française between 1715 and 1789. There was no shortage of work cast in the mould of taste. Yet this abundance did not allay, it intensified rather, feelings of dissatisfaction and dismay. Discerning critics suspected that the French theatre was being cherished to death. The conventions, the rules, the reverence seemed to be fostering plays that were imitative and lifeless: false alike to history and to nature. In 1768 Mme du Deffand, after reading Shakespeare, wrote to Horace Walpole: 'He almost makes me believe … that the rules are a hindrance to genius … They chill, they extinguish …' A few years later the dramatist Louis-Sébastien Mercier said that France's much vaunted tragedy was no more than 'a phantom dressed up in purple and gold'. It was widely criticised for its stereotypes, platitudes, predictable dénouements, and repetitive working of the theme of love. There was *amour, amour,* and yet more *amour.* The baron de Grimm complained that the French tragic stage had become inundated with *mauvais goût,* and was puerile when judged by the standards of ancient Greece. 'Theatre', said Mme de Staël, 'is noble life – but it must be life.'[33]

After the discovery of Shakespeare some tentative efforts were made to vary the traditional formula. Plays began to appear with 'Shakespearean' innovations, such as plots from modern history and exotic settings. Diderot and Mercier proposed abandoning conventional tragedy altogether, and experimented with a new, hybrid form of serious theatre called *drame.* Much had been done by the early 1820s, when Stendhal published *Racine et Shakespeare,* a provocative call for an overhaul of the classical theatrical tradition. But Shakespeare himself still had not made his entry on to the French stage. Voltaire, and the ghost of Voltaire, had seen to that.

Voltaire was the tutelary presence in the French theatre during much of the eighteenth century. He was guardian of its mysteries and sacraments, and his spirit lingered there long after his death. It is remarkable how the world outside the theatre and the world within brought out two very different aspects of his complex personality. In the light of common day he challenged authority and tradition, lambasted tyranny, spoke in the accents of the Enlightenment. The lamplight of the stage revealed an intolerant autocrat, an unrepentant potentate of the *ancien régime.* No pontiff in a pulpit was more dogmatic than Voltaire in the theatre, the temple of his vocation.

Often, he despaired. He acknowledged the mediocrity of French drama since Racine. 'Our host of feeble tragedies is frightening', he wrote. 'There are nearly a hundred volumes of them. It's an enormous storehouse of boredom.' He tried to revitalise the exhausted *genre* by writing tragedies with modern subjects and American, Arabian, and even Chinese settings. He pruned the rampant superfluity of *galanterie* and *amour*. He increased the number of characters, introduced more action, and cut back descriptive *récit*. In *La Mort de César* he featured a plebeian mob and had a corpse brought on to the stage. Once, in *Mariamne*, he risked a death on stage – but only once, since audience reaction made it obvious he had gone too far. His *Adélaïde du Guesclin* made French theatrical history by exhibiting a wounded hero and requiring a cannon to be fired. He borrowed cautiously from Shakespeare. The ghost in *Hamlet* especially impressed him, and he used the idea in *Eriphyle* and in *Semiramis*. He always insisted, however, that stage productions of Shakespeare's own work were unthinkable. They would undermine civilisation, because once bad taste had been allowed to enter the theatre, it would be impossible to get rid of it. In other fields of art, barbarity spontaneously withered; but in the theatre it took root and flourished. In the theatre one often saw 'the worst works of every type enjoying prodigious success', buoyed up by 'the cabal and the stupid enthusiasm of the vulgar'.[34]

Chateaubriand linked the age of Romanticism with that of Voltaire by following in this way of thinking. He feared that Shakespearean theatre would be especially subversive in France. 'I'm not sure', he said,

> how far a nation which has masterpieces of every genre can revert to a liking for the monstrous without risking its morals. It is for this reason that the penchant for Shakespeare is so much more dangerous in France than in England. In an enlightened country, the good morals of a very polite people are more dependent on good taste than one thinks.

Judging by the history of Rome, the adulteration of 'les grands modèles' by foreign strains would hasten, not arrest, the national decline. Was not 'a confusion of dialects in the Roman Empire' the cause of the fall of Latin literature?[35] Even Stendhal, standard-bearer of the Romantic revolutionaries, jibbed at the idea of Shakespeare, or plays in the Shakespearean manner, on the French stage. 'It is essential', he emphasised, 'to steer well clear of the Shakespearean style.' Modern drama could have no truck with stage combat or stage executions. 'In the nineteenth century the spectator finds the horrible repugnant.' Verbal licence was no longer acceptable ('language, which is a matter of convention, must be respected ... and we should try to write like Pascal, Voltaire, and La Bruyère'), and authors must not 'lapse into tirade'. The modern ear was attuned to restraint and understatement in speech.[36]

No one blamed Shakespeare for the barbarism in his work. It was universally agreed that this derived not from Shakespeare himself but from the age in which he had lived. His misfortune had been to be born at a time when genius was not perfected, but corrupted, by the spirit of the age. 'Nature gave him all her diamonds', wrote Voltaire, 'but in that age it was impossible that they should be polished ones.' On another occasion he commented: 'He would have been a perfect poet if he had lived in the time of Addison.'[37] Villemain, in his essay of 1827, explained that in judging Shakespeare's faults it was necessary to bear in mind the period in which he worked. 'In all the countries of Europe except Italy, taste was at once rude and corrupted.'[38] Verlaine was still arguing in this way in the 1890s. He decided that in Shakespeare's work 'excess despotically rule[d] the immense ensemble', but that excess was a sign of his times.[39] This view of the matter preserved the kudos of genius. Since it was a force of nature, genius was essentially innocent. 'The closer a man is to nature', wrote Marmontel, 'the more ingenious he is ... Nature is always true, and everything which is exaggerated, mannered, forced, and out of place, derives from art.'[40] Genius was, as Voltaire said, 'respected', and it remained so for as long as the intellectual world was content, following the lead of the *Encyclopédie*, to recognise it and not define it. But in the middle years of the nineteenth century genius was defined, in terms supplied by the new science of psychiatry. The concept of decline was extended and medicalised, and in this new phase of the debate genius was discredited. From being proposed as part of the solution, it now figured as part of the problem.

The old idea (as old at least as Aristotle) that genius was a malediction, a mental disease, was revived and fortified in France by the erratic, feverish art of Romanticism, and by the example of Byron particularly. Byron helped to formulate in French minds the image of genius as tormented, deluded, and self-destructive.[41] Byron, says a character in Dumas' play *Teresa*, 'was a sort of fallen rebel angel, on whose brow God's finger had written: *Genius and Misfortune* [*Génie et Malheur*]'. Medical attention was directed to the eccentricities of art and literature by the prevailing concern about decadence. It redefined this as a global, rather than a national problem, and formulated the theory of *dégénéres-cence*. This postulated progressive physical and mental deterioration of the human species operating through heredity. Genius – literary genius especially – featured in this theory as a morbid symptom. In 1859 Jacques Moreau, a future director of the insane asylum at Salpêtrière and an emi-nent authority on mental medicine, published *La Psychologie morbide*, in which he claimed to demonstrate that genius was psychopathic. The genius was neurotic, 'un fou sublime' exhibiting aberrations fundamen-tally akin to those of insanity.[42] This polemic attracted a large audience in France, especially after the books of Cesare Lombroso (an Italian criminal psychologist) and of Max Nordau (his German populariser) had been translated into French. Shakespeare, inevitably, was drawn into its orbit, since there was much in his writing that suggested psychosis and moral degeneration. French opinion resisted, however, the attempt to pathologise him. In fact, he served to undermine the theory of genius as morbid. French psychiatry never fully accepted (as Lombroso did) that genius was madness, and one reason may well have been because Shakespeare, the archetypal genius, resisted such diagnosis.

The way to pathologisation had been opened by Rousseau, the Romantics, and the prominent literary critic Sainte-Beuve, who all pro-posed that art was autobiographical, an expression of the inner self;[43] and the substance, as well as the manner, of Shakespeare's work pushed the debate in this direction. The ability convincingly to portray madness was itself reckoned to be a symptom of madness.[44] Shakespeare was therefore made suspect by his most celebrated dramatic *tours de force*. Paul Bourget, whose medical training drew him to psychiatric specula-tion, deduced from the literary evidence a mental state akin to insanity. 'One shudders', he wrote,

> to think of the emotional crises that Shakespeare must have passed through when he was composing [*Hamlet* and *King Lear*], because both are con-cerned with that indefinite and transitory state of mind in which suffering is so intense that it borders on madness. The very short distance that separates devastating grief from mania is here documented with a precision that is frightening.

The note of homosexual obsession in the Sonnets indicated a moral per-version of the type that featured in the semiotics of degeneration. 'There are some which are very strange', wrote Bourget of these poems, 'and which seem to suggest that this man of genius was a victim of the most singular deviance of the heart and the imagination.'[45]

But this sort of inferential, speculative psychobiography served in the end only to increase ambivalence and uncertainty. For if Hamlet and Lear and the author of the Sonnets offered themselves as self-portraits, so too did Prospero – and who could be more sane, more redemptive and regenerative than he? 'Prospero is certainly Shakespeare', declared Emile Montégut. Like countless others, he read *The Tempest* as Shakespeare's literary testament, his valediction, in which he recapitulated and took his leave of the teeming universe of his creation. The whole play, Montégut maintained, was an allegorical autobiography. Like Prospero, Shakespeare had come as an impoverished fugitive to a primitive and hostile region (the London theatre), and like Prospero he had overmastered its bestial denizens (Marlowe and his like) and reclaimed it for the empire of light and art:

> Then the brambles began to bloom, the thickets of brushwood were transformed into luxuriant groves of verdure where people loved to meet, the horrible obscurity of the primitive forests was suddenly dissipated by the light of glittering apparitions, the thick mephitic air became sonorous and filled with melodies irresistible even to Caliban and his loutish companions and which will retain their power for as long as there exist on earth souls responsive to music and to poetry.[46]

Sainte-Beuve, who staked his reputation on his ability to read the lives of authors in their works, likewise discerned a sane, gentle, and unimpeachably sober Shakespeare – 'the most free of the creative geniuses and, without realising it, the greatest of the classics'.[47]

Because all the conflicting inferences were equally plausible, there was no escape from ambiguity and enigma. It therefore seemed more and more likely that the underlying assumption of critics like Sainte-Beuve was wrong. He, Rousseau, and the Romantics had been misguided in believing that authors' souls were imprinted on what they wrote. Acquaintance with Shakespeare's work made French critics aware not of authorial presence, but of authorial absence, at the centre of the literary text. The instance of Shakespeare indicated that in art the creative personality was divisible to the point of disintegration; that a great author was no one because he was everyone. His alone was the silent voice. No more was indisputable than the operation of an overreaching, mutating intelligence, echoing and invoking existential uncertainty. Germaine de Staël had noticed how Shakespeare's characters

> cause quite different reactions in the spectator during the course of the same play ... Shakespeare needs only a few words to capture the souls of his audience and bring them round from hatred to pity. The infinite diversity of the human heart constantly renews the source on which talent draws.[48]

Flaubert, in a letter of 1846, asked: 'Who can really tell me what Shakespeare liked, what he hated, what he felt?' No one could, because Shakespeare was among those few supreme artists who 'without being preoccupied with themselves, or with their own passions, throw aside their own personality in order to become absorbed in that of others [and] reproduce the universe'. Six years later, while rereading *The Merchant of Venice*, it became clear to him that 'an author, in his work, should be like God in the universe – present everywhere and visible nowhere'; and that an author, like Shakespeare, must not usurp God's privilege. He must not draw conclusions.[49] To Alfred de Vigny, Shakespeare's was a vagrant, volatile genius, constantly migrating through avatars of beauty and sadness:

> Rien ne trahit son cœur, hormis une Beauté
> Qui toujours passe, en pleurs, parmi d'autres figures
> Comme une pâle rayon dans les forêts obscures. *[50]

It was futile, warned Alfred Mézières, to interrogate the work of Shakespeare in order to discover Shakespeare himself. Shakespeare's writings were not an index to his psyche. Shakespeare, in Hamlet's words, held a mirror up to nature, and there were innumerable faces within its vast reflecting surface that could have been his own. 'If the poet is lurking behind Hamlet, why not also behind Othello? ... What state of mind has he not depicted in a striking manner?' There were as many Shakespeares as there were Shakespearean characters:

> Like the lawyer who defends today someone he will, if need be, accuse tomorrow, he experiences in turn the contradictory feelings of his heroes. He

---

*   Nothing betrays his heart, save a Beauty / Which is forever moving in tears among other forms / Like a pale ray in dark forests.

identifies with each of them, and although he creates their features after his own image, their image does not give us back his own.

Not even the Sonnets were a witness to the man, since they were 'rhé-torique artificielle' in the Petrarchian manner.[51] The novelist Jules Barbey d'Aurevilly could see in Shakespeare's work no sign of its author except the measure of coldness and callousness that was implied by his 'superb impassivity' ('superbe impassibilité'). This led him to conclude that the most moving art comes from the artists who are least moved, or whose emotions are most inscrutable. 'Shakespeare', he wrote, 'does not dogmatise. He exposes … and in such a powerful way, that your heart is wrung, and your brain is struck as by a discharge of thunderous electricity.'[52]

When Shakespeare entered the kingdom of Taste, it was shaken by a crisis of belief and of self-confidence. The dogmas and edicts by which it had been comforted and ruled lost much of their authority, and the faithful were forced from a sanctuary into unfamiliar and disturbing ways of thought. French cultural life entered an era of shifting founda-tions, varying parameters, and divided truth. What was guilt before one tribunal became innocence before another; judgements were reserved as strategies of evaluation collapsed; the Cartesian self fragmented and dis-solved; Proust refuted Sainte-Beuve; Barthes proclaimed the Death of the Author. French inquiry had probed the mystery of Shakespeare and retrieved only three certainties. It was impossible to recognise in his work either the Taste that civilisation demanded, or the madness that science deplored. But it was also impossible not to recognise the genius that no one could define, and without which art was sterile and a nation unprosperous and abject. Of that pentecostal afflatus there was no more compelling evidence anywhere.

3

Stranger within the Gates

Eighteenth-century French talk of Shakespeare as a barbarian was not just idle invective. It accorded with the prevailing interpretation of history. The common assumption was that civilisation had vanished with the end of Classical antiquity, and had not reappeared until the burgeoning of culture in France in the seventeenth century. The barrenness of the intervening 'Middle Age' (described by d'Alembert as 'a long interval of ignorance') had been relieved only in Medicean Florence, where a local resurrection of Classical art and learning had anticipated, on a less triumphant scale, the splendour of the French ascendancy.

During the nineteenth century, this view of history changed. The Gothic and feudal Middle Age became less dark, more richly endowed with art and spiritual life; and it contracted, making room for a fully developed prelude to modernity. This prelude involved much more than just the Florentine experience. It was an enlargement of European consciousness: a 'Renaissance' that not only recuperated the ancient world, but opened the way to the New World too. This idea of the Renaissance enhanced understanding of the history of civilisation, and served to restore its unity. 'Renaissance' denoted a distinctive style of European art, thought, literature, and conduct which, by both recalling the past and anticipating the future, mended the broken continuity of European culture and fortified the idea of progress.

The French discovery of Shakespeare preceded the discovery of the Renaissance and probably assisted it. Much of the early historiography dealt with the Renaissance in Italy; but the Renaissance was never conceived as something exclusively Italian. The writer who popularised the term was, as is the term itself, French; and he used it to designate a phase not of Italian but of European history. Michelet, in the ninth volume of his *Histoire de France* (1855), defined the Renaissance as 'the discovery of the world, the discovery of man'. It was the work not only of the

Italian humanists, painters, and architects, but of Columbus, Coperni-
cus, Galileo, Rabelais, Luther, Montaigne, Shakespeare, Cervantes, and
Calvin as well. They had unmasked both the earth and the heavens, and
'plumbed the deepest depths of human nature'.[1] The term 'Renaissance'
caught on, because the notion of intellectual and cultural rebirth was by
now familiar. It had appeared in rudimentary form thirty years before
in an essay on *Hamlet* by Guillaume-Prospère Brugière, baron de
Barante. 'We are dealing with a period', wrote de Barante, 'in which the
human spirit, long arrested, and captive in the trammels of an imper-
fect civilisation, begins to take flight, full of movement, curiosity, and
ardour.' In the 1840s, Philarète Chasles, again in an essay on Shakespeare, had sketched a portrait of what would later be recognised as a
'Renaissance man'. Chasles did not use the term, but once the term had
been coined it fitted closely the model he had constructed. According to
Chasles, Shakespeare's mind was of its time in its range and rationality.
It was steeped in Continental humanism. Shakespeare had read
Plutarch; he was familiar with the work of Ariosto, Tasso, Boccaccio,
and Petrarch; and he had, Chasles was convinced, made a close study of
Michel de Montaigne. He thus personified what would shortly become
known as the Renaissance: man's reconquest of dignity and freedom
through the agency of culture and reason. In Shakespeare, what Chasles
called 'the mysterious echo of the expiring Middle Ages' mingled with
the embryonic stirrings of ideas that would change the world.[2]

The role of Shakespeare in the discovery of the Renaissance remains
uncertain; but there is no doubt that the discovery of the Renaissance
assisted the appreciation of Shakespeare. It provided a new context in
which to place him; a new light by which to read him. He became a
European rather than a local phenomenon; a proto-modern rather than
a retarded barbarian. In his *Kultur der Renaissance in Italien* (1860),
Jacob Burckhardt compared Elizabethan England to the states of Renaissance Italy and claimed that Shakespearean drama was the Northern
equivalent of the Southern schools of painting. Alfred Mézières, in the
study of Shakespeare which he published the same year, adopted a similar argument. Shakespeare, he said, spoke in and to a society that had
irretrievably lost the simplicity of the archaic ages. He was part of 'a
learned and refined civilisation' which had made human relations
sophisticated and complex, intensified the conflict between man and the

natural world, and created new needs and expectations. Shakespeare's locution, with its jarring juxtapositions, overload of metaphor, and daring reaching out for new registers, new octaves of expression, represented sensibility and intelligence confronting the multiplied passions, illusions, and temptations of 'a society in labour'. Shakespeare stood at the intersection of the old and the new, and interpreted the one in the terms of the other. He took the rough, misshapen vessels of chronicles and popular tales, and filled them with vitality and fresh meaning. Shakespeare's characters, unlike those of Racine and the French theatre, lived before and beyond the events narrated, and their psychological verisimilitude imposed consistency and coherence on the old ramshackle scenarios. Furthermore, they created their own destiny. In place of the Classical scheme of pre-ordained necessity, Shakespeare depicted humanity perturbed by manifold possibility, both for good and for evil. He subjected his primitive material to the 'révolution intellectuelle' that was achieving liberty and humanistic dignity for his contemporaries of Northern Europe. Henry V, the most finished and charismatic of his heroes, was the archetype of the 'homme des temps modernes'.[3]

Chasles and Mézières were critics of weight and authority. Nevertheless their presentation of Shakespeare as a common heritage of the Renaissance long remained neglected in France. It was overtaken by racialist ideology, which permeated all levels of critical thinking from the middle of the nineteenth century until the First World War. During this time the dominant idea in intellectual responses to Shakespeare was not that of cultural affinity, but that of ethnic variance. He was much more readily understood as an Anglo-Saxon peculiarity than as a Renaissance humanist. His was the most intractably foreign of all the foreign presences in the French cultural firmament. Racialism referred to Shakespeare in order to substantiate the notion of otherness and antithesis that was the essence of its thinking about the hinterland beyond the Channel. According to racialist doctrine, there was an *esprit français* which was fundamentally incompatible with the Anglo-Saxon, or Germanic, spirit of Shakespeare. Where Shakespeare flourished, the *esprit français* withered; where the *esprit français* flourished, Shakespeare was resisted and would remain so for as long as the French were French.

Three attributes constantly recurred in the inventories of difference:

fog, the Bible, and Shakespeare. The ubiquity of these things across the Channel made that narrow strait a frontier as indelible as any that was ever drawn on a map. Every French schoolboy knew that the English were shrouded in perpetual fog, always reading the Bible, and fanatically addicted to Shakespeare. And it was known that when they left the fog behind, they took the Bible and Shakespeare with them. Paul Bourget, who claimed to understand them as well as any Frenchman could, wrote in 1882 of Englishmen embarking for India 'with a Shakespeare and a Bible in their baggage'.[4] On this triple foundation was erected the stereotype of the islander: pious, poetic, introverted, splenetic, and driven by circumambient gloom either to retreat into lamplit domesticity, or to break through, and conquer the sunlit world beyond. Even as late as the end of the twentieth century there lingered a vestige of this image in French depictions of Britain. The fog and the Bible had by then been dropped, as a concession to clean-air legislation and post-Christian hedonism. But the assumption about Shakespeare remained. English was (and is) still referred to as 'la langue de Shakespeare', and the axis of the English mentality was still reckoned to run through London and Stratford.

Bardolatry featured as the English form of atavism as early as the early eighteenth century. French visitors to London who went to the theatre – and most, it seems, did – inferred from the frequency with which Shakespeare was still performed that he was a truly national poet whose work had become inextricably absorbed into the national way of life and way of thinking. The jubilee organised by David Garrick in 1769 to commemorate the bicentenary of Shakespeare's birth was widely reported in the French press as a characteristically English event. The French public was assured that the celebrations were an endorsement by the whole nation of its greatest poet.[5] Voltaire's diatribe against Le Tourneur's translation of Shakespeare aroused anxiety and dismay. The *Correspondance Littéraire* assured its readers that the implications for Anglo-French relations could not but be 'infiniment graves'. Was it conceivable, it asked, in view of 'the idolatrous cult of the genius of Shakespeare professed by the whole English nation', that this insult would pass unrequited?

> Will [the English] allow the Académie Française calmly to debate the validity of this cult? Will they recognise the competence of these foreign judges?

Will they not contrive to set up their own party at the very heart of our literary world? Has it been forgotten how much hatred, sectarianism, and fury have been produced by quarrels of this nature, and for causes much less worthy?[6]

Voltaire himself had acknowledged that there was a *culte* of Shakespeare in England.[7] Germaine de Staël reckoned that such veneration of an author was unique: 'The English feel for Shakespeare the most profound enthusiasm ever felt by any people for a writer.'[8] Villemain, writing of the canonisation of Shakespeare by English critics, observed that 'the admiration of his genius [had] become, as it were, a national superstition'.[9] A century later, Henry de Montherlant included English worship of Shakespeare among the 'idolâtries intolérantes' of modern times.[10] As late as 1979 a French scholar was claiming that Bardolatry defined English culture at both the higher and the popular level, and that the English response to Shakespeare compounded reverence with worship: 'One commits oneself to Shakespeare by an act of faith, formalised by the frequentation of his plays.' Stratford had become a site of pilgrimage, replete with shrine, ritual, hordes of votaries, and a thriving trade in relics. 'In the department stores editions of the works lie beside keyrings with images of Falstaff.' Inveterate attachment had been made even closer by the loss of worldly eminence. Always associated with English patriotism, Shakespeare had become the comfort of a nation in decline. The English now cherished him because they saw in his global reputation 'proof of Albion's empire over the universe'. He was their consolation for the loss of India; the solace of their post-imperial abjection.[11]

The idea of an obsession itself became obsessive, and contradictory evidence went unnoticed. The Garrick jubilee had in fact aroused widespread ridicule and satire in England, and the crowds who were flocking to Stratford 200 years later had clearly been set in motion not by national *angst* and atavism but by the phenomenon of international tourism. Nevertheless, there is much to be learnt from the French conviction. It shows how in France Shakespeare and his nationality became so closely identified that hardly anyone could think of either except in terms of the other. Critics were unwilling, or unable, to separate the writer from England, or England from the writer. 'Never', wrote Villemain, 'was poet more national.' Shakespeare was, he said, typical of his nation in his 'force and lofty bearing, his severity, his profundity, and his melancholy'. In Shakespeare's characters, whatever their ostensible nationality, Englishmen and Englishwomen could always recognise themselves; and the originality, spontaneity, and republican nonconformity of his style clearly bespoke the English temperament.[12] Bourget, likewise, called Shakespeare 'the most English of all the poets ... profoundly, intimately English'; and he judged that Shakespeare's drama, 'with its audacities of blood, carnage, and triviality, combined with the most suave, the most delicate of poetic aspirations', mirrored the English personality, which was 'uncouth to the point of brutality, fierce to the point of violence, and hard to the point of cruelty' – but also 'visionary', 'meditative', 'poetic', and prone to 'deep reflection'.[13]

The discovery of what was apparently a symbiosis between a writer and a people, of a nation seemingly enthralled by a dramatist's art, was very significant. It opened up in France a new area of social-scientific inquiry, and it helped to shape a new understanding of the art of writing. In the ferment of this discovery the modern concept of 'literature' was born.

Before the French knew of Shakespeare, wherever French was spoken or known the word *littérature* had no specific meaning.[14] It was used interchangeably with *lettres* and *science* to denote knowledge, or learning in general. The *République des lettres* comprised all who were in any way erudite or studious. Until 1765, the Dictionary of the Académie Française defined *lettres* as 'toute sorte de science et de doctrine'. The adjective *littéraire* meant 'intellectual' in the broadest sense. Poets, mathematicians, historians, jurisconsults, *savants* of every type were known as *gens littéraires*. There were vague and loose divisions within the *République des lettres*. The term *belles lettres* was sometimes used to distinguish the writings of humanists from those of divines. There were, however, no national or disciplinary frontiers. No one talked about 'foreign' literature, or 'English literature', or 'French literature' – or about 'literature' as opposed to 'science'.

It was during the second half of the eighteenth century that the word *littérature* was pluralised and restricted. It came to mean imaginative and non-utilitarian writing – poetry, drama, novels, and essays. 'A distinction is made', explained Jaucourt when writing about *lettres* in the *Encyclopédie*, 'between *gens de lettres* who cultivate a varied and graceful erudition, and those who dedicate themselves to *sciences* which are more abstruse and more obviously useful.' La Harpe, in the preface to his *Cours de la littérature ancienne et moderne* (1799–1805), linked *littérature* to 'the arts of the spirit and the imagination'. By now, too, the notion of a Literature was being supplanted by that of many literatures. Each literature was made within and for a single nation, and consecrated not the collective voice of humanity but the language in which it was written. This fragmentation seems to have been part of a reaction, in Catholic circles especially, against the Cartesians (or *géomètres*) and *philosophes*, who assumed that mankind was always and everywhere the same. By encouraging the belief that humanity was universally *raisonnable* and *conséquent*, they were, declared the abbé Du Bos, preparing a havoc comparable to that once wrought by the Goths and the Vandals.[15] The discovery of a distinctive, national literature in England accelerated the intellectual change and made it clear that there was no equivalent literature in France. There was literature in French; but there was no French literature. In an essay on dramatic art published in 1773, Louis-Sébastien Mercier observed that French classical tragedy, the most noteworthy genre in the language, was not popular: 'Shakespeare is much more of a national poet for the English than Corneille is for us.'[16] Mme de Staël agreed. 'French poetry', she wrote,

> is the only poetry that has no popular appeal ... Our French poets are admired by all cultivated minds at home and throughout the rest of Europe; but they are completely unknown to the common people and even to the bourgeoisie of the towns, because the arts in France have not, as they have elsewhere, developed from the native beauties of the country itself.[17]

A truly French literature was precluded by the absence of a truly national language. French was an international tongue. It was spoken by educated people throughout Europe and Russia, but in France itself it was largely confined to the Ile-de-France, the northern area around Paris. Elsewhere the prevalence of *patois* and of regional vernaculars, such as Basque and the Occitan dialects, meant that until the First World War communication was often more difficult between two Frenchmen than it was between a Frenchman and a German, Russian, or Pole. In a world increasingly configured by self-aware and self-confident Anglo-Saxons, this lack of a national language and a national

literature became ominous. It seemed to suggest a deficiency of patriotic purpose and resilience. The French intelligentsia therefore laboured
to invent what they could not discover. Histories of 'la littérature
française' proliferated in the nineteenth and twentieth centuries, all
heeding the summons that Désiré Nisard had issued in his prototype
of the 1840s: 'What we have to study, to delineate with precision, is the
very foundation, the soul of our France, as it is manifest in surviving
writing.' Generations of academics guided generations of students
through the literary deposits of centuries, rummaging, sifting, comparing, and classifying, in an urgent concern to reveal 'that which [was]
constant and immutable in the *esprit français*'.[18]

Literature, thus redefined, became prominent among French intellectual concerns, and the supposed synergy between Shakespeare and
his nation intrigued those who would understand why literature existed;
why writers wrote and why they wrote in the way they did. French opinion roamed speculatively over the relationship between the English and
English literature. It tended now to the view that the nation had created the literature; now to the view that the literature had created the
nation. Louis Riccoboni, director of the Comédie-Italienne in Paris,
argued in the 1740s that the sanguinary violence of English tragedy
was determined by the phlegmatic, ruminative temperament of the
English. If the stage were not continually deluged in blood, they would
fall asleep.[19] Rousseau reckoned that a nation's theatre was more directly
expressive of the collective humour: 'An intrepid, grave, and cruel
people demand deadly and dangerous festivals ... A ferocious and
hot-headed people demand blood and combat ... A voluptuous people demand music and dancing.' Drama therefore merely reflected
and reinforced the national disposition.[20] This theory offered a plausible explanation for the distinctive colouring of Shakespeare's plays. In
France these were classified as *sombre*. Shakespeare's work, according
to the eighteenth-century poet Jacques Delille, was filled with 'debris ...
shadows ... tombs ... ghosts ... assassins ... fear, pain, and mourning'
which made it strongly redolent of the English climate and the English
character as they featured in French accounts.[21] Villemain reckoned
that the famous soliloquy of Hamlet could have been conceived only
in a land of fog and spleen. Likewise, the darkness and cruelty in
Macbeth and *King Lear* recalled the bloody history of the English, and

their passion for sadistic sports and pastimes.[22] Hamlet, said Bourget, was

> an Englishman, and conceived as such ... The 'fat' and sturdy Hamlet, madly keen on violent exercise ... who is the first to leap on board when a pirate vessel attacks his ship, is at the same time an inveterate scrutiniser of his own conscience. Put a Bible into his hands and you at once transform him into a puritan of the time of Cromwell.[23]

French commentaries were littered with such linkings and analogies. Yet Shakespeare was a genius – that was axiomatic – and the essence of genius was originality. It was determining, not determined. The genius as demiurge was not coerced by period and circumstance. He was a sovereign whose acts of imagination created new forms, proposed new models, and shaped a society and an age via the work and thoughts of disciples and admirers. Geniuses were authors of themselves. 'Ils se sont formés de leurs propres mains', wrote Du Bos.[24] If Shakespeare had been born in France, said Delacroix, the whole history of French taste would have been different. Art and literature were not moulded by national character. They were created freely by outstanding individuals. It was they who moulded the national character, by leading opinion and setting literary fashions.[25] According to this way of thinking, Shakespeare had created the Englishness of the English – above all by forging the language that became the vehicle of English religion and the matrix of English consciousness. 'It is great poets', declared Voltaire,

> who have determined the spirit of languages ... It was Shakespeare who, barbarous as he was, gave to English the strength and the energy which it has ever since been impossible to increase without overstraining and consequently weakening the language.[26]

It was Shakespeare who had fostered the English sense of nationality. By bringing the country's history out of obscure chronicles and on to the public stage, by attracting all degrees of rank and fortune into the community of the theatre audience, he had nurtured the collective memory and patriotic sentiment. Furthermore he had been his nation's schoolmaster. His plays abounded in striking maxims, aphorisms, and precepts. They were a common fund of proverbial wisdom. And by forsaking art for nature, he had held up a mirror wherein the English could observe themselves and discover familial links and resemblances across rifts of time and circumstance.

Discussion along these lines was important in the intellectual affairs of nineteenth- and twentieth-century France because it exposed, and reinforced, a difference of opinion about literature and the way it should be studied. If Englishness had, so to speak, created Shakespeare, then literature moved in the orbit of the social sciences – history, ethnology, sociology, social psychology. It was the expression of a collective consciousness, and great writers were paradigmatic, voices of their age. If, on the other hand, Shakespeare had created Englishness, then literature was a metaphysical, inexplicable phenomenon. It derived from some mysterious, autonomous force that operated not within but upon history, subjecting it to the random impulses of inspiration and imagination.

Between the ebbing of Romanticism in the 1840s and the seismic shocks of the 1960s, the notion of literature as spontaneous and independent was in abeyance. The pedagogical hierarchy in French lycées and universities interpreted the literary work as essentially a paraphrase of its time and its environment; as a distillation of sources, influences, and traditions. Senior patriarchs of this academic tribe were Ferdinand Brunetière, who taught at the Ecole Normale Supérieure and became editor of the *Revue des Deux Mondes* in 1893; and Gustave Lanson, a professor at the Sorbonne. Brunetière insisted that writers should be studied not in isolation but within a literary-historical sequence. No work of literature was so unique that it did not relate to the works that had come before and those that came after. 'In literature as in art', he told his students in 1889, 'after the influence of the individual, the principal action in operation is that of works on other works.'[27] Lanson, whose *Histoire de la littérature française* (1894) served many generations of school and university students, taught that 'literature is the expression of society', and that the great writer is 'in large measure a repository of previous generations, a gatherer of contemporary movements'. The writer of genius, he insisted, is 'the product of an environment and the representative of a group'. It was the function of genius 'to sum up and to symbolise the life of an epoch and a community'.[28] Brunetière and Lanson and their followers expounded literature as a 'discipline' requiring to be studied historically, sociologically, and comparatively. Nothing was entirely *sui generis* or coincidental. A national literature was an organism, an elaborate tissue of 'movements', 'schools', 'genres', 'periods', 'sources', and 'influences', which it was the function of criticism to distinguish, describe, and relate.

The agenda for this long debate had been set by Germaine de Staël as far back as the early 1800s. In her essay *De la Littérature* she proposed 'the influence of religion, manners, and laws on literature' as a topic of critical investigation. In *De l'Allemagne* she claimed that the difference between French and English poetry originated in 'the primitive sources of imagination and thought'. But it was Hippolyte Taine who made the decisive break with traditional connoisseurship, by treating literature as something scientific rather than aesthetic.

Taine's *Histoire de la littérature anglaise*, published in five volumes in 1864, belongs with those magisterial surveys that were the nineteenth-century contribution, brave and doomed, to the perennial Western effort to reduce the cosmos to system and syntax. Taine's leading idea was that genius was more determined than determining, and that a literature was meaningful only if read in the light of natural and social conditions. History, he maintained, was a matter of psychology. It was states of mind that made things happen. But no state of mind was random or isolated. No man is an island ('l'homme n'est pas seule dans le monde'), and it had been the cardinal intellectual error of previous generations to believe that history was made by exceptional individuals – by heroes, criminals, and geniuses. It was the case, rather, that the heroes, criminals, and geniuses were made by history. Taine's psychology discounted idiosyncrasy. It postulated that states of mind are not spontaneous but an index of the circumstances it summarised famously as *race, milieu,* and *moment.* Race was the constant in the equation. It connoted the 'innate and hereditary dispositions' of a human group. These never varied. 'In every age, under every civilisation, a people is always the same.' *Milieu,* or environment, subsumed 'differences of sky and soil', 'political circumstances', and 'social conditions'. *Moment* referred to a historical period and its 'conception dominatrice'. There is no state of mind, said Taine, no chemistry of consciousness, that is not governed by these three contingencies. A work of genius is a transcription of a general state of mind, since genius is the brilliant epitome of the collective mentality. It is the voice of the 'hidden world';

of 'invisible humanity'. Manifestations of genius – as literature, art, religion, or philosophy – therefore explain the past and unlock the secret of those general laws of psychology that ordain the future. Taine reckoned he could have substantiated his thesis from the evidence offered by any one of three literatures: Greek, French, and English. All were mature, extensive, and richly expressive. He had chosen English literature because it was living and therefore easily available to students, and because as a Frenchman he could view it from the distance which disclosed its distinctive patterns and contours. Furthermore there existed within English literature evidence of a state of mind of unparalleled fertility and intensity. The Elizabethan drama, with Shakespeare as its supreme master, indicated a sudden and full expansion of human nature: a rebirth so complete that it rendered obsolete the medieval past. It registered the whole spectrum of human passion; encompassed life in all its superabundance and complexity.[29]

For all its revisionist posture and scientific jargon, Taine's book had a familiar ring. The influence of climate on national character and the progress of the arts had been mooted by Du Bos and Montesquieu over a century before. Moreover, Taine drew heavily on the fund of stereotypes and commonplaces about England and the English that had been beguiling the French public for 150 years and more. All the ingredients of the myth reappeared in Taine's work – the barbarism and brutality, the fog, the Bible, the domesticity, the sluggish sensibility requiring strong stimuli, the palates excoriated by red meat and pharmaceutical beverages. The fog he worked to death. *Brouillard* is such a dominant presence in his book that it threatens to undermine the primacy of race. It alone, it seems, explains Englishness. It induces introspection, which emphasises subjectivity, which stimulates abnormal strength of will, which leads to intractability and an urge to roam and conquer:

> the sky disgorges rain, the earth sends back mist, the mist creeps through the rain; everything is drowned ... This is truly the Cimmerian country of Homer ... A climate such as this ordains action, forbids idleness, develops energy, counsels patience.[30]

Taine's detailed account of English literature, likewise, does little more than amplify the clichés of French opinion. He writes of a rank, overgrown wilderness; of 'surabondance et dérèglement'.[31] English literature wanted finish, smacked of improvisation, eschewed abstraction, and traded in images rather than in ideas. Its prevailing qualities were excess, incoherence, coarseness, prolixity. The polished productions of Pope, Dryden, and Addison occupied a brief interlude between the formless fecundity of Shakespearean and Jacobean drama, and the equally form-less and fertile eighteenth- and nineteenth-century novel.

The essentials of this verdict were perennial. They still had a long life after Taine and were repeated by Montégut, Anatole France, Paul Claudel, and André Gide, among others.[32] Taine's description of the Anglo-Saxon people, however, was already seeming out of date at the time it was published. Taine had read an enormous amount of English literature, but his knowledge of the English hardly extended beyond what he had read. His understanding of the *race* and the *milieu*, as well as of the *moment*, was itself derived from literature, since his book was virtually complete before he made his first, brief excursion across the Channel.[33] He had constructed an England from the literature, and then explained the literature by the construction. This hermeneutic circular-ity was made obvious by the accounts brought back from Britain by a new generation of travellers. These revealed not a correspondence but a contradiction between the race and the literature. The unruly writing had been produced by an orderly people. Taine diagnosed Anglo-Saxon psychology in the chaos, excess, and recalcitrance of Shakespeare's work; yet the French visitors who came to Britain in ever increasing numbers in the early decades of the nineteenth century had discovered no such equivalence. The Anglo-Saxons struck them as remarkable for their self-mastery, social discipline, political moderation, and obedience.[34] The English of the old myth – heretics, regicides, and revolutionaries – had given way to a people orderly in disorder, and calmly turbulent.

Philarète Chasles (who lived among them for many years) wrote of 'la liberté réglée et l'ordre passionné' of the island race. 'In England', he said, 'regularity is habitual and liberty is in the soul.'[35] The exemplary conduct of the British troops who had occupied Paris after the defeat of France in 1815 seems to have predisposed French observers to a gener-ous view, and they now commented less and less on the coarseness and violence, and more and more on the restraint and decorum of Englishness.[36] Many travellers remarked on the absence of unkempt nature in England. They found a landscape that was like a garden, and gardens that were like a landscape. Outdoors and indoors alike, the country was all contrived informality – or informal contrivance.[37] Even Chateaubriand, whom years first of exile then of ambassadorial service in London had left unreconciled to the materialism and mercantile opportunism of the English, admired the even tenor of their ways. In England, he explained, social and political change was moderated by tradition, the past prefigured the future, and republican sentiments were contained within monarchical institutions.[38] The English, wrote Montégut, were 'truly free people, fiercely independent, yet more submissive, more obedient, than if they had been trained all their lives under a paternal absolutism or according to the code of the Jesuits of Paraguay'.[39] Taine was aware that the modern Anglo-Saxons seemed to be incongruous with the spirit of their ancestral literature, yet it remained a fundamental article of his creed that racial psychology never changed. He dealt with the paradox by insisting that the ancestral characteristics were still there, beneath the surface. 'Even today,' he wrote, 'the militant passions, the sombre humour, subsist beneath the regularity and well-being of modern manners.'[40] Ostensible conformity and amenability masked an innate, inveterate unruliness. The work of recent authors such as Byron and Dickens, clamorous with protest and dissent, demonstrated clearly that the instinct of revolt was in the race.[41]

Taine was often accused of selecting and manipulating his evidence. He was generally judged as more plausible than convincing.[42] His most prominent critic was Sainte-Beuve, who complained of his relentless emphasis. He found Taine's lapidary, rigidly symmetrical prose a poor substitute for 'the discursive manner ... of those promenades in the style of Montaigne, where you seem to move straight ahead to the pleasures of adventure and serendipity'. Taine was 'tiring to follow and heavy reading'. His monumentality, his invocation of 'a great universal power which includes an infinite variety of beings and accidents', bludgeoned, it did not persuade, the reader – because it left the essential mystery ('the how of creation or of formation') intact. Taine found the evidence he was looking for and ignored the rest. He said nothing of what came between general causes and specific effects.[43] That was difficult to gainsay; yet fifty years later it was Sainte-Beuve's reputation, not Taine's, that was in eclipse. The Histoire de la littérature anglaise reached its eleventh edition in 1903.

The reproach levelled against it in academic quarters was not that it had transformed literature from a delightful pastime into a dismal science, but that it had neglected Darwin. Brunetière commented that in stressing the inexorability of race, Taine had lost sight of evolution. Race was not immutable. It was modified by natural selection, which occurred as a result of chance variation. Idiosyncrasy remained at the margin of Taine's theory, whereas it was at the centre of Darwin's.[44] Louis Cazamian, a leading scholar of the next generation, told his students at the Sorbonne that 'the philosophy of *race, milieu* and *moment* [had] collapsed', since it had failed to take into account evolution and adaptation. The English race had developed psychologically as its environment had changed ('le type même de la race se modifie'). Nevertheless, Cazamian retained Taine's idea of a deep permanent substratum of racial psyche, and it was in this that literature had its source. Literature was a 'revenge of instinct' against moral constraints and external influences. A 'histoire littéraire nationale' was racially determined in its broad configuration and merely modified in its accidentals by the 'multiple effects of circumstances of all kinds'.[45]

The prospect of submergence, of absorption into a cultural hegemony not of its own making, weighed all the more heavily on French educated society in that such an eventuality seemed to lie in the logic of evolution. 'There is no doubt', said Cazamian, 'that a European psychological rhythm has for a long time been developing ... brought about by growing convergence between the general conditions of civilisation.'[46] Taine's *Histoire* continued to command respect probably because it was a powerful antidote against such implications. The whole work is an extended fabric of comparisons and contrasts. It harps continuously and heavily on the theme of difference. Arresting phrases and trenchant aphorisms, fluent paragraphs and copious quotations all reinforce the contention that what is Anglo-Saxon, or Teutonic, is, and must always be, the antithesis of what is French, or Latin. 'People over there', declared Taine, 'are other than they are here' ('l'homme là-bas est autre que chez nous').[47] The Revolutionary and Napoleonic Wars had been the clash not of two governments, but of 'two civilisations and two doctrines'.[48] The French were often told that they were a nation, not a race; nevertheless, viscerally enthralled by this perception of England as the Other, the anti-France, they continued to think of themselves as both. 'The more I have travelled', wrote Paul Bourget,

> the more evidence I have found that, between one people and another, civilisation has not modified the radical differences pertaining to race. It has merely covered with a uniform varnish the exterior aspects of those differences ... Ninety-nine times out of a hundred there is between an Anglo-Saxon and a Gallo-Roman a mutual incomprehensibility, an invincible diversity of mentality and feeling.[49]

Cazamian confirmed this. 'The sentiment of difference', he said, 'is in our bones after prolonged contact with the rough originality of the British.'[50]

During the two decades that followed the controversial conviction of the Jewish Captain Dreyfus of treason (1894), when French writing and thinking were steeped in 'the Affair' and intellectual nationalism resounded from printed page and public tribune, Taine's book remained popular because it told the French quite clearly who they were. The acrimony and recrimination of these years were extraordinary even in the context of French intellectual life. Educated Paris tore itself apart. But although patriotic militants of the Action Française, the Ligue de la Patrie Française, and the Ligue de la Culture Française often lacerated one another, they found a common inspiration in Taine. His racial anthropology had identified in classicism a shibboleth of Frenchness. The clarity and scientific precision of his style served as a Gallic rebuke to the allusiveness and intuitionism of Teutonic-Semitic Romantics and mystics.[51] In an atmosphere poisoned by diatribe, invective, aggression, and emotion, the reader of Taine was reassured that 'French' meant ordered, restrained, decorous, coherent, and intellectually rigorous.

All sense of irony was lost as the ideology of Taste was subsumed in the fiction of race. Relativism had become the new orthodoxy of critical thinking. In 1884 Paul Bourget was signalling the terminal decline of Cartesianism. 'Is not the variety of intelligence', he asked, 'one of the discoveries – dangerous perhaps, but certainly definitive – of our age?' The philosophical foundation of traditional criticism, the Cartesian dogma of the 'identité des esprits', had, he said, collapsed in the reassessments that followed the discovery of foreign literatures in the early years of the nineteenth century and the adoption of racialism by 'scientific' thinkers such as Taine. 'It became evident ... that there are many legitimate ways of thinking, of feeling, and, consequently, of attaining to a sense of Beauty.' One catalyst of the change had been the discovery of Shakespeare, which had discredited the old juridical school of criticism and its manual of aesthetics: 'Shakespeare had composed superior poetic dramas by following procedures quite the opposite of those used by Racine in writing his tragedies. But had not [Shake-spearean] drama and [Racinean] tragedy an equal claim to admiration?'[52] French standards now replaced universal standards as the criteria by which Shakespeare was judged. Shakespeare, wrote Georges Pellissier in 1886, offended the 'génie national' of France by violating the 'goût classique'.[53] Another scholar asserted in 1921 that it was 'a funda-mental tendency of our race' to require 'clarity and simplicity in all things'. In France, therefore, 'however enthusiastic we may feel about Shakespeare, we shall always prefer Racine'.[54] To Germaine de Staël and her generation *classique* had signified the predilection of a cosmopolitan élite. To the generations taught by Taine it signified a racial habit and cast of mind. They referred constantly to 'l'esprit classique français'. This French classical spirit was, according to the cultural historian Emile Faguet, composed of 'clarity ... order ... logic, and ... a certain taste for liveliness and alertness'. Its presence in France had been evident as far back as the Middle Ages; it had revived during the Renaissance; and it had triumphed in the seventeenth-century theatre. French classical drama was the expression of a national temperament 'more sensible than passionate, more logical than imaginative, more disposed to com-pose than to invent'. It showed the French to be a people who, 'while very artistic, have done the most to make art rational'.[55]

Shakespeare figured prominently in this therapy of self-definition and self-assertion. As the quintessentially Anglo-Saxon author, he became the measure of what a French author was not, and could not, be. He was not merely different; he was alien. This was the gist of a genial though serious book published in 1894. Its title was *Shakespeare en France sous l'ancien régime* and its author was Jean-Jules Jusserand, a scholar and diplomat who became French ambassador to the United States in 1903. Jusserand claimed that the crude and colourful French drama of the six-teenth and early seventeenth centuries – that of Hardy, de La Serre, Schélandre, La Calprenède, and others – had been banished from the stage by popular disapproval. The old plays, with their battles, murders, arbitrary treatment of time and space, national and medieval subjects, and intermixture of comedy and tragedy, all written in extravagant, unbridled language, fell out of favour because 'the whole nation, chiefs and all, thirsted for regularity and good order'. Even Corneille had been compelled by public opinion to abide by the classical rubric. This was clear evidence that 'beneath the various elements of which French minds [were] formed, the Latin substratum [would] always remain'. A French mind, wrote Jusserand, was 'inamoured of straight lines, [and] too strongly tempered to be metamorphosed'. For this reason Shakespeare, 'so different, so powerful, so universal', would never be acclimatised in France. 'All the care in the world will not make fine olive trees grow in Scotland, nor fir trees in Algeria.'[56]

In Jusserand's view French resistance to Shakespeare was a symptom of strong and salutary multiculturalism. Others were less confident of the resilience of Frenchness. They regarded Shakespeare as a threat, and argued that he should be kept out of French schools and universities. 'There is no better weapon for youth', wrote Anatole France, 'than Latin strength.' He conceded that *Hamlet* was a work of cosmic magnitude; but what was a French schoolboy to make of it?

> How can he grasp those phantasmal ideas, more elusive than the phantom wandering on the battlements of Elsinore? How can he find his way through the chaos of those images, as uncertain as the clouds whose changing forms are pointed out to Polonius by the melancholy youth? ... This can never be a 'classic' for us.[57]

A similar reaction came from André Gide, despite his low opinion of Taine. Gide believed that behaviour is governed by influences so subtle and so inscrutable that our working hypothesis can be only that we are free. Genius, as Oscar Wilde had said, was always ahead of its time, answering questions that others have not yet asked.[58] Furthermore, Gide – owing perhaps to his Protestant education – had a hankering after historical truth. He acknowledged that French had not always been the chaste, crystalline medium that was now so impermeable to Shakespeare. In his preface to the Pléiade edition of Shakespeare's works, published in 1938, he recalled that the language of Ronsard and Montaigne had possessed a 'plaisante plasticité' which permitted 'merveilleuses inventions verbales'. And when he sounded his own note of caution about the use of Shakespeare in French schools, he seemed to concede that Frenchmen and Frenchwomen were not born, but made: 'With Shakespeare a child may be stirred, feel his heart swell with sublime emotion – but he will learn neither to reason well, nor to write well.' Yet it was Gide, again in the Pléiade preface, who contrived to summarise in a single sentence the intellectual retreat from Literature to literatures, from the Republic of Letters to disparate ethnic mentalities. 'Shakespeare', he wrote, 'has little heed for that logic without whose support our Latin spirits stumble.'

The illusion was that Shakespeare was being resisted because he was alien. The reality was that he was being resisted because he was familiar. No generation of French intellectuals so routinely laundered the national history and the collective memory in order to foster the hallowed myth of difference. To Gide's seniors and contemporaries, history in France was unique, was French, because amidst the platitudes of social and political disarray, a *rappel à l'ordre* had again and again been heard and obeyed. This was the ancestral summons, redeeming tragedy and turmoil. France, to this generation, did not mean the Wars of Religion and the war of the Fronde, the atrocities of the Revolution, the devastation and carnage of the Commune, the public displays of *sensibilité* and emotion. Nor did it mean petticoats, black stockings, and raucous *joie de vivre* in Parisian music halls. It meant the Catholic monarchy; the cults of Reason and Taste; the Napoleonic epic of regeneration; the heroic defiance of Prussian barbarism; the theatre of Molière and Racine. Seventeenth-century drama they revered as Frenchness in its purest manifestation. Gustave Larroumet, lecturing at the Odéon in 1888, called it 'an admirable art, a unique moment, in which the faculties of our race, having reached their plenitude and perfect equilibrium, found expression in works that equal or surpass all their rivals'.[59] They ignored the well-documented indifference of the wider French public to this art. Rousseau had testified that the Comédie-Française had difficulty in attracting audiences of more than 300.[60] Alfred de Musset had written of theatres half empty when the classics were performed:

> J'étais seul, l'autre soir, au Théâtre-Français,
> Ou presque seul; l'auteur n'avait pas grand succès.
> Ce n'était que Molière ... *[61]

---

* I was alone, the other evening, in the Théâtre-Français / Or almost alone; the author was not having much success. / It was only Molière ...

But two million people lined the streets for the funeral of Victor Hugo. Sarah Bernhardt could fill huge theatres over and over again with plays by Sardou and with *La Dame aux camélias* by Dumas fils. Not even Bernhardt, however, the most popular and celebrated actress in French theatrical history, dared risk Racine in her standard commercial repertoire. Phèdre was one of her legendary roles, but she only ever played it at special matinées.[62] The 'esprit classique français' had no existence save as the figment of a marginalised intelligentsia. By identifying the 'classical spirit' with what was French, they were aiming to invalidate a world order that was no longer French. They were humanists who no longer believed in Humanity, who retreated into the idea of many races as the actuality of one culture worked more and more to undermine them. Terms like 'esprit français', 'âme française', and 'âme latine' bespeak a fear of submergence and annihilation. They were arms against the agents of the alternative internationalism – especially those defined by Charles Maurras, leading polemicist of the Right, as 'the four confederated estates': Jews, Protestants, Freemasons, and dagos ('métèques'). Less specific but no less insidious for French intellectuals was 'the spirit of the North', encroaching on the territory of their significance with the relentlessness of glaciation. This was the spirit that Shakespeare personified.

So much is made clear by a book on Shakespeare written by Léon Daudet early in his career. It was in this work that Daudet hatched the ideas about France, classicism, and the Latin/Teutonic divide that would later fuel the hatreds of *L'Action Française*, the newspaper he founded and edited. *Le Voyage de Shakespeare*, published in 1896, depicts the young English poet hovering on a shadowy frontier between two eras and two hemispheres. Shakespeare is wooed but not won by the Renaissance. He sleeps the disturbed sleep of unreason, because he belongs by racial affiliation not to the South, but to the murky, antipodean North. Taking the often debated subject of Shakespeare's travels as his theme, and prompted by the allusions and images that seemed to link Shakespeare's texts to the weird visions of Hieronymus Bosch, Daudet assumed a journey not to Italy, but to the Netherlands, North Germany, and Denmark. His book, half novel and half biographical polemic, recounts how in 1584 the young William embarks on a voyage of exploration and self-discovery, through regions still benighted by sorcery, astrology, monstrosity, and primitive custom. At sea, he reads North's translation of Plutarch, and is momentarily enraptured by the epic of Classical achievement. But when a furious tempest breaks, these visions vanish, and nightmares arise from the turbulent deep. Which voice, he wonders, should he heed? That of civilisation, or that of the storm? Should he create 'a theatre of bestiality; tragedies wherein all would be instinct – animality almost – and blood?' Or 'a theatre of exquisite ideas, of refined sentiments, which would conceal the biped beneath a flow of harmonious words?' In Leyden a student asks him: 'Why are you wandering in the North? Do you not feel more drawn to Italy?' The question again turns his aspirations in the direction of beauty, reason, sunlight, and 'the race but half dominated by feeling, and half-committed to the rule of clarity ... Race of calculation and harmony'. Ancestral inclination, however, draws him irresistibly to 'the girls whose supple skin is salty, and who have an ulterior motive in pleasure'; to the company of the Jews, Protestants, students, mariners, artists, actors, and witches who haunt the fringes of the Northern cities; to sights from which the refined gaze is averted – physical deformity, the torture and execution of criminals. At Elsinore, after an encounter that prefigures the plot of *Hamlet*, his spiritual orientation becomes clear and he abandons humanism for mystical Teutonic transcendentalism: 'I no longer separate the idea from the form, nor destiny from chance, nor the highest wisdom from instinct.'

Daudet's book was perhaps the most vivid and widely read presentation of Shakespeare as a stranger instinctively detained outside the Latin cosmos. It directed towards him many of the fears and resentments of educated France. It registered that descent of the intellectuals into the arena of political causes and animosities, that surrender to transient, temporal urgencies, which was so bitterly deplored by Julien Benda. Benda's *La Trahison des clercs* (*The Treachery of the Learned*, 1927) was fervently anti-racialist. It endorsed Renan's dissent from racial determinism: 'A man belongs neither to his language nor to his race; he belongs only to himself, because he is a free being, that is to say, a moral being.'[63] Taine now seemed discredited. The rift that had opened up under the pressures of history had failed to correspond to the divisions and oppositions of his theory. Under the stress and trauma of the First World War the conception of England as anti-France, as the Other, had been confounded by a rediscovered sense of closeness and community. It transpired that English literature represented not the values that France was fighting against, but those she was fighting for. The ideology of humanism was rediscovered, and Shakespeare the Teutonic alien was superseded by Shakespeare the pre-eminent European, heir of the Renaissance.

This was the Shakespeare portrayed in a best-selling critical biography published in 1931. The author was Louis Gillet, a French Academician who was well known in Paris between the wars as a teacher, journalist, and art historian. Gillet explained that the purpose of his book was 'to show that there is no reason to insist more on what divides than on what unites'. There was, he said, 'a family common to all the sons of humanism, to the children of Christianity and of the Renaissance'. Shakespeare was therefore neither the product of an alien civilisation, nor 'an isolated phenomenon'. He was 'the Renaissance made man, the full-blown flower of Europe'.[64] Gillet blamed the Germans for the racialisation of Shakespeare. 'Germany', he protested, 'has annexed Shakespeare as she has seized Rembrandt. She has made him the symbol of the Germanic races, the type of the anti-Latin.' For a hundred years Shakespeare had been disfigured in French eyes by the 'poison' of German-Romantic misrepresentation.[65]

But the popularity of Benda's and Gillet's books (both many times reprinted) indicated no more than a brief flirtation with humanist values. Humanism was often a mask for nationalism, and nationalism in France continued to feed on a deep, stable, substratum of racialist thought and feeling. This was made evident in the decade from the mid-1930s until the end of the Second World War. The leaders of French opinion now confronted the fear and the reality of invasion: invasion first by immigrants (chiefly Jewish), then by Nazis, following France's catastrophic military collapse in 1940. These events kept intellectuals and politicians thinking and talking in terms of nationality and race. They also consecrated the idea of 'resistance' as a principle of intellectual and political behaviour. Both the immigrants and the Nazis were resisted, the one openly, the other clandestinely; and in each case humanist rhetoric about the defence of Civilisation was mixed up with violent hostility to what was foreign. It was this racialist aversion to both Jews and Nazis that made intellectual and political life in France at this time so fissured and agonised. There were no simple choices when resistance to one national enemy implied collaboration with the other.

Ideological tension and confusion fragmented wartime resistance against the Nazi occupation of Paris and northern France.⁶⁶ The Resistance envisaged a future built on humanist values, but it spoke with a nationalist voice. In its rhetoric Frenchness was not transcended by humanism, but equated with it. Taine's dogma of race was still audible in its theme of an *esprit français* confronting the barbarity of foreignness. And there should have been an empty place in honour of Taine in the cafés on the boulevard St. Germain where the Parisian intelligentsia congregated in the years of uncertain dawn that followed the war. His theories of literature and of Shakespeare were still far from dead, even though Jean-Louis Barrault was declaring that Shakespeare was more popular in France than Racine,⁶⁷ and Jean-Paul Sartre was expounding existentialism as the modern humanism.

For Sartre sounded remarkably like Taine when he talked about the nature of literature. Existential freedom, Sartre discovered, has no meaning outside history. Since freedom connotes choice – that is, commitment, *engagement* – it takes different forms at different times and in different places. 'Strictly speaking', he wrote, 'freedom does not *exist*: it is conquered in a historical situation ... It is an essential and necessary feature of freedom to be situated.' Writers are free individuals addressing other free individuals. Nothing compels them to write in the way they do. Nevertheless, it is the time and circumstances in which they live that reveal their freedom to them. 'Every book proposes a concrete liberation from a specific state of alienation.' Every book therefore implicitly refers to 'a whole world which the author and the reader have in common'. The writer remains in this sense historical. Like the audience he addresses, he is inseparable from a situation created by memories and perceptions that are peculiar to his age and collectivity.⁶⁸

It was reserved to the next generation finally to sever the line of communication with Taine and banish the old theory of *race, milieu*, and *moment* to the museum of extinct ideas. In the late 1950s and in the 1960s Paris burgeoned with banners inscribed boldly with the word 'new'. It was the age of La Nouvelle Critique, Le Nouveau Roman, La Nouvelle Vague. This modern renaissance declared redundant the traditional academic approach to literature and art. It set up an apparatus of critical theory and critical terminology that ignored the old national and racial references. It thereby won for itself celebrity abroad. Not since the seventeenth century had French critics been so influential beyond the French-speaking world. Barthes, Lacan, and Lévi-Strauss pronounced, and an international audience listened. University students throughout Europe and North America wrestled with their elusive concepts and cryptic language, and countless theses and monographs echoed their neologisms and their peculiar arabesques of dialectic. Like the humanists of the earlier Renaissance, they were free-ranging scholars expounding a recovered heritage. They liberated texts from authors, and authors from history. Texts were given back to readers; authors to themselves. Literature, they said, was not just about writing; it was also about reading. But the acts of writing and reading were performed neither in an existential vacuum nor in an historical situation. They were performed within socio-linguistic structures, for the self was an object, not a subject; acted, not acting.

The historical method was attacked, most notoriously, by Roland Barthes, leading rebel of La Nouvelle Critique and trail-blazer for structuralism. In three essays on Racine (1963), Barthes disputed both the neutrality and the sufficiency of historicism. He argued that ultimately literature always eluded history. Analogies never held up and paradoxes abounded. Insofar as it was an 'institution', a literary work was the effect of a cause; but insofar as it was a 'creation', it was a 'sign', a signifier of something other than the sum of its parts. It was not therefore explicable in terms of 'sources, influences, and models ... events, conditions, collective mentalities'. This meant that criticism, too, was paradoxical – both historically determined and subjective. And since no critical language was innocent, the truth about literature could not be told.[69] The furious reaction from academic quarters revealed the strength of the commitment to *lansonisme*. Nevertheless, even in the universities teachers from now on talked less and less about 'literature' and 'the history of literature'. They talked instead about the 'phenomène littéraire' and about 'histoire littéraire' – by which they meant all literary activity, including reading and publishing.

The weary weaver was still weaving. Structuralism was yet another fabric produced by the endless search for cosmic system and syntax. It was soon unravelled, pulled apart by the cyclical return of analysis after synthesis. The era of the aftermath was at hand, when post-structural-ists and postmodernists frowned on all 'structures' and 'master-narratives' that claimed to encompass history and reduce it to order. Following the upheavals of 1968, Jean-Louis Lyotard declared that such totalising *grands récits* were characteristic of modernism, and that the postmodern response must be to reject them. They were untrue; and, in that they stifled speculation about justice and truth with dog-matic valuations and hierarchies of privilege, they were repressive. The concern of postmodern intellectuals like Derrida and Foucault was to demonstrate the fallibility of all general laws, and to redistribute the power subsumed in cartels of knowledge.

Nevertheless, structuralism had altered French literary perspectives. It did not bring back into cultural anthropology the 'subject' – the stable, free-standing Cartesian self – and for that reason it has been accused of anti-humanism.[70] But it did eradicate the old nationalist and racialist conception of literature. One of its lasting legacies was its new critical lexicon. After structuralism, the leaders of literary debate, at least, had no further use for the term *esprit français* and the ideological baggage that it carried.

4

A Story without an Ending

French translations of Shakespeare are a landmark on the surface of modern Western literature. They lie in a huge mound, accumulated over more than 250 years and testifying to one of the most strenuous attempts ever made to transfer an author from one language to another. The eighteenth-century versions were the first of a sequence that has never tarried. In France, translating Shakespeare became a labour of Sisyphus, each generation recommencing as soon as the previous one had laid down its pen. Between the middle of the eighteenth century and the middle of the twentieth, the canon was translated wholly or substantially ten times – about once in every twenty years. Most of the plays were also translated individually. For each of eight plays the published French translations (including stage adaptations but excluding opera libretti and scenarios for puppets) exceeded twenty. *Hamlet* and *Macbeth* were each translated 39 times; *Romeo and Juliet* was translated 36 times; *Othello* 31 times. The next most frequent were *Julius Caesar* (30 translations), *King Lear* (22), *The Merchant of Venice* (21), and *A Midsummer Night's Dream* (20).[1] The whole range of French literary talent was involved in this gigantic endeavour. Eminent and famous authors, as well as amateurs high-ranking and obscure, contributed their toil. Voltaire, Alfred de Vigny, Alexandre Dumas, Pierre Loti, George Sand, Louise Colet, Maurice Maeterlinck, André Gide, Albert Camus, Pierre-Jean Jouve, Jules Supervielle, Marcel Pagnol, and Yves Bonnefoy all feature among the ranks of the translators. Probably no other foreign writer ever received so much attention in France, and no other activity did more to promote Shakespeare's international fame. In the eyes of a reverential Europe, each new translation into French was another stone on a votive pile.

Translation has been an essential function in the literary economy of Europe ever since the Renaissance, and the Renaissance itself was in a

fundamental sense the work of translators, assisted by printers. Without
the massive conversion of Greek and Latin works into vernacular languages, followed by their distribution in printed copies, there could
never have occurred that enlargement of popular consciousness, that
general correction of myopic vision, whereby the Renaissance acquired
its brilliant *éclat* and historical momentousness. Without these stimuli,
it must have remained a esoteric and sterile affair, inhumed in universities and scholarly cloisters. Translation was a symptom of the linguistic
fragmentation that had developed as Latin retreated from literary creativity. Since the laity was becoming less and less familiar with Latin, the
replication of Latin texts and Latin translations of Greek works could
not in itself have ensured a wide audience for the Classics. Only vernacular versions made possible the popularisation of the recuperated
heritage, its absorption into the substance of modern art and literature.
This was especially true in France, where vernacular versions of the
Classics – such as Amyot's translations of Plutarch (1559 and 1572) –
enhanced the prestige of the French language and established translation
as a genre in its own right.[2] It was also the case in England, where
North's translation (made from the French of Amyot) gave Shakespeare
access to Plutarch, just as vernacular versions of the Latin Vulgate Bible
gave his generation access to scripture.

But the traffic in translation followed more than one route. It was a
means not just to recovering the sacred and secular past, but to pos-
sessing the wider world as well. It became an adjunct of travel. Accounts
of voyages were followed by translations of works gleaned from foreign
lands, and minds were assisted across frontiers of space, as well as of
time. To translations from the Classics were added translations between
vernaculars – Italian, French, English, and Spanish. It was in John Flo-
rio's translation (1603) that Shakespeare read Montaigne. In the
eighteenth century the way even to Arabia was opened up. The so-called
'Oriental Renaissance' began with the publication in twelve volumes of
Antoine Galland's French version of popular Arabian tales (*Les Mille et
une nuits*) between 1704 and 1716.[3]

During the Enlightenment, translations from the English became a
mainstay of the Parisian publishing industry. Between 1740 and 1790, 222
English novels were translated into French, and a further 46 were spu-
riously advertised as 'traduit de l'anglais' in order to boost their

commercial appeal.[4] It was translation, much more than travel, that made Britain familiar in France in the eighteenth century.

Because the French discovery of Shakespeare was so long delayed, he came late in the chronology of this activity. Sidney, Ben Jonson, Milton, Swift, Pope, and Addison were all published in French before he was. But the discovery once made, translation quickly followed. It would have been unthinkable to leave untranslated the writer universally recognised as England's most celebrated poet, given prevailing anglo-mania and the French pursuit of linguistic self-sufficiency. Even Voltaire, whose admiration was so strongly qualified, tried his hand at turning Shakespeare into French. When he published his edition of Corneille's works, in 1764, he included a French version of the first half of *Julius Caesar* in order to point the contrast between the French and the English way of staging a conspiracy. What is surprising is not the translation of Shakespeare, but the scale and persistence of the exercise. Why should the French have aspired so relentlessly after an author who was widely regarded in France as the Other, the alien, the personification of everything that Frenchness was not and could not be? The fact seems even more paradoxical in that every act of translation made the foreignness of Shakespeare not less but more apparent. He receded ever further as translator after translator advanced. The attraction lay, without a doubt, mainly in the difficulty. Everybody knew that to translate Shakespeare was difficult. It became a commonplace of literary wisdom that it was all but impossible. For that reason it became everybody's ambition. The challenge was irresistible in that it had never been met. No French version ever achieved authority comparable to that of Schlegel's and Tieck's in Germany. The obscure and the famous laboured; France waited still; and the kudos reserved for success grew ever greater as the miracle was again and again postponed.

The difficulty was partly owing to the divided sensibility of the French educated public. In France in the eighteenth century, as well as in the nineteenth, there was a hankering after art and literature that were strong and emotionally charged. The popularity of poetry and fiction that was fabulous, exotic, and *sombre*, and of music that was passionate and unconventional, signified a thirst for bizarre and hyperbolic effects. A public avid for sensation consumed Ossian, Shakespeare, the *Thousand and One Nights*, and Italian opera, just as it would later consume

Victor Hugo's evocations of the Orient – 'grand, riche, fécond', and suffused with 'la vieille barbarie asiatique'.[5] The aristocratic *salonnière* Marie du Deffand, friend of d'Alembert, Voltaire, and Montesquieu, suddenly developing when blind and in her seventies an addiction to Shakespeare, English novels, and the youthful Horace Walpole, bespeaks a world of privilege unfulfilled and frustrated at some deep level of its psyche. Yet the prison of the spirit was also its refuge, and there was no mandate for rebellion that threatened its security. Translators knew that they catered for people who, though bored, were also easily shocked and alarmed. They therefore had to transfer meanings not only from another tongue, but from another code of civility as well. The Orient presented by Galland, and the Shakespeare presented by early translators (especially those working for the stage), were designed to match rather than test the inherited limits of tolerance and receptivity. They put a bridle on the bizarre and the hyperbolic; made what was odd and menacing more obedient to the edicts of propriety and sophisticated taste. What the translators received as exotic they gave back as exotic still, but at the same time familiar and innocent. Often they adopted theoretical positions at odds with their practice, and so sustained that pressure of dissatisfaction, that sense of the provisional, which imparted to the history of Shakespeare in French its movement of eternal return.

In addition to these social and commercial constraints, translators encountered ideas that compounded the artistic difficulties of their task. As Cartesian notions of uniformity and universality retreated, so too did belief in a generic grammar of human consciousness. The theory took hold that languages were autonomous: rooted not in some underlying prototype, but in disparate cultural and historical circumstances. Languages were generated by (and helped to generate) not that which made peoples alike, but that which made them distinct. Linguistic frontiers were no less real than ethnic frontiers, and history had been fragmented by changes in habits of speech.[6] In the light of such ideas (propounded by Vico, Hamann, Herder, and others) the possibility of true translation seemed less and less assured. The possibility of translating poetry, which was language at its most densely meaningful, seemed virtually extinct. Leibniz, in an essay of 1697, had argued that thought and language were inseparable; that thought is not merely carried by language, but is inherent in it. If this was the case, it followed that a poet's meaning could not be replicated outside his original utterance. Such was the conclusion drawn by Marmontel. After explaining that the palette of the poet was rich in nuances, and that these nuances were 'in most cases exclusive to the language in which he [had] written', he added: 'I almost said in which he has thought, because an idea, in coming to birth, searches for the word that will express it, and without that word it dies.'[7] Voltaire argued that the emotions of tragedy were common to all languages and cultures. Humanity remained united in its tears. But he conceded that it was divided in its laughter. 'There is no laughter in a translation', he wrote. 'The subtlety of witticisms, allusions, aptness – all this is lost to a foreigner ... Good comedy is a talking picture of what is ridiculous in a nation, and without a profound knowledge of the nation you are in no position to judge the picture.'[8]

No translators deemed themselves so fiendishly martyred as those who tried to convert English literature into French. Jean Baretti said it was like trying to make African date palms fructify on the coast of Genoa.[9] Jules Barbey d'Aurevilly compared it to shipping a wine that refused to travel.[10] The restricted vocabulary of French, combined with its nasal phonetic register and its resistance to inversion, created an environment that was especially inhospitable to English works. Their characteristic roughness and deformity became smooth and straight; their chiaroscuro was transformed into an even illumination. The pride of French-speakers was the clarity of their language. Rivarol explained that this was owing to the 'uncorruptible' syntax of French, which banished ambiguity. But it made French unsuitable for poetry, and turned translation into an analytical process of elucidation. The qualities that made English writing so richly allusive – the suspensions of meaning, the subtle calibrations and modulations of colour – it was impossible to replicate in French.[11] Germaine de Staël reckoned that the peculiar sonority of spoken French allowed no scope for vivid emotion, and that the language could attain to a tragic level only intellectually, through elevated diction.[12] A twentieth-century veteran of translation, the poet Yves Bonnefoy, observed how, in the passage from English to French, the contingent became timeless and the irrational became intelligible.[13]

Since Shakespeare was regarded as the most quintessentially English among prominent anglophone writers, of all the meanings that were present in English literature, his were judged the most restive. In the

1840s Philarète Chasles embarked on a translation of the Shakespeare canon but retired defeated after taking a whole year to produce an unsatisfactory *Roméo et Juliette*. He doubted that translation of this writer's work could ever be successful, given that Germanic languages were as alien to French speakers as Chinese or Japanese:

> To struggle with Shakespeare, the spirit of the North personified, armed in the fight with the weapons of a half-Roman idiom born of imitation, formed by it and for it, disciplined by academics and founded on a system of conventions absolutely foreign to the civilisation of sixteenth-century Britain, is a rash enterprise in which success is virtually impossible; it is a noble labour which offers as reward only the pleasure of following the English poet into the remotest corners of his thought, of grasping their most fugitive nuances, and of admiring with a sort of fear the profound abyss which forever separates the nations of Teutonic extraction from those of Roman origin.[14]

Georges Duval, unlike Chasles, managed to finish a translation of the complete dramatic works. His version was published in eight volumes between 1908 and 1909 – but only after an exhausting toil. 'You would never believe', he told his readers, 'with what difficulty our language adapts to certain English usages.' He had encountered images and jests repulsive to the Latin mind; grammatical liberties forbidden in French; allusions and puns that drove him to despair.[15] No writer, said André Gide, better deserved translation than Shakespeare, and none was more difficult to translate and more prone to disfigurement in the process. The fault was partly Shakespeare's. His texts were hastily written, almost improvised at times, and

> it's always the worst-written phrases, those which the author has most rapidly written, which cause the translator most trouble. He has frequently to cover up the faults of logic which are so frequent with English authors. Nothing shocks a French mind so much as metaphors which 'do not follow' ... Nothing shocks an English mind less.

The Shakespearean metaphor was the bane of the conscientious French translator. 'The images overlap and clash; the unfortunate translator is flabbergasted by the superabundance ...' Furthermore his vexation was often redoubled by hermeneutic uncertainty. 'Numerous passages in Shakespeare are either incomprehensible or can be interpreted in two, three, or four different ways.' Which should the translator choose?

Or should he choose none, and attempt instead to reproduce the ambiguity and the incomprehensibility? But the French language was also to blame for the translator's ordeal. Gide said that when he set about translating Shakespeare he became aware as never before of the 'résistances ... réticences et refus' of French. Its stubborn inflexibility meant that the translator could remain faithful both to his own language and to Shakespeare only by means of 'continual petty ruses and paltry trickery'. French was 'a rigid, intransigent language, making strict grammatical and syntactical demands; a clear, precise, and prosaic language'.[16] When Yves Bonnefoy confronted the problem, he discovered that it was as much cultural as syntactic and hermeneutic. Shakespeare remained unFrench even when he was lucid and direct. When translating *Hamlet* Bonnefoy was confounded by the word 'jelly' in Horatio's description of the two sentries terrified by the ghost ('distill'd / Almost to a jelly with the act of fear'). 'Jelly' is a French word ('gelée') and it has the same sense in both languages. Yet to Bonnefoy it seemed inappropriate for a French text because it had been lifted straight from life – 'used carelessly: without accretion of meaning'. He discovered that, as a Frenchman, he required that 'such contexts heighten knowledge, and thereby economise meaning'. He required language that was called 'noble', or 'literary', but which was in effect merely 'taut' ('tendue'). He inferred that the English expected less of language than did the French. 'They require more direct observation of simple psychology ... than heroic reconstruction.'[17]

Gide and Bonnefoy were late recruits into a long battle between Shakespeare and a language that had been burdened with classical prescriptions and racialist ideology. When French translators first tackled Shakespeare, their lexicon was divided into words that were sanctioned for literary use and those that were not. Etiquette demanded that words classified as 'low' be avoided, especially on the tragic stage. These words included the names of most lower forms of life – plants, animals, and insects – and what one eighteenth-century translator referred to as 'expressions designed to signify actions or employments which [were] publicly unsuited to people of distinguished rank'. The proscription extended to words and expressions denoting manual labour and the mechanical arts, since these were almost invariably associated with the lowness of those who exercised them.[18] English too, it was conceded, distinguished between what was low and what was noble, but the translator striving to convert English works – especially Shakespeare's – into French found himself dealing with languages in which the lines of demarcation were differently drawn. Often he had to resort to substitution or periphrasis in order to avoid transforming noble English into low French. 'How fatiguing it is for him', wrote Marmontel, 'to follow through the brambles of barbaric language the tortuous passage of a writer who, in his own language, is walking a straight path strewn with flowers!'[19] But generally English writers valued expressiveness above decorum. Abel Boyer, who translated Addison's *Cato* in 1713, discovered that in comparison with literary English, literary French was 'enervated and impoverished by refinement; always timid and always the slave of rules and usage'.[20] Later, nationalism added new constraints. As 'la langue de Racine' became 'la langue française', patrimony of the nation and vehicle of its literature, it became enveloped in a protective mentality, and translators found themselves playing a crucial role in its defence. Operating at its point of contact with the language of the Anglo-Saxons, they had a special duty to police the incoming traffic and arrest harmful influences.

Protestations of fidelity and accusations of betrayal were common currency in the debate about translation in France. The leading question always was, fidelity to what, to whom? Part of the answer was, not to words – not to profane words, at least. It was axiomatic from the first that for all texts except scripture the translator should weigh words and not count them ('peser les mots et non pas les compter'). But the translator dealing in profane literature confronted the conflicting claims of the author and the text. Fidelity to the foreign author meant correcting his 'faults' and bringing his work into conformity with the canons of beauty and propriety (*bienséance*). Loyalty to the text meant reproducing its crudities and blemishes as written, and submitting to the discipline of exactness and self-effacement.

During the Renaissance and through the seventeenth century translators were almost invariably loyal to authors. They felt it incumbent upon them to 'improve' the original. It was generally accepted that too close an adherence to the text would produce not translation but transliteration – something beneficial to neither party. In the translator it signified *servitude* – an abject and slavish cast of mind. For the foreign author it meant exposure to the censure of a refined public. Since the ideal translation should read like a sophisticated original, the translator was expected to prune the metaphors and the hyperbole in modern – especially Italian – works, and to refine the crudity of the Classics. Perrot d'Ablancourt's improved versions of Tacitus and Lucian were referred to as 'belles infidèles'. Their infidelity was recognised as a higher form of fidelity, since it safeguarded the reputation of the ancient authors and allowed them the benefits of modern advances in aesthetics and morals. Houdar de la Motte, whose verse translation of the *Iliad* appeared in 1715, argued that a version close to the original would be unreadable in French. He had aimed 'to give a reasonable French poem'.[21] No translators, not even those who criticised the embellishing infidels, risked uncompromising exactness. Mme Dacier, a distinguished Hellenist, made a great issue of the 'fidelity' of her translation of the *Iliad* (1699), but she had in fact abbreviated, rearranged, and purified Homer's text.[22] The assumption behind this approach was that solecisms were never knowingly or willingly committed. To correct them according to the universal criteria of taste and beauty was therefore a favour owed by the translator to his author.

These principles were often restated in the eighteenth century, when the public's appetite for English works was matched only by its intolerance of their uncouthness and discursiveness. Elie Fréron, writing in the *Année Littéraire* in 1755, defined translation as 'the fine art of embellishing and perfecting'. It was the translator's mission 'to establish order, curtail superfluities, correct features, and finally allow to be seen only what really merits admiration'. To treat his work in this way was not to betray a foreign author. It was to render him 'grands et éminents services'. It was the only way, in fact, to ensure a favourable reception in France, where the standards of universal taste had become a national preference. In perfecting a text, said the academician Charles-Pierre Colardeau in 1779, the translator gave it 'a national appearance'. He 'naturalise[d], after a fashion, this foreign plant'.[23] From the 1730s the abbreviating, purging, and general gallicising of English novels and English poetry was the main activity of the Parisian publishing industry. 'I have given his work', wrote Prévost in the preface to his translation of Richardson's *Sir Charles Grandison*, 'a new look, by cutting drawn-out excursions, overloaded descriptions, useless conversations, and inappropriate reflections.' He reduced to four the seven volumes of the English edition (which he reckoned would fill fourteen volumes in the standard French format). Likewise, Fielding's *Tom Jones* was shrunk from six volumes to four by Pierre-Antoine de La Place. Pierre Le Tourneur said that in translating Young's *Night Thoughts* he treated the text 'as an architect would a mass of building materials, shaped and ready, but heaped up haphazardly in eight or nine different places and intermixed with rubble'. He explained that his intention had been to extract a French Young from the English one, and he advised all translators dealing with English works to follow his example. The advice was widely followed. In the early nineteenth century Dickens was abridged and tided up by Amédée Pichot. *Childe Harold's Pilgrimage* was 'completed' by Alphonse de Lamartine, who wrote a new ending more in keeping with French piety and less damaging to Byron's reputation.

By now, however, the whole subject was engulfed in controversy. Objection to the ventriloquial style of translation had been building up throughout the eighteenth century, especially among *érudits* and *philosophes*. In the 1730s rival translations of Pope's *Essay on Man* had provoked a literary storm, and when Voltaire took up the matter he argued strongly for fidelity to the text:

> If the poet has employed a metaphor, another metaphor should not be substituted; if he uses a word which is low in his language, it should be rendered by a word which is low in ours. It's a picture whose arrangement, postures, colours, faults, and beauties should be copied exactly, otherwise you give your own work instead of his.[24]

Turgot, eminent as an economist and statesman, but deeply interested in literature and translation, was scornful of 'those individuals who imagine that they are embellishing their author by lending him their own ideas'. Translating did not mean turning a foreign author into a French one. In his own translations of Salomon Gessner's poetry (1760–61) his practice had been 'to employ the right word, even if low, rather than a noble one which [was] vague and incompatible with the meaning'. The marquis de Saint-Simon, in an essay on translation of 1771, demanded scrupulous textual exactness: 'A translator should reproduce faithfully the images, the phrases, and even the punctuation of his author.' In 1785 the *Année Littéraire* was calling for 'authors as they really are'. Translators were constantly exhorted to efface themselves and allow their authors free speech.[25] One of the most notable nineteenth-century examples of translation according to this formula was Chateaubriand's *Paradise Lost*. This imitated Milton's prosody and syntax even at the cost of contorted and unidiomatic French. Another example was Gérard de Nerval's *Faust*, which attempted to replicate the occlusion of Goethe's idiom. 'It's better, I think', wrote Nerval, 'to risk leaving some passages peculiar or incomprehensible than to mutilate a masterpiece.'

French literary theory then, and French literary practice, allowed alternative methods of translation. In the case of Shakespeare both methods were used, because for a long time France demanded not one Shakespeare but two. France required a Shakespeare for the printed page, and a Shakespeare for the stage. Translators for the page quickly pledged their allegiance to the text. Translators for the stage struggled for much longer to preserve Shakespeare's reputation. They indulged in 'correction' on a draconian scale. The plays were lopped, regularised, and sanitised, and they were rendered into French verse. Until well into the nineteenth century, Shakespeare, so far as the French theatre was concerned, meant tragedy; tragedy meant verse; and verse meant twelve-syllable lines (alexandrines) in rhyming couplets. In the eighteenth century a few efforts were made to write blank verse in French – most notably by Voltaire, in his partial translation of *Julius Caesar*. This was, however, done with a view to demonstrating the unsuitability of Shakespearean prosody for the French stage. Voltaire's opinion was that blank verse in the French theatre would mean the end of French tragedy. Such verse was, he said, unworthy of this superior genre because it was 'born of inability to conquer difficulty, and the urge to finish quickly'.[26] On this matter Voltaire was in complete agreement with his old enemy the abbé Desfontaines, translator of *Gulliver's Travels*. Desfontaines had argued that French verse without rhyme was indistinguishable from prose. The cadence of French verse was weakened by the frequent articulation of the 'e' mute (*e atone*) at the ends of words. Without rhyme, verse would not therefore sound like verse. It was also a matter of habit – but, he insisted, the French were partial to novelty, and habit alone would not have preserved rhyme if this had not been necessary for other reasons. Rhyme was consequently indispensable, even though 'a long sequence of rhymes [was] fatiguing and oppressive'.[27]

This monopoly of verse precluded anything resembling authentic Shakespeare on the French tragic stage. The dynamic of rhyming alexandrines is quite different from that of Shakespeare's verse, which is structured not in syllables but in feet. Shakespeare's pentameters give free range to his meaning, which surges across the scansion – 'always flowing', as Coleridge said, 'from one [line] into the other, and seldom closing with the tenth syllable':

> Like to the Pontic sea
> Whose icy current and compulsive course
> Ne'er feels retiring ebb, but keeps due on
> To the Propontic and the Hellespont,
> Even so my bloody thoughts with violent pace,
> Shall ne'er look back, ne'er ebb to humble love,
> Till that a capable and wide revenge
> Swallow them up.

In the classical French alexandrine the meaning is contained by the versification. It is regularly checked by the break within the line (the caesura), and is either closed or pulled back by the rhyme. Always pausing, returning, and beginning again, French tragic verse evokes the circularity of passion and reason in equal combat:

> Mourrons: de tant d'horreurs qu'un trépas me délivre!
> Est-ce un malheur si grand que de cesser de vivre?
> La mort aux malheureux ne cause point d'effroi:
> Je ne crains que le nom que je laisse après moi.
> Pour mes tristes enfants quel affreux héritage!
> Le sang de Jupiter doit enfler leur courage;
> Mais, quelque juste orgueil qu'inspire un sang si beau,
> Le crime d'une mère est un pesant fardeau.*

In the hands of a genius like Racine, this instrument produced ravishing

---

* Let us die: may a decease deliver me from so many horrors! / Is it such a great unhappiness to cease to live? / Death causes no fear to the unhappy; / I fear only the name that I leave behind me./ What a terrible inheritance for my poor children! / The blood of Jupiter must swell their courage; / But however justified the pride inspired by such fine blood, / The crime of a mother is a heavy burden. Racine, *Phèdre*, III, iii.

music. In the hands of lesser talent, it sounded monotonous and meagre. François-Thomas de Baculard Arnaud, an eighteenth-century dramatist who specialised in works of terror and horror, longed for a form of versification free from 'this distressing uniformity', which loaded an author with chains. He noted enviously how Shakespeare's metre varied; how his style was always matched to the occasion; how minor characters differed in their expression from leading ones.[28] In 1830 Philarète Chasles complained of 'the alternating monotony of lines which fall one by one, following each other in procession charged with their regular rhyme'. He likened it to 'a handbell ringing at regular intervals and sending you to sleep with the inevitable return of the cadence'.[29] While these conventions prevailed, 'Shakespearean' texts concocted for the French stage were clearly bound to be remote from Shakespeare. For this reason they were generally referred to not as translations, but as imitations or adaptations.

Gradually, the need for two Shakespeares lessened. As theatre audiences grew more tolerant of unconventional and exotic effects, the old rules of taste and prosody were relaxed, and the process of adaptation became bilateral rather than unilateral. That is to say, there was less and less adaptation of Shakespeare to the French theatre, and more and more adaptation of the French theatre to Shakespeare. Translators for the stage switched their allegiance to the text, and the gap between the two Shakespeares narrowed. But until this theatrical revolution was accomplished (and it was a long time in the making) it was only through the efforts of literary translators that the French public could hope to know what Shakespeare was really like.

The first effort had been cautious. It remained loyal to the author rather than to his text, even though it was intended solely for the reading public. Between 1745 and 1748 Pierre-Antoine de La Place, a man of letters who had been educated at the college of the English Jesuits at Saint-Omer, published an anthology of English theatrical works in eight volumes. Four of these were devoted to Shakespeare. La Place had ruled out integral and literal translation. This, he said, was impossible, given the fundamental differences between the two languages. Instead, he selected 'all the scenes and ... passages which lend themselves to tolerable translation'. One play (*Richard III*) he translated in its entirety. Nine others were partially translated, with synopses replacing the omitted segments. The remaining plays were merely summarised. La Place used prose for *Richard III*. Elsewhere he used a mixture of prose and alexandrines in an attempt to replicate the variety of Shakespeare's idiom. He freely acknowledged that he had taken 'great liberties' and had produced 'feeble imitations' rather than 'exact translations'; but he argued that without such presumption it would have been impossible to 'bring out fully the beauties of [his] original'. The object of his exercise was to demonstrate that though Shakespeare's work was tarnished by 'superfluous scenes', 'a lack of *vraisemblance*', and 'misplaced details', his merits, when winnowed from these faults, vindicated his great reputation. They were a rebuke to those blinkered French critics who judged the whole by those parts they deemed 'faibles, ridicules, ou déplacées'. Such critics should, said La Place, beware of condemning what their descendants would one day applaud.[30]

The critical reception showed that there was still plenty of support for La Place's principles. The abbé Le Blanc maintained that complete translation, or even faithful translation of the best plays, could only have harmed Shakespeare's reputation. 'It's a pity', he wrote, 'that he falls so often into lowness and puerility. One would be just as pained by reading a tragedy of his from beginning to end as one is gratified by seeing a detached morsel.' Pierre-Joseph Fiquet du Bocage, a well-established translator of English works, congratulated La Place on the prudence and discernment with which he had handled a worthy but scabrous author. He reckoned that he had selected 'what [was] presentable from something which would soon have changed public curiosity into repugnance had it been revealed as it really [was]'. Anything closer to the original would have upset the altar at which La Place worshipped.[31]

Others, however, objected to a bland paraphrase in which there was little recognisable as Shakespeare's except the names of the characters and the broad outlines of the plots. Voltaire complained that the French public had been misled, and he undertook to expose the real Shakespeare by translating some of the most scurrilous passages from *Othello*.[32] Pierre Le Tourneur regretted that La Place had been obliged 'to allow us only cautious glimpses of Shakespeare, to refashion, so to speak, to polish, and to whittle down this foreign giant'. Convinced that 'one must, and can, accommodate and bend the French language to the plays of Shakespeare', he gave up his court position as censeur royal and secrétaire général de la librairie in order to devote all his time and energy to a new translation. No longer was he aiming, as he had been when he translated Young, to turn an English author into a French one. The public was now promised 'a complete translation, the most faithful it will be in my power to provide'. He and his collaborator, the accomplished Breton aristocrat the comte de Catuélan, recruited assistants from among the amateur and professional men of letters in Paris, and in 1775 published a prospectus soliciting subscriptions for the great literary monument, to be published in twenty volumes.[33]

The response showed how radically circumstances had changed in thirty years. La Place's Shakespeare had enjoyed no official favour nor even sanction. It had had to be produced anonymously and with a putative London imprint, in order to protect a publisher who had not obtained a royal *privilège*. Le Tourneur's first two volumes came from the press loaded with every honour that supreme authority and high society could bestow. The edition was dedicated, by special permission, to the young Louis XVI, and Voltaire was almost certainly justified in believing that the project had the personal support of the king. Louis had a good knowledge of English, and a deep interest in matters literary and theatrical. He may even have contributed to the labour of translation. The list of almost a thousand subscribers blazed with rank and eminence. It included members of the court nobility, army officers, ecclesiastical dignitaries, academicians, ambassadors, and ministers of the crown. Only 200 or so of the 800 French subscribers were unrelated to the *noblesse*. The 200 foreign subscribers were headed by George III, the Prince of Wales, Lord North, and the archbishop of Canterbury. By the time the third and fourth volumes appeared, in 1778, another 150 people had subscribed and the commercial success of the undertaking was assured. Probably something like 2000 sets of the complete edition were sold.[34]

Le Tourneur omitted the poems and chose prose rather than verse for the plays. This indicated clearly that he did not have performance in mind. Absolved from the rigorous constraints of the stage, he deemed himself free to produce 'une traduction exacte et vraiment fidèle'. 'We have', he claimed rather grandiosely in his dedicatory epistle to the king,

> courageously disencumbered [Shakespeare] of the paste diamonds which had been substituted for his true richness, and snatched away the mask

which, by smothering the living expression of his features, endowed him with only a dead and characterless image.

An 'exact and truly faithful' translation was not, however, the same as a literal one. Literalism, Le Tourneur argued, would have adulterated the original, since words that were 'noble' in English were often 'bas' in French. There were only very few low words and expressions in the language of Shakespeare. True equivalence was not therefore lexicographic. 'The duty of fidelity', he explained,

> imposes on us that of substituting for a metaphor which, in French, would become mean and vulgar, an equivalent which preserves the dignity of the original; of searching for another word to render the word which would turn out to be low in our language were it translated according to the dictionary.[35]

These adjustments were not needed in the comedies; but in the tragedies and histories Le Tourneur and his collaborators made many changes for the sake of linguistic nobility. In *Macbeth*, 'man' became *guerrier, noble companion,* or *illustre collègue.* The witches were *magiciennes;* the Devil, *l'oracle des enfers.* In *King Lear*, 'the sky' became *le firmament;* 'the cold wind', *la bise aiguë.* Throughout the tragedies, 'marriage' was translated as *hymen,* and the names of animals, birds, and insects were changed in order to avoid vulgarisation. 'Lion', 'bear', 'tiger' and 'eagle' were directly translated; but 'horse' became *coursier;* 'camel' and 'weasel' (in Hamlet's teasing of Polonius) were both rendered as *corbeau;* and the mouse mentioned by the sentry in the first scene of *Hamlet* ('not a mouse stirring') was transformed into an insect (*pas un insecte n'a remué*). The rat in Hamlet's exclamation on hearing an intruder behind the arras ('How now, a rat?') was promoted into a burglar (*Comment, un voleur?*). In *Othello*, 'dog' was translated variously as *le ver qui rampe* and *vautour.* Insects, too, were dignified. 'Cricket' was replaced by *l'insecte du foyer;* 'fly' by *insecte;* 'flea' by *mouche.* Only crustaceans flummoxed these refiners of base creation. There was no way of ennobling a crab, so in Hamlet's banter with Polonius ('yourself, Sir, shall grow as old as I am, if like a crab you could go backward') the simile was simply omitted (*Seigneur, vous deviendrez aussi vieux que moi, quand même vous reviendrez en rétrogradant dans la vie*). Shakespeare's images and metaphors were radically modified or even deleted in order to avoid lowness or incongruity. War that 'opens his vasty jaws' in

Henry V was transformed into *la guerre qui menace de sa dent affreuse*. Hamlet was oppressed not by 'the slings and arrows of outrageous fortune', but by *les traits poignants de l'injuste fortune*; and he did not 'take arms against a sea of troubles' (the metaphor would sound absurd in French) but, *se révoltant contre cette multitude de maux, s'oppos[ait] au torrent*. Lewdness was discreetly censored. In the first act of *Othello*, for example, Iago was not allowed to refer to 'an old black ram / ... tupping your white ewe'. The image of copulation was retained, but the mammals were changed into birds (*noir vautour* and *jeune et blanche colombe*).

Yet it was no part of Le Tourneur's intention to conceal what he had omitted or modified. In his copious notes he explained how he had departed from the original and gave alternative literal translations. Errors of comprehension were very few. Le Tourneur had never been to England, but his literary knowledge of English was supplemented by the linguistic expertise of a collaborator who had. The comte de Catuélan was well known in intellectual and high social circles of London. Together they made it possible for the French public to know the architecture and the detail of Shakespeare's plays – if not in their artistic mutuality, then at least as component parts. For this reason, and because it included a full résumé of English and German critical and biographical scholarship, Le Tourneur's edition was a cardinal document in the history both of Shakespeare abroad and of French publishing. Voltaire realised this, and was hostile partly because he had been excluded.

The first two volumes were the talk of Paris. Everybody was reading them, and only Voltaire withheld his welcome. 'It's making a big impression', reported the *Mercure de France* of the new Shakespeare. 'It's therefore a good thing, and much needed.'[36] Nevertheless the boldness and the scale of the enterprise caused some reservations and even a slight sense of shock. The most favourable reactions were mixed with relief that Le Tourneur had not gone any further. The least favourable betrayed a fear that he had gone too far. When she read *Othello* in the new version, the marquise du Deffand realised that La Place's Shakespeare was a mere skeleton; but she appreciated Le Tourneur's tact. He had been right, she explained to Horace Walpole, to translate 'Othello's occupation's gone' as *la tâche d'Othello est finie*, since the word *occupation* had base connotations in French. It would, she insisted, 'be suitable for things of small importance, and certainly not for the things of which Othello has been speaking ... "Tâche" generally means "occupation", but a hard and painful one, so this word suits Othello's state of mind.'[37] Less sympathetic readers complained of flattering falsification. Le Tourneur had polished Shakespeare's characteristic ruggedness, concealed his unprepossessing nakedness. Marmontel was heard to remark that the Shakespeare of this translation resembled 'a savage dressed up in lace, a bit of embroidery, and an ostrich plume'.[38] La Harpe objected that the grossness of the grosser passages had been obscured. But he also complained that the nobility of the noble passages had been compromised. Why, for example, had Le Tourneur translated the word 'thigh' in Othello's speech in Act V ('Behold! I have a weapon / A better never did itself sustain / Upon a soldier's thigh') as *cuisse*? 'It's part of the special delicacy of our language', expostulated La Harpe, 'not to admit into the noble style words which denote certain parts of the body ... This word *cuisse* would spoil, for French ears, the most beautiful phrase.' How much better it would have been to turn the thigh into a hand and render the passage as *Jamais arme plus sûre ne fut dans la main d'un soldat*! Like Voltaire, La Harpe was worried lest Shakespeare in French be used to undermine the great French dramatists.[39] He forgot that Le Tourneur's versions of the plays were never intended for French ears – for performance, that is. They were intended for the solitary reader in the library, the study, the boudoir, or – as Le Tourneur suggested in his preface – the romantic wilderness of nature.

The commercial success of the new Shakespeare was assured, and critical hostility curtailed, by a combination of royal support and editorial shrewdness. In contriving to observe linguistic rules of exclusion without actually concealing anything, Le Tourneur had managed to satisfy readers who wanted novelty and sensation, but who preferred the grosser elements of life to be exactly as he had made them – discretely segregated away from the public gaze. If tolerance was stretched, it was stretched less by the content than by the scale of his translation. French educated society already had a good idea of the sort of thing that Shakespeare's writing contained, but it was less generally aware that he had written so much. As volume after volume came from the press, even well-wishers began to wilt, and to wonder whether it had been advisable to translate him entire. 'I never did think that everything in Shakespeare was good', wrote the chevalier de Rutlidge rather fretfully to Le Tourneur. The *Année Littéraire* qualified its commendation by regretting the inclusion of so much that was trivial or uninteresting. 'Well-made extracts', it protested, 'would have been a true treasure for our literature'; but 'twenty volumes of boredom by subscription' were another matter.[40] It was in order to meet these objections that Paul Duport published, in 1820, his *Essais littéraires sur Shakespeare*. He claimed that in these two volumes men and women of fashion would find everything they needed to know about the subject. 'It has', wrote Duport, 'become almost indispensable for us to have a good knowledge of Shakespeare ... But what reading for people of the world!' Thirty-seven five-act plays, each of which was almost double the length of the longest French dramas, tested the endurance even of professional literary folk. Bearing this in mind, he ventured 'to offer a complete and detailed analysis, scene by scene, of each of the plays of Shakespeare'.

The instance of Pierre Le Tourneur clearly indicated how far a translator's practice was liable to be diverted from his intentions by the preponderant obsessions of pre-Revolutionary France. In a culture so fundamentally conditioned by inequality and rules of precedence, it was inevitable that Shakespeare should be ennobled before being exposed even in reading matter intended for private consumption. It was impossible to dispense with the lace, the embroidery, and the ostrich plume until Revolutionary ideology had democratised French literary language. One of the first indications that rank had been abolished came in 1821, when François Guizot published the thirteen volumes of his 'revised and corrected' version of Le Tourneur's translation. Guizot was an obvious candidate for this work of the Revolution. As an academic, he pioneered the modernisation of historical studies in France, by reconnecting historiography to archival scholarship and encouraging the collection and editing of national records. He was the French Ranke. In his political career he was a liberal, a democrat of the vintage of 1789. For these reasons he was averse to leaving Shakespeare as he had found him – dressed up in the finery of the *ancien régime* and reflecting its rituals of discrimination and exclusion.

In collaboration with his wife and two other liberal intellectuals, Amédée Pichot and the baron de Barante, he overhauled Le Tourneur's text. Segregated material was reinstated, paraphrases were unscrambled, passages that had strayed from the original were retranslated. The result was an idiom noticeably more demotic than Le Tourneur's. Burglars had reverted to rats, vultures to dogs, magicians to witches, insects to flies and mice, multitudes of evils to seas of troubles, and frightful teeth to vast jaws. Even the banished crustacean was readmitted – though at first only as an *écrevisse* (crayfish). Not until 1860, when he published a second edition of his revision, did Guizot use the word *crabe*. This was citizen Shakespeare, all his appurtenances of nobility laid aside. He was not, however, exempt from the edicts of taste. Guizot, minister and even briefly prime minister of bourgeois France, cherished bourgeois propriety. So there was no black ram tupping a white ewe in either of his editions. Instead, Le Tourneur's white dove and black vulture continued with their surrogate copulation. The crude jocularity of Shakespeare's comic characters remained diluted, too. 'In order to make this passage bearable in French', wrote Guizot in a note to *Henry IV Part Two*, 'it has been necessary to tone down the realism of Falstaff's language.'[41]

Guizot's attempt to salvage the old translation was sabotaged by Romanticism, which demanded not just democracy, but expressiveness – poetic language of a type not written before. It hijacked Shakespeare: carried him off to supernal regions well beyond the range of sublunary locution. Only another Shakespeare, it seemed to say, could translate Shakespeare. In June 1826 *Le Catholique* disparaged Guizot's version as 'that bad parody in prose which is going around calling itself a translation of Shakespeare'. Devoid of all poetic sentiment, this was 'Shakespeare rendered by the words, but without his poetic soul and the harmony of his creative style'.[42] Others tried to do what Guizot and his collaborators had failed to do. In 1839 two further revisions of Le Tourneur were published. One, in three volumes, was by the historian and literary scholar Francisque Michel. The other, in two volumes and containing only the dramatic works, was by Benjamin Laroche, a journalist who had spent time in England as a political exile. Both took advantage of the resources of Romantic diction, and Laroche's version had considerable commercial success. By the end of the century it had gone through ten editions, and it was still in use in the 1940s. Yet there was no sense of progress. The drive for authenticity seemed only to expose the inadequacy of the French language. In the 1840s Philarète Chasles reviewed the available translations and was forced to the conclusion that, a century after his name had become familiar, Shakespeare's work was still unknown in France. By a frustrating irony, the more the French desired him, the more elusive he became. Despite a hundred years of painstaking effort, those who did not know English remained excommunicated from the company of the blessed: 'Most translations have made Shakespeare speak a feeble, bizarre, often unintelligible prose.' In their passage from the Teutonic to the Latin medium, some sort of embalming chemistry had annulled 'the uninhibited passion, the naive story-telling, the direct expression of emotions common to all humanity, of universal ideas' that were the miracle of Shakespeare's art. What was extraordinary had become quotidian and jejune. Laroche's offering, conscientiously literal, was a distressing witness to the chasm that must apparently always separate a translator's intention from his achievement: 'The pathetic has become trivial, the sublime is no longer anything but absurd pathos. What cultural relation is there between these disconnected thoughts?' Le Tourneur's laboriously compiled and expensively produced volumes harboured a relic: something shrunken, desiccated, and colourless. 'A picture by Raphael has become a wood engraving, executed without taste.' This 'Cicero-Shakespeare' was unrecognisable to those who knew the original. 'The depiction of our soul accused, described, analysed, pardoned, exalted, and crowned ... has been reduced to a few agreeable periods.'[43]

Authoritative pessimism such as this served only to raise the stakes and redouble determination. Furthermore the view was gaining strength that the nineteenth century should have its own Shakespeare, rather than a patched up eighteenth-century one. The translations based on Le Tourneur savoured of mould and obsolescence. They remained rooted in the mentality of the pre-Revolutionary years – an era that now seemed, as the historian Augustin Thierry said, immeasurably remote. Retranslating Shakespeare thus became a symbolic gesture: a renunciation of the old dispensation and its values.

In the 1850s, François-Victor, the youngest son of Victor Hugo, set about providing his age with the Shakespeare it needed. His translation was the most ambitious yet undertaken, and the one that remained longest in print. It survived for 140 years as France's nearest equivalent to the German version of Schlegel and Tieck. Hugo's texts, unlike those of the Germans, were seldom performed; but they became an indispensable work of reference for anyone in any way connected with Shakespeare in France – including actors. The star tragedian Jean Mounet-Sully, when preparing to play Hamlet in a stage version by Dumas and Paul Meurice, discovered that it was only from Hugo's translation that he could construct a consistent and convincing interpretation of the role.[44] This Shakespeare was exhaustive in that it included not only the Sonnets (never before translated into French) but the apocrypha as well. It was courageously faithful to the text in that it deleted nothing, concealed nothing, and resorted to paraphrase and substitution only when exactness would have led to incomprehensibility. Hugo abandoned nobility and defied taste. The periphrasis, the metaphors were not shirked. The scabrous passages were unblushingly exposed; the obscenities were boldly rendered either by direct translation or by equivalent word-play, as indecent in French as in English. There was a reference to male varlets and masculine whores in *Troilus et Cressida*; a clown punning about erection in *Tout est bien qui finit bien*. Hugo honoured his intention to make it possible, so far as the French language and modern scholarship would allow, for the French-speaking world to know exactly what the English dramatist had written. He spoke not of 'translating', but of 'reproducing' Shakespeare, and his work took Shakespeare – and translation – to their furthest point from the redemptive, protective principles of the seventeenth-century masters.

It was the product of remarkable dedication. Hugo began work in 1853, at the age of twenty-four, after spending six months as a political prisoner in the Conciergerie in Paris. On his release he joined his parents in Jersey and remained with them in exile for eighteen years. Twelve of those years he devoted to the mammoth task, translating on average three plays a year. He worked directly from the 1623 folio in the Redstone library on Guernsey, but consulted too all the available quartos. Because the text of *Hamlet* varied so widely between the folio and the first quarto edition, he translated the play twice. All the work of translation was carried out in Guernsey and Jersey, where he was assisted by his fiancée Emily Putrou. Editorial research took him once a year to the

British Museum in London, and in 1858 he made a tour through England which included a visit to Stratford. His editorial was as prodigious as his literary effort, and when he sent to Paris the manuscript of his final volume he probably knew as much about Shakespeare as anyone then alive. Each play was glossed with explanatory notes and with translations of Shakespeare's sources and related historical documents. Each was introduced by a lengthy preface which analysed the author's themes and stressed their topicality in terms that recalled Victor Hugo's political utterances and ideological poems. It was in these polemical essays that François-Victor Hugo revealed his personal identification with Shakespeare as the dramatist of usurpation, tyranny, exile, and the indomitable heroic spirit.

The Hugo translation, swollen into fifteen volumes by the supplementary matter, was initially published between 1857 and 1865, then reissued in a second, revised edition between 1865 and 1873, the date of Hugo's death. Subsequently the plays were reprinted many times without the editorial material, and twenty-seven of them were selected in 1938 for the complete works of Shakespeare in the prestigious Bibliothèque de la Pléiade, published by Gallimard.[45]

Victor Hugo was undoubtedly right when he claimed that his son had given Shakespeare to the French unmuzzled ('sans muselière').[46] He was less justified in asserting that this translation was definitive. In one crucial aspect it did not – could not – differ from those it claimed to have superseded. François-Victor Hugo gave to the francophone world Shakespeare's meaning, more or less intact. What he did not give it was the Shakespearean experience. His prose, which was originally interspersed with dashes to indicate where Shakespeare's lines of verse had ended, is versatile: clever when coping with puns and tropes and ambiguities; lyrical or weighty as required. But it is hard-wearing rather than memorable. It does not date, but its riches are soon exhausted. Its meanings are at once apparent, and not withheld as Shakespeare's constantly are. It takes no risks, forces no frontiers; does not contract, twist and fracture under the pressures and urgencies of consciousness. It is not a text to be revisited, or to start a conflagration in the mind. Hugo makes few demands, and is parsimonious with his gifts. He is, in short, easy and safe, whereas Shakespeare is difficult and perilous. He is also uniform, whereas Shakespeare is multifarious. In this translation the language of *Love's Labours Lost* is much the same as that of *Cymbeline*. Hugo could not resist the force of gravity that was forever pulling translation in French from complexity to simplicity, from knottiness and opacity to smoothness and transparence. He did not therefore bring about a sense of arrival. He merely sustained the ever-recurring sense of departure. No sooner was his work published than the process resumed. Translators continued to refine and adjust, tear up and start again; and in 2002 the long-standing classic status of Hugo's Shakespeare was finally withdrawn. Gallimard then began replacing the old Pléiade *Œuvres complètes* with a new collaborative bilingual edition.

So the story remains without an ending. Yet for that reason Shakespeare remains in a metaphysical sense alive. Each new translation is a resurrection: a reprieve from the slow but inexorable death that is decreed by the gradual extinction of Shakespeare's own tongue. The English language is no longer the language of Shakespeare, and the famous promise of literary immortality in the Sonnets is as mortal as the language in which they are written. But for the Shakespeare who speaks in French, summer's lease is ever and again renewed. The history of the Classics has shown, and the history of Shakespeare will doubtless show again, that for a writer there is no immortality save that conferred by foreign tongues. Beyond this, survival is a myth – for literature as for all art. No masterpiece truly outlives its moment. Each is a valediction, and 'heritage', in all its applications to art, is a matter of translation – of counterfeit, that is, and compromise.

5

Desdemona's Handkerchief

The protocol of taste and the theory of race were a heavy drag on Shakespeare's dramatic career in France. It took him much longer to reach the French stage than to reach the French page. A wide and long-lived variance between what was printed in his name and what was performed shows how fundamentally educated Paris could be at odds with its own intrepid self. Until late in the nineteenth century even bold modern spirits, men and women of the world, were overpowered by notions of tradition and nationality when they encountered drama as performance. These notions were especially associated with the state theatres. Once inside those venerable precincts, the cosmopolitan Parisian became self-consciously French, and thought of Shakespeare as an alien, archaic Leviathan whose right of admittance was forfeit to some gallicised surrogate.

George Sand, a Romantic novelist and proto-feminist, notorious for her flouting of sexual and literary conventions, capitulated to the forces of orthodoxy when, in 1856, she translated *As You Like It* for the Comédie-Française. 'There is no way', she declared, 'that you can translate Shakespeare literally for the stage. If ever it was permitted to summarise, extract, and expurgate, it is with regard to this savage genius who knows no curb.' To resolve to do it was 'to commit murder, without a doubt', but the evil was as unavoidable as it was regrettable. The 'impetuous dash' and the 'delicious caprices' of Shakespeare, like his 'singular and apparently inexplicable' switching between, on the one hand, 'the divinest grace and chastity', and, on the other, 'the most frightening cynicism', were now disallowed by 'certain indisputably legitimate spiritual needs'. These needs she defined, predictably, as 'l'ordre, la sobriété, l'harmonie, et la logique'. The clock could not be put back. Progress in dramatic art had exposed in Shakespeare's work 'a negligence and an audacity which are no longer of our time and which our taste would not tolerate'.[1] Apologising for the sacrilege she was committing, she therefore gutted Shakespeare's play and stuffed its skin with Molière. Her *Comme il vous plaira* is a sentimental pastoral comedy inspired by *Le Misanthrope*. The self-exiled melancholy Jacques, nursing a broken heart in the forest of Arden, is reawakened to the happiness of love by the tender ministrations of Celia.

This was one of the earliest attempts to bring Shakespearean comedy to Parisian audiences. Hitherto theatrical interest had been focused on the tragedies. But since, in France, the tragic stage was such a jealously guarded sanctuary of national values and national taste, the attempt to domesticate Shakespeare had involved adjustments even more drastic than those made by George Sand. In order to qualify for performance, Shakespeare's tragedies had had to be made classical – regular, that is, and edifying, and adapted to the prescriptions of *vraisemblance, convenance,* and *bienséance.* These adaptations brought Shakespeare's name before the theatre public, but they were never regarded as anything other than unsatisfying compromises, and they became less and less acceptable as racialist ideology refined its dogma of types and antipathies. If Shakespeare was quintessentially unFrench, then, *a fortiori,* the attempt to gallicise him was unFrench too, since it was by definition absurd and irrational. It was impossible to frenchify what was essentially unFrench. The logic of racialism therefore demanded that Shakespeare be either left to the Anglo-Saxons, whose genius he was, or exposed without mitigation or apology to the incomprehension of French audiences. The result would in either case be the same. Shakespeare would be relished by a few students, and rejected by the instincts of the wider public. In fact, the casualty of the exercise turned out to be not Shakespeare but classicism. Its hegemony collapsed as authentic Shakespeare became established and racialist assumptions proved false.

This consequence was always implicit in the attempt to domesticate Shakespeare, because from the very first the theatre looked to him for something that was different. It required that he be French, but it also required that he be *shakespearien* – a word that entered the French language in the 1780s.[2] It signified amplitude, emphasis, energy, and explicit emotion, and it registered the difference between the tragic theatre of France and that of England: between a theatre of repose and stasis, and a theatre of life in motion. As often as it was said that French tragedies contained nothing but conversations and narrative, it was said that Shakespeare abounded in spectacle and action. In purely dramaturgic terms, the advantages of Shakespeare were freely acknowledged. He was often offensive, but never tedious. The verbal drama of Racine, said Grimm in 1776, could never deliver the same theatrical impact as the kinetic drama of Shakespeare. 'The action of the English stage often offends taste, [but] the narratives of the French stage almost always weaken interest.'[3]

With a view to producing tragedy that was both French and *shakespearienne*, the linguistic register of the plays was lowered while the pictorial register was raised. The procedure routinely followed was to reduce and regularise the text, while multiplying the cues for spectacle and ostentation. French Shakespeare was, in a word, operatic, and it entered the theatre through the breach that opera had made. Visual and emotional stimulus were provided by big stages, elaborate and realistic scenery, and supplementary pantomime and ballet. At the time when Shakespeare's name began to circulate in France, fashionable Paris was addicted to the Italian opera, and his work was taken up by the theatre because it could be a vehicle for this sort of entertainment. Voltaire wanted to modify tragedy in accordance with the new art form, and his initial interest in Shakespeare was undoubtedly owing to the operatic possibilities offered by his work. In 1778 the *Année Littéraire* summarised the theatre's current need when it called for 'une fable décente et régulière' incorporating the 'action, spectacle, mouvement [et] variété' that were the hallmark of Shakespeare's craftsmanship.[4]

The most noteworthy of the many *gens de théâtre* who adopted this formula was Jean-François Ducis, poet, popular dramatist, and inheritor of Voltaire's *fauteuil* in the Académie Française. Ducis was one of the first and the most ardent of French *shakespearomanes*. He judged Shakespeare 'perhaps the most vigorous and amazing tragic poet who ever lived'.[5] Legend has it that a portrait of the English bard had a place of honour among his possessions, alongside the portraits of his mother and father. He has a permanent footnote in the history of literature in France as the man who introduced Shakespeare to the French stage, and for over half a century he dominated the market for performing editions of the dramatist's work. Ducis was never bothered by the problems of translation, because he never experienced them. He could neither speak nor read English, and his knowledge of Shakespeare was derived entirely from the translations of La Place and Le Tourneur. Emboldened by this linguistic innocence, he brought to the theatre five tragedies with Shakespearean titles: *Hamlet* (1769), *Roméo et Juliette* (1778), *Le Roi Léar* (1783), *Macbeth* (1784), and *Othello* (1792). Three of them were remarkably successful. *Hamlet, Léar,* and *Othello* were still in the repertoire in the middle years of the next century, and Sarah Bernhardt made a fledgling appearance in *Léar* as late as 1867 at the Odéon. The archives of the Comédie-Française record 489 performances of Ducis' Shakespearean plays, and they were also frequently seen in the provinces. His only failure in the genre was *Le Roi Jean sans terre* (*King John*), premièred in 1791 but never revived.[6]

Although Ducis' name remains indissolubly linked with that of Shakespeare, the differences between his plays and their English namesakes are far more evident that the similarities. Anyone who knew Shakespeare's work would have found even its best-known features missing from the French versions. Ducis' *Hamlet* had no ghost, no Rosencrantz and Guildenstern, no players, no gravediggers, no fencing match, and no dead hero at the end. In his *Roméo et Juliette* the brawling, the ball, the nurse, Friar Laurence, the balcony were all missing, and after the first performance a happy ending was substituted for the lovers' suicide. *Macbeth* had no witches (except as an optional extra, never used), no porter, and no banquet, and it was many years before a sleepwalking scene was added. In *Othello* there was no sign of Cyprus, no mention of a handkerchief, and no marriage of the hero and heroine, though quite possibly there would be wedding bells at the end, since theatre managers were offered an alternative to Shakespeare's distressing dénouement. In *Le Roi Léar* there was no fool and no final catastrophe, since the abused king recovered both his sanity and his throne. The characters in Ducis' plays were far fewer than those in Shakespeare's, and they mostly carried unfamiliar names. There was nowhere any mention of Horatio, Laertes, Mercutio, Cordelia, Goneril, Gloucester, Banquo, Macduff, Iago, or Desdemona. A few sounded vaguely Shakespearean (Volnérille, Thébaldo, Hédelmone), but the majority answered to names unknown in the Shakespeare canon (Norceste, Elvir, Albéric, Flavie, Helmonde, Norclète, Frédegonde, Iphyctone, Loclin, Séver, Lorédan, Pézar). Furthermore what happened to these people was often quite different from what happened to Shakespeare's characters. So Ducis' reputation as Shakespeare's henchman had very little substance. There was no more to it than a few basic themes, the occasional well-known phrase, a loose treatment of time and place, and operatic stage effects. 'He is seen in the far distance', runs one stage direction in *Léar*, 'lit by lightning, through the trees of the forest, alone, lost, looking agonised and agitated about him ... Thunder erupts, lightning sets the horizon ablaze, the wind howls, hail falls upon the bald and uncovered head of Léar.' Such windows for histrionic display made these plays *shakespearien*, but Shakespeare himself was no more than a faint, oneiric presence: the dim halo of a light eclipsed by protocol.

In order to secure performance, Ducis had constantly to sacrifice his own inclinations and better judgement. He told David Garrick that, since a speaking ghost, strolling players, and a fight with foils were 'absolutely inadmissible' on the French stage, his *Hamlet* was necessarily quite different from Shakespeare's: 'I have therefore been compelled to create, in one way and another, a new play. I have simply tried to make an interesting role of the parricidal queen and above all to depict in the pure and melancholy soul of Hamlet a model of filial tenderness.'[7] Even so, his play was rejected by the celebrated tragedian Henri-Louis Lekain, who lectured him on the dangers of literary innovation and the difficulty of making the crudity of Shakespeare acceptable to audiences accustomed to 'the substantial beauties of Corneille and the exquisite refinement of Racine'.[8] Ducis frequently revised his texts in response to objections and suggestions, and *Hamlet* in its final form owed much to the advice of François-Joseph Talma, the actor who took up the title role in 1803 and made it a staple of his repertoire. Always striving to please and fearful of offending, 'le bon Ducis' sacrificed his own more daring ideas and sought the safety of the beaten track. He used rhyming alexandrines; he introduced *confidants* and *confidantes*; he eschewed comic relief; he honoured the edicts of taste, *politesse*, and moral propriety. His Roméo and Juliette abstain from all physical contact except a final embrace. His *Othello* was a story about the terrible consequences of filial disobedience. In *Macbeth* he avoided 'the always revolting impression of horror', and diluted terror 'by mixing it artistically with what could make it bearable'. He would contemplate an innovation and then retreat, alarmed by his own temerity.

He gave Léar back his sanity because, he said, he 'trembled more than once … in thinking about bringing on to the French stage a king who has lost his reason'. He changed the ending of *Roméo et Juliette* into a flurry of timely explanation and joyful resuscitation in order to avoid the topic of suicide, about which everyone was very touchy following the appearance in French of Goethe's *Werther* (1776). He decided to stay the hand of Othello by a last-minute revelation because he had been worried by the strong reaction to the killing of Hédelmone at the first performance. ('Never was such a terrible impression made. The whole house rose, and uttered a single cry. Several women fainted.')[9]

These concessions and compromises brought Ducis immediate success and subsequent extinction. A few literary figures congratulated him on having made Shakespeare appropriately decent and regular; but most critical opinion was hostile from the start, and it became steadily more so after his death (1816). Initially he was accused of having polluted French theatres with Shakespeare.[10] Later he was arraigned for having disfigured Shakespeare beyond recognition. The baron de Barante, who translated *Hamlet* for Guizot's revised edition of Le Tourneur's Shakespeare, scathingly dismissed Ducis' version. 'The play and the characters', he wrote,

> have been forced into a sort of uniform and conventional mould, whereby all distinctive colouring, all originality, all grandeur of conception, all living truth, have disappeared. A sequence of scenes that embraces human nature … has been replaced by a tyrant, a conspiracy, *confidants*, and a young princess – all very familiar and apparently taken straight from the theatrical stockroom.[11]

When *Othello* was revived at the Comédie-Française in 1839 in a benefit performance for the actor Frédérick Lemaître, Gérard de Nerval reported in *Le Messager* that the play 'made a poor showing'. He wrote of 'the profound boredom prevailing in the auditorium during the old-fashioned speeches'. Saint-Beuve registered the general verdict of this generation when he described the works as 'travestissements sentimentales', unread and unreadable.[12]

They are not, in fact, travesties, since they were never intended to be copies of Shakespeare. Nor are they adaptations, given that they owe so little to the Shakespearean scenarios. They are imitations – but not in the modern sense of the word. In eighteenth-century aesthetic theory *imitation* had no connotations of pastiche or deception. It meant not crafty mimicry, but the sort of open, creative replication that involved dismantling and reassembling: recasting a given idea in a different cultural mould. 'Good imitation', wrote Diderot in the *Encyclopédie*, 'is continual invention.' It meant, said Marmontel, 'taking an old work and reproducing it either in the same form with new beauties, or in a new form with beauties that are foreign, ancient, or modern introduced'.[13] Ducis had no intention of deceiving, nor indeed was deception possible. As he pointed out, the publication of Le Tourneur's translation made it clear to everyone how far his plays differed from Shakespeare's. They were deliberately of their own time, both in their prosody and in the issues they addressed. Ducis extracted Shakespeare's 'modern' subjects from his 'barbaric' idiom and made them contemporary. He used them as pegs on which to hang topical concerns and shibboleths. *Hamlet* and *Le Roi Léar* are political plays of the *ancien régime*. They vindicate the claims of legitimacy by depicting the defeat of subversion by consecrated authority. Prince Hamlet survives an attempt at usurpation by Prince Claudius and assumes the burden of the succession. Léar's return to sanity and to sovereignty signifies the triumph of divine right. *Roméo et Juliette* is saturated in *sensibilité*. It treats the conflict between parental authority and love in the manner of a *drame bourgeois*. *Macbeth* began as a play of the *ancien régime* and acquired a revolutionary slant when it was revived in 1790. Both versions show Macbeth, the usurper, overcome by the rightful heir to the throne of Scotland; but in the later version the victorious Malcome (*sic*) becomes a constitutional monarch. He is crowned as 'first citizen' ('premier citoyen'), and bound by oath to observe the book of the law ('le livre de la loi'). *Othello* absorbed the ideology of the Revolutionary years. The hero owes more to Rousseau than to Shakespeare. He is a noble savage in conflict with a corrupt aristocracy, and he attributes the apparent infidelity of Hédelmone to the vile environment of Venice:

> C'est l'effet du climat. Il faut, pour tant d'horreur,
> Que tout l'art de Venise ait passé dans son cœur.*

---

* It's the effect of the climate. So much horror could not be / Had all the cunning of Venice not entered into her heart.

It was argued in Ducis' defence that he gave the French theatre as much of Shakespeare as it could tolerate. Pierre Lami said in 1824 that 'in their natural state, that is to say more closely resembling the originals', nobody in France would have cared to see these plays.[14] But during the Revolution it was noted how the French public were becoming inured to scenes of horror and terror;[15] so by the 1820s those impatient to clear a space in the theatre for themselves or their friends were able to claim that Ducis was superseded. His polite conversations and happy endings had been cut off from modern sentiment by the deluge of blood and fire that had swept the *ancien régime* to its grave. The duc de Broglie argued in 1830 that people who had lived through a Shakespearean cataclysm could not be content with anything less than real Shakespeare on the stage. 'We ourselves', he wrote,

> have taken part in terrible events. We have witnessed the fall and rise of empires ... We have known great men – conquerors, statesmen, conspirators – men of flesh and blood powerful by their arms, by their genius, and by their eloquence; and in order to be interested we must be pointed to men equally real, to men who resemble them in all respects.[16]

How could the puppets of conventional classical drama satisfy minds thus alerted to the tremendous facts of history and destiny? The clamorous ovations that greeted the English actors in Paris in 1827 and 1828 suggested a new appetite and a new capacity for strong theatrical meat. How much longer therefore could the public be denied raw, unprocessed Shakespeare? 'It is time', cried Emile Deschamps,

> that the French public were shown the great Shakespeare as he really is, with his magnificent sweep, his varied characters, his well-judged mixture of comic and tragic styles ... and even with his faults ... It is time that these masterpieces were reproduced faithfully on our stage.

Among the 'faults' that should no longer be concealed were 'obscene buffoonery' and 'those chilling horrors of the time of Elizabeth'. Alfred de Vigny declared that the age of *imitations* was past. 'An imitator of Shakespeare would in our time be as false as the imitators of [Racine] are.' The critic Charles Maurice argued that Shakespeare was better left to the English, but that if the French insisted on taking him up they should accept him for what he was: 'Don't deprive him of his colouring, his character, his peculiarities.' Théophile Gautier, likewise, demanded unadulterated Shakespeare. There was no longer any reason to neutralise his 'couleur étrangère et même étrange'.[17]

There was no lack of Shakespeare in the public domain in Paris during the periods of the Restoration, the Second Republic, and the Second Empire. He seemed to be everywhere – in the music of Berlioz and Ambroise Thomas, in the art of Delacroix, in the work of almost everyone who wrote for the stage: from leading Romantics like Hugo, Dumas, and de Vigny, to academic classicists like Casimir Delavigne and jobbing playwrights like Eugène Scribe. However, this was still muted and diluted Shakespeare. After seeing *Othello* in English, performed by William Macready on a return visit to Paris in 1844, Gérard de Nerval deplored the anaemic substitutes that still passed as Shakespeare in French. 'What is feared in Paris', he wrote, 'is the right word, true action.'[18] Theatres humoured their public; and the Parisian public generally preferred the sheltered side of the frontier between what was customary and what was not. It was a moving frontier. The limits of tolerance were widening as the spirit of Penelope, forever at work, again shifted the boundary between what was totem and what was taboo. Things deemed inadmissible, in art as in morals, would become routine. But the drift of opinion away from the Catholic-classical prohibitions was neither quick nor uniform, and the survival of modified Shakespeare was favoured for some time yet by ebbs and eddies in the stream. These imitations and adaptations were generally ridiculed by sophisticated critics – Gérard de Nerval and Jules Barbey d'Aurevilly, most notably; but they were welcomed by the champions of tradition and 'le répertoire', whose leader was Francisque Sarcey. Sarcey lived for the theatre and virtually in it. He contributed a weekly column to *Le Temps* for more than thirty years and gained immense authority by telling the Parisian public what they should patronise and why. His was the voice of commonsense, decency, and *le goût français*. Discussing an adaptation of *King Lear* at the Odéon in 1868, he praised the translator for having intercepted the full impact of Shakespeare's nastiness:

> How grateful I am to M. Jules Lemaître for having spared me that abominable Edmond, such a cold, resolute hypocrite, adulterer, and parricide! How I thank him for having delivered me from that Edgar, cursed by his father – as if there wasn't enough malediction already in this infernal drama ... There are enough horrors left, far more than I can cope with.[19]

The role of authors in the long resistance to authentic Shakespeare is ambivalent and complex. They were not always unwilling accomplices of tradition. Often they were far less revolutionary than they claimed to be. Not even the Romantics were entirely innocent of collaboration with the *ancien régime*. When they translated Shakespeare for the stage, de Vigny, Deschamps, and Dumas all discovered, not just in their audiences but also in themselves, nostalgia for the 'fable décente et régulière'.

De Vigny often said that he was uncomfortable in the theatre. He complained of being cramped by its conventions and limitations. Yet his encounter with Shakespeare suggests that in this portrayal of himself as an artist fettered by a philistine theatrical public there was a good deal of Romantic posture. The preferences and inhibitions that constrained him were as much his own as those of his audience. His translation of *Othello* (*Le More de Venise*) received its première at the Comédie-Française at the end of October 1829 – a significant time in the history of the French theatre generally and of the Comédie-Française in particular. The actor Joanny, who played the title role, insisted that this was the real *Othello*, the *Othello* of Shakespeare, and an aura of revolutionary importance gathered around the work. De Vigny was a writer of the first rank, and his translation, together with Dumas' *Henri III et son cour* and Hugo's *Hernani*, came to be regarded as the heavy artillery of Romanticism. Its arrival at the Comédie shortly after Dumas' play and shortly before Hugo's seemed to symbolise the collapse of classicism before the forces of innovation. De Vigny himself promoted this idea, by presenting his translation as a challenge to French tragedy – that anachronism, that lifeless monument to routine and *politesse*.[20] In fact, *Le More de Venise* delivered much less than a full-scale assault on the old-style theatre. *Othello* was already more than half classical in its observation of the unities and its concentration on a single character and a single passion. De Vigny made it almost wholly so, by having careful regard for *bienséance* – or, as he put it, 'the changes which the progress of the general intellect has brought about in the philosophy and mentality of our age, in some of the usages of the stage, and in the chastity of speech'. Discussing Shakespeare's 'somewhat too energetic expressions', de Vigny explained that he had retained them when they were 'imperatively called for by the situation' – which meant that they were almost all suppressed.[21] Othello addresses Desdemona as *prostituée* in Act IV; but elsewhere euphemism takes over and brutal scurrility is transformed into tepid innuendo. 'These Moors are changeable in their wills', says Shakespeare's Iago. 'The food that to him now is luscious as locusts, shall be to him shortly as bitter as coloquintida. She must change for youth: when she is sated with his body, she will find the error of her choice. She must have change, she must.' De Vigny converts this direct, heavily loaded language into an inoffensive jingle:

> L'amour d'un More est très frivole
> Et sa flamme brûlante au bout d'un mois s'envole.
> Pour sa femme elle est jeune; elle devra changer,
> Elle le doit.

Iago's explicit complaint against Othello ('it is thought abroad that twixt my sheets / He has done my office') becomes prudishly vague: *On dit partout que, sans scrupule, / Il m'a stigmatisé d'un affront ridicule.* Without the notes of lechery and sexual cynicism, symptoms of general turpitude, the sense of Othello's tragic isolation is lost. What was a play about martyred innocence has become a play about a moral flaw, about jealousy. De Vigny was clearly concerned to spare his audience the nihilism of Shakespeare. Suffering had to be justified – Desdemona's, as well as Othello's. Three references to the culpability of her disobedience of her father were carefully inserted.

De Vigny used prose for his own plays (*Chatterton; La Maréchale d'Ancre*) – but these he classified as *drames*. He baulked at abandoning rhyming verse in tragedy. Transplanted into French, the Shakespearean mixture of prose and verse would, he thought, bring operetta to mind, and he was later confirmed in this suspicion when he saw *Julius Caesar* performed in August Barbier's translation. 'When a character, like the tribune Marcellus, after having grumbled in prose, suddenly starts to reason in verse, it seems that he is about to sing a couplet ... You are waiting for the music to begin.'[22] Epic prose alone was unsuitable because in the theatre it sounded inflated, rigid, and melodramatic.[23] He therefore rehabilitated the alexandrine, by making it more supple, and replicated the alternation in Shakespeare's diction by moving between what he called 'récit' and 'chant'. In passages of 'récit' he followed Hugo's call for verse that was rhyming but flexible. Thus when Desdemona begs Othello to grant an audience to Cassio ('Why then, tomorrow night; or Tuesday morn; / On Tuesday noon, or night; on Wednesday morn: / I prithee name the time ...') she speaks lines daringly asymmetrical and open-ended:

> Ah si ce n'est demain, que ce soit donc bien vite!
> Demain soir, ou mardi matin, ou vers midi,
> Du mardi soir, ou bien, au plus tard, mercredi
> Dès le matin! Fixons le moment, je t'en prie.

But for the big passionate moments of what he called 'chant', de Vigny employed the academic alexandrine with its end-of-line closure and midway caesura. The result was to transform a poetry of private anguish into the rhetoric of public declamation. When he translated Othello's valediction to happiness and pride –

> O! now for ever
> Farewell the tranquil mind; farewell content!
> Farewell the plumed troop and the big wars
> That make ambition virtue! ...

– de Vigny deliberately set out to make the language 'less prosaic' than Shakespeare's, and 'better conforming to the grandeur of the African warrior'. He thereby, as a modern French critic has pointed out, falsified the instrumentation of the drama by requiring Othello to sound 'noble' at precisely the moment when he is laying nobility aside:[24]

> Et maintenant adieu!
> A tout jamais adieu, le repos de mon âme!
> Adieu, joie et bonheur détruits par une femme!
> Adieu beaux bataillons aux panaches flottants!
> Adieu guerre! Adieu, toi, dont les jeux éclatants
> Font de l'ambition une vertu sublime!

Suffering defeats Shakespeare's Othello. It brutalises him and discomposes his language:

> But there, where I have garner'd up my heart,
> Where either I must live or bear no life,
> The fountain from the which my current runs
> Or else dries up; to be discarded thence!
> Or keep it as a cistern for foul toads
> To knot and gender in!

De Vigny's Othello masters his suffering, and alchemises it into eloquence:

> Mais l'asile adoré, le tabernacle d'or
> Où j'avais de mon cœur déposé le trésor,
> La source ou je puisais et rapportais ma vie,
> M'en arracher moi-même et me la voir ravie,
> Ou bien la conserver lorsque son flot d'azur
> Est tout empoisonné comme un marais impur!

Le More de Venise is full of classical reminiscences, but they are nowhere more evident than in the episode of Desdemona's handkerchief. Innocently lost by Desdemona, then unscrupulously acquired and 'planted' by Iago in order to incriminate her, this simple but crucial accessory was a major headache for French translators. 'Mouchoir' was a word which well-bred French people could not bring themselves to utter – or to hear – in public. It was emphatically 'low'. The poet Ponce-Denis Lebrun, when adapting Schiller's *Marie Stuart* for performance in France, had felt unable to use it even though the handkerchief in this play had been embroidered by a queen. He had substituted the word 'tissu' (*prends ce don, ce tissu, ce gage de tendresse*).* Desdemona's handkerchief was even more problematic in that it was 'spotted with strawberries', because 'fraise' ranked even lower than 'mouchoir' in the lexical hierarchy. Consequently for almost two hundred years no translator for the stage dared to ask actors to say – or audiences to hear – exactly what it was that Desdemona had lost and Iago had made atrocious use of. Translations intended for readers made no secret of the matter. Le Tourneur gives *mouchoir brodé de fleurs* but includes the exact term in a note ('*strawberries* – fraises'). In 1837 a prose translation by Philippe Le Bas featured a *mouchoir parsemé de fraises*. François-Victor Hugo preferred *mouchoir brodé de fraises*. But until well into the twentieth century translators working for the stage made do with euphemism and periphrasis. Ducis introduced a *bandeau de diamants* ('diamond headband'). Others opted for a *mouchoir parsemé de fleurs rouges*, a *rare et beau mouchoir brodé de fleurs*, or a *mouchoir singulier*

---

* Nimm dieses Tuch! Ich habs mit eigner Hand / Für dich gestickt in meines Kummers Stunden.

tout brodé de fraisiers en fleurs. De Vigny broke the taboo on the name of the article itself. When he saw a handkerchief he called it a handkerchief. He took credit for having been the first to cause the word to be uttered in the French theatre. Mlle Mars, playing Desdemona, had objected; but her scruples had been overcome and history had been made. Her *mouchoir*, however, remained without *fraises*. It was *orné de fleurs asiatiques*. Writing in 1925, a British scholar observed that it had taken a hundred years for Desdemona's handkerchief to be called by its proper name on the French stage, and that a further hundred had elapsed without accurate mention of its distinctive decoration.[25]

The story of *Le More de Venise* shows what happened when a leading Romantic writer decided to translate Shakespeare 'faithfully' and the chief French theatre put all its resources at his disposal.[26] It shows that the poet and the theatrical public were united rather than divided in their reservations. The public were more tolerant than the poet of Ducis, whose *Othello* was still being played at the Comédie-Française in the 1840s; but neither was yet ready for the real thing. Literary Paris acknowledged the significance of de Vigny's experiment. It welcomed what it judged to be a qualified artistic success. The *Revue de Paris* summed up the critical response when it decided that de Vigny had not really translated Shakespeare, but that he had, here and there, given a recognisable and striking equivalent. Audience reaction suggests that the play offended many of the regular patrons of the Comédie-Française, but failed to attract the wider, less fastidious bourgeois public who gobbled up melodrama in the boulevard theatres. The first night was turbulent, with noisy interruptions during the drunkenness of Cassio, Othello's repeated demand for *le mouchoir*, Desdemona's bed-time toilette, and the harrowing dénouement. The cast performed nervously and uncertainly, their confidence undermined. But the approval of the pro-Romantics was equally vociferous, and the evening ended with loud applause drowning the cat-calls and whistles. De Vigny made further cuts to what was already an abbreviated text, and subsequent performances were quieter. The actors settled into their roles, and the work was given a fair hearing. But interest waned as the scandal and excitement died down. After half a dozen performances receipts began to diminish and houses to grow thin. *Le More de Venise* was financially much more successful than many classical tragedies, but it lacked the appeal of other

Romantic plays. After the seventeenth performance it disappeared and was never revived, save very briefly at the théâtre Historique in 1862 and at the Odéon in 1895.[27]

The fortunes of *Le More de Venise* were closely followed by other Romantic writers, and they drew from de Vigny's experience the lesson that the time was not yet ripe for authentic Shakespeare in the Paris theatre. One of these writers was de Vigny's friend Emile Deschamps, whose Shakespearean ventures included collaborating with de Vigny on a new translation of *Romeo and Juliet.* Harriet Smithson's triumph had made this tragedy the talk of the town, and Deschamps and De Vigny decided to produce a French theatrical version that would replace the old 'imitation' of Ducis. Their text was accepted by the Comédie-Française in 1828, but no arrangements were made for performance. The leading lady of the Comédie, Mlle Mars, was now forty-nine and feared ridicule if she appeared as Juliet. De Vigny thereupon lost interest, but Deschamps translated the whole play and published his text in 1844.

It then became clear that despite his call for Shakespeare 'as he was', Deschamps himself was not prepared to deliver so much. He confessed to having omitted 'a great number of characteristic scenes', 'an infinity of curious and picturesque details', and 'many forceful expressions', since these would have slowed down the action and 'shocked our theatrical customs'.[28] The only version of *Romeo* by Deschamps that was ever heard in public was his libretto for Berlioz's dramatic symphony (1839); but his *Macbeth* did reach the stage and met with remarkable success. It was produced at the Odéon in 1848 and ran for 120 performances. Its advantages were not literary. Deschamps used blank verse in an effort to mimic Shakespeare, and his crippled alexandrines make it obvious why de Vigny lost interest in collaboration:

> Ainsi demain, demain encore, puis un autre
> S'avance vers le gouffre; et tous nos jours passés
> N'auront fait qu'éclaircir de tristes insensés
> Sur la route qui mène où tout s'abîme ensemble ... *

---

* Tomorrow, and tomorrow, and tomorrow / Creeps in this petty pace from day to day / To the last syllable of recorded time; / And all our yesterdays have lighted fools / The way to dusty death ...

The play succeeded because it was rigidly regular and circumspectly decent. Made wise by de Vigny's mistakes, Deschamps decided that presenting Shakespeare 'as he was' did not preclude 'delousing' him. (He used the word 'écheniller', which means 'remove the caterpillars'). Translation thus purified would, he explained, remain 'literal', because although it would not contain all of Shakespeare, it would contain only Shakespeare.[29] Having thus conceded the right to subtract and withheld the right to add, he had proceeded to do both. In *Roméo et Juliette* he not only eliminated the coarse language, he also substituted Garrick's ending for Shakespeare's. Juliet wakes from her death-like sleep while the poisoned Romeo is still alive, and they embrace in a final farewell before she stabs herself. In *Macbeth* he disinfected the dialogue and added a dénouement of his own. Macduff and Macbeth are both mortally wounded in their final combat, and they hail Malcolm as king before they expire. The three witches then reappear, cackling with triumphant laughter. *Amis!* cries Malcolm to his soldiers as the curtain falls, *Vive l'Ecosse et ne croyons qu'en Dieu!*[30]

Clearly, when French writers insisted on real Shakespeare in performance, they did not mean what they said. They reserved for translators the right to make Shakespeare French – even while they maintained that frenchification was neither possible nor desirable. Emile Montégut revealed himself to be a scrupulous, even pedantic translator. For many years his prose version of Shakespeare's dramatic works (first published between 1867 and 1870) rivalled that of François-Victor Hugo. Yet on the stage he preferred his Shakespeare reconstructed. Discussing a version of *Macbeth* by Jules Lacroix, produced at the Odéon in 1863, he began by asserting that the French public were now blasé, open-minded, able and willing to tolerate exotic aberration. 'Classical prejudices', he affirmed,

> have disappeared – or just about. Our modern public have seen so many literary efforts of all sorts, have been subjected to so much rashness, that they can hardly bring themselves to be surprised by anything at all ... Shakespeare is no longer for this public a drunken savage, an invading barbarian who must be repulsed at all costs ...

He then went on, however, to approve the deletions which Lacroix had made in deference to 'le goût français'. These included the first scene with the witches, the porter, and the on-stage murder of Banquo and

1. Voltaire, by Houdon. (*Victoria and Albert Museum*)

2. *The Triumph of Truth*, by Sir Joshua Reynolds. (*University of Aberdeen*)

3. Jean-François Ducis.

4. Harriet Smithson.
(*British Museum*)

5. Harriet Smithson as Ophelia, Paris 1827. Lithograph by Devéria and Boulanger. (*British Museum*)

6. Hamlet and the Ghost. Lithograph by Delacroix.

7. Hamlet in the Graveyard. Lithograph by Delacroix.

8. Sarah Bernhardt as Hamlet. (*Victoria and Albert Museum*)

9. André Antoine as Lear, 1904. (*L'Illustration Théâtrale*)

10. A scene from Antoine's production of *Jules César*, 1906. (*L'Illustration Théâtrale*)

11. André Gide. (*Medlar Images*)   12. Jean-Louis Barrault. (*Medlar Images*)

Lady Macduff. His justification for the last omission was that the events were subsequently narrated. There was no need to depict what was described – as Racine had demonstrated so convincingly in *Phèdre*.[31]

Alexandre Dumas père, after achieving first national, then international fame with his historical dramas and novels, followed de Vigny and Deschamps down the Shakespearean road. He decided to translate *Hamlet* – a formidable challenge, given the immense amount of critical and artistic attention that this work had by now received throughout the Western world. Ducis' version was still in use at the Comédie-Française, but because it was now judged less on its own merits than in comparison with Shakespeare's, it was seeming more than ever inadequate. Dumas needed a collaborator, since he knew no – or very little – English, and he chose Paul Meurice, a young writer from his wide entourage of assistants and protégés. Meurice had been jointly responsible for *Falstaff*, compiled from both parts of *Henry IV* and performed at the Odéon in 1842. Together Dumas and his associate devised a *Hamlet* in rhyming verse which had a long stage history after its first performance in 1846. It entered the repertoire of the Comédie-Française in 1886, and remained there until the First World War. It was played at Angers as late as 1954. During this long life, the translation underwent revisions which reflect the slow conversion of the French theatre to the cause of authentic Shakespeare. Almost all the changes, however, were made on the initiative of Paul Meurice, and the most fundamental date from after 1870, the year of Dumas' death. Despite his reputation as a Romantic firebrand, which was generated by his historical dramas in prose, Dumas was governed by the box-office and never took risks for the sake of artistic ideology or theory. So when, with *Hamlet*, he entered the tragic repertoire, he was very mindful of the special significance of tragedy for the theatre-going public. He was reminded by de Vigny's experience that it was not good business to move away from the time-honoured forms and rituals. In its original version, therefore, the Dumas-Meurice *Hamlet* was a 'fable décente et régulière', constructed with careful regard for taste and *bienséance*. It moved back from de Vigny towards Ducis, rather than forward from de Vigny towards Shakespeare. Dumas had seen a performance of the Ducis imitation in his youth, and he claimed to have been so deeply impressed that he learnt the leading role by heart and never forgot it.[32] Probably it is this lasting impression which

explains many of the peculiarities of his own *Hamlet*. Meurice seems initially to have done little more than provide a literal translation for
Dumas to shape and versify. His own inclinations may have been less
conservative. According to press reports, his *Falstaff* had 'dared everything', and 'recoiled before no far-fetched expression'.[33]

Dumas recast what was in France still widely regarded as a ramshackle
masterpiece, and pulled and pummelled Shakespeare's imagery to make
it fit into rhyming alexandrines:

> Quels rêves peupleront
> Le sommeil de la mort, lorsque sous notre front
> Ne s'agiteront plus la vie et la pensée?
> Doute affreux qui nous courbe à l'ornière tracée!
> Eh! qui supporterait tant de honte et de deuil,
> L'injure des puissants, l'outrage de l'orgueil,
> Les lenteurs de la loi, la profonde souffrance,
> Que creuse dans le cœur l'amour sans espérance,
> La lutte du génie et du vulgaire épais?
> Quand un fer aiguisé donne si bien la paix!*

Fortinbras disappeared, and the whole of the opening scene on the battlements of the castle was scrapped because there was no gainsaying old
wisdom – it was superfluous to depict what was subsequently narrated.
But in the first act a scene was added in which Hamlet courted Ophelia
and left her exclaiming, breathless with rapture, *Il m'aime! Il m'aime!
Oh! que je suis heureuse!* Hamlet was not banished to England, so his
treacherous companions, Rosencrantz and Guildenstern, did not perish
there. Instead, they lived to witness a dénouement wildly different from
Shakespeare's, but more in conformity with the requirements of justice.
Providence, in this rendition of the play, was equitable in its arrangements. At the climactic moment, after the fatal fencing match, when

---

* For in that sleep of death what dreams may come / When we have shuffled
off this mortal coil, / must give us pause. There's the respect / That makes
calamity of so long life; / For who would bear the whips and scorns of time,
/ The oppressor's wrong, / The proud man's contumely, / The pangs of dis-
priz'd love, the law's delay, / The insolence of office, and the spurns / That
patient merit of the unworthy takes, / When he himself might his quietus
make / With a bare bodkin?

Hamlet, his adversary Laertes, his mother the queen, and his stepfather the king all lay bleeding or expiring, it was not the heroic, redeeming figure of Fortinbras who appeared, but the ghost of Hamlet's father, returned to deliver condign punishment to each of the stricken protagonists. Spectators who knew a little Shakespeare must have thought, for a disconcerting moment, that this errant spirit had lost its way, and turned up in Elsinore when it should have been at Bosworth Field. Sentencing the culprits, it took up the refrain of the phantoms who torment Richard III on the eve of his final battle. *Désespère et meurs!* ['Despair and die!'] it enjoined the regicide Claudius. *Prie et meurs!* ['Pray and die!'] it told the treacherous Laertes. *Espère et meurs!* ['Hope and die!'] it commanded the lascivious queen. Only when it addressed Hamlet himself did it become clear that there was no ghostly disorientation, merely a little picking and mixing to tidy up Shakespeare's messy ending. *Et quel châtiment m'attend donc?* ['What punishment, then, is reserved for me?'] asked the wounded prince. To which the ghost replied, as the curtain fell: *Tu vivras!* ['Thou shalt live!'].

Dumas defended this drastic metamorphosis by arguing, along academic lines, that Shakespeare's dénouement was defective because it violated *vraisemblance*, offended propriety, and upset the dramatic symmetry. 'Since Hamlet', he insisted, 'is not guilty to the same degree as the others, he should not die the same death as the others.' Four corpses on the stage, furthermore, created 'the most unpleasant effect'; and given that the ghost had been conspicuously present at the beginning of the play, 'it must necessarily reappear to be present at the end'.[34] Dumas' belief that Shakespeare could, and should, be 'improved' by the application of rules and formulae, together with the dramaturgical tactics of de Vigny and Deschamps, expose serious limitations to the Romantic commitment to Shakespeare and weaken the whole idea of a Romantic revolution in the French theatre. In their dealings with Shakespeare these self-proclaimed partisans of change and renewal revealed themselves to be accomplices of classicism and exponents of Frenchness. Probably they did more to retard than to hasten the entry of their idol on to the French stage. It was only when Romanticism was extinct that efforts to adapt Shakespeare to the French theatre were finally overtaken by efforts to adapt the French theatre to Shakespeare.

The Dumas-Meurice *Hamlet* was first performed privately in the little theatre at Saint-Germain-en-Laye, where Dumas lived, in 1846. It then transferred to Paris, playing at the théâtre Historique, the Odéon, and the théâtre Beaumarchais in 1847, 1855, and 1861, with the celebrated tragedian Philibert Rouvière in the title-rôle. But it was caustically disparaged for having falsified Shakespeare,[35] and in 1864 Meurice published a revised version. The first scene was reinstated, Fortinbras brought back, and the original ending restored. Fortinbras was the last of these recuperations to reach the stage. There was no sign of him in 1867 at the théâtre de la Gaité, where the actress Mme Judith appeared as the melancholy prince. Twenty years later, at the Comédie-Française, cuts had to be made to allow time for shifting the elaborate scenery, so Fortinbras was again omitted. The curtain fell after Hamlet's final words (*le reste est silence*). His absence, however, was only temporary. Paradoxically it was now, when racialism was entering into the most strident phase of its presentation of Shakespeare as alien to the Latin cosmos, that artistic pressure for full acceptance of his work became irresistible. The literary figures who clamoured for the real thing now meant what they said, and they got what they asked for when Jean Mounet-Sully and Sarah Bernhardt, dazzling stars of the theatrical firmament, added their influence to the campaign.

The removal of Fortinbras had always been one of the most controversial of the alterations made by Dumas and Meurice. Gautier had pointed out in 1847 that the loss of this character destroyed an essential tension in the psychological dynamics of the drama.[36] Paul Meurice fully appreciated the argument, and in a note to the published version of the 1886 text he expressed the hope that 'the admirable episode of Fortinbras' would one day find its way back to the stage:

> The character of Fortinbras illuminates and throws into relief, by opposition, the character of Hamlet ... Shakespeare has expressed ... this contrast, and brought it out in an even more striking way, in the dénouement, which shows us Hamlet dead in the midst of his victims and Fortinbras king in the midst of his soldiers.[37]

The cause of Fortinbras was taken up by Mounet-Sully, who was Hamlet in the revival of 1886 and who subsequently played the role more than 200 times. Fortinbras, the Norwegian soldier-prince who incarnates Hamlet's ideal of humanity ('What a piece of work is a man ...!'), is, Mounet perceived, essential as a measure both of Hamlet's existential paralysis and of the rottenness of Denmark:

> The court of the king is sunk in sensuality and intrigue while the enemy is on the march ... I should like it to be the main purpose of the stage presentation to make the public aware of the abandon, the disorder, and the perpetual orgy in which the king, the queen, and all the court live ... It is this appetite for sensual pleasure, this compulsive need for noisy distraction, that give the drama all its intensity.[38]

Mounet had his way. When the production was revived in 1896 the text had undergone further revision and Fortinbras finally made his entry on to the stage of the Comédie-Française. Furthermore, Hamlet's banishment was reintroduced, and the spurious scene of courtship dropped. These modifications meant that a French *Hamlet* was at last being performed whose configuration matched that of Shakespeare's and which concluded, like Shakespeare's, not in a classical equilibrium transcending time, but at a point of re-entry into the onward flow of time and contingency. When he saw the play in its new shape, Stephan Mallarmé realised that it was Fortinbras and his soldiers who made it crucially different from its classical surrogates. They introduced a contrast not just between hesitation and action, but also between an esoteric paraphernalia of death (poison, a stream with lilies, an unbuttoned foil) and the mundane destructiveness of an army on the march: the movement of history which purged the stage and released the spectator from 'une somptueuse et stagnante ... exagération du meutre'. Shakespeare required the audience to see what the classical author concealed – the dismantling of the tragic apparatus; just as, in *Macbeth*, by beginning with the witches, he revealed its being set up.[39]

By now *Hamlet* was overlaid with so much association, memory, interpretation and, in France, reconstruction and variation, that it had become all but invisible. Watching Mounet-Sully's performance, critics were conscious of a disabling loss of innocence. They experienced a crushing weight of inhibition when they tried to write about a character in whom the origin and the culmination of so much had been identified. 'It is difficult to think of any piece of theatre', wrote Jules Lemaître, 'which can awaken in us such a quantity of remembrances and impressions ... Of what does *Hamlet* not make us think? We have to think of so many things that we hear it as if in a dream.'[40] Sarcey confessed to a failure of comprehension in the passage from page to stage: 'When I read it, there is no problem ... but ... in the theatre I no longer understand Hamlet ... The commentaries merely make me more confused. Volumes have been written in order to explain Hamlet, and the more he is explained, the less intelligible he is.'[41]

Never did a clearing away of lumber, a return to fundamentals, seem more urgent, and this was now reckoned to be impossible while the theatre insisted on Shakespeare in classical French verse. Sarah Bernhardt knew from painful experience that the marriage was doomed. In 1884 she had appeared at the théâtre de la Porte-Saint-Martin in a translation of *Macbeth* by her lover, the novelist Jean Richepin. It was the last of the stage versions to use rhyming alexandrines, and not even Bernhardt's charisma could save it from disaster. Richepin's text was savagely trounced, both when it was first performed and in 1914, when the Comédie-Française made a vain effort to revive it. Jacques Bainville called it 'une sinistre caricature' which distorted Shakespeare almost as much as Ducis did. He complained that the versification was not just barbarous, but insipidly so. It ruined the beauty of the original. The rhythm was ungraspable; there was a deplorable abundance of padding. It was a hotchpotch: the 'style pompier' rubbed along with the 'style flamboyant', and tatters of Romanticism were mixed with classical odds and ends.[42] Richepin, like so many others, had been defeated by the stubborn refusal of French rhymes to accommodate Shakespeare's imagery:

> Eteins-toi, éteins-toi, clarté brève ... La vie
> N'est qu'une ombre qui passe, un acteur qu'on envie
> Pauvre diable, pendant que le monde en fait cas,
> Alors qu'il va et vient, superbe, avec fracas,
> Sur la scène, emplissant son heure de délice,
> Et puis qu'on n'entend plus, rentré dans la coulisse ... *

After this unhappy experience Bernhardt abandoned verse and made

---

* Out, out, brief candle! Life's but a walking shadow, a poor player / That struts and frets his hour upon the stage, / And then is heard no more; it is a tale / Told by an idiot, full of sound and fury, / Signifying nothing.

theatrical history by introducing to French audiences Hamlets who spoke in prose. The venture began with more disaster. In 1886, still at the Porte Saint-Martin, she appeared as Ophelia in a prose translation specially commissioned from Lucien Cressonois and Charles Samson. Paris was impatiently waiting for Mounet-Sully's Hamlet at the Comédie-Française and booed off the stage the mediocre Philippe Garnier, another of Sarah's paramours.[43] This ill-starred production was the prelude to a legend, nevertheless. In 1899 Bernhardt herself played Hamlet at her own theatre (the old théâtre des Nations) using a new prose translation by Marcel Schwob, a young writer who was attracting attention with his delicately crafted essays and biographical miniatures.

The *Hamlet* of Dumas-Meurice and that of Marcel Schwob were both products of their time, and to move from the one to the other is to move from the cultural milieu of the Second Empire to that of the *fin de siècle*. The Dumas-Meurice version bespeaks an age of structures and systems, sharp outlines and diatonic melodies; of strong light, dark shadow, and a Cartesian division between the self and the world. It says science, Positivism, Parnassianism, grand opera. Schwob's *Hamlet* comes from the time when art and literature were entering the misty regions. Its age was the age of vanishing contours, twilight, solipsism, and chromatic harmonies. It says Decadence, Symbolism; Wagner, Schopenhauer, Bergson. Schwob made a quantum leap. He exploited the resources of prose to release Shakespeare from the Procrustean bed of French classicism and reconnect him with the Elizabethan late Renaissance. Like so many writers of his time, he was fascinated by the pathology of lateness. He was attracted to the mutations of language and sensibility that characterised and linked the late epochs of history – the Byzantine epilogue to the Roman empire, the Baroque aftermath of the Renaissance, the modern *Götterdämmerung*. He was therefore most responsive to those aspects of Shakespeare's writing that had been erased by the classical furbishers – the ornateness, the euphuism, the arcane and occult allusions. He and his collaborator, Eugène Morand, made it their special concern to transpose these into French. They declined to paraphrase. Instead, they followed the Decadent stylists into the remotest corners of the French language, and rummaged there for esoteric terminologies and forgotten locutions that would replicate Shakespeare's Baroque orchestration. 'Words', they explained,

> are represented by words, and phrases by phrases … The style of the six-teenth century is not that of the present. Fitting a Shakespearean period into the fashion of today would be rather like aiming to translate a page of Rabbelais into the language spoken by Voltaire.[44]

They laid under contribution *argot* and archaism, and they resorted to neologism where *le mot juste* eluded their erudition. They used words like 'féal', 'mitan', 'lige', 'nenni', 'icelui', 'ru', 'joyeuseté', 'hanap', 'enrib-auder' – words that lived in lore, liturgy, and ballad. When Hamlet stabs him through the curtain, Polonius cries: *Je suis occis!* During their noc-turnal watch on the battlements of Elsinore, Hamlet and his companions hear sounds of revelry within the castle. Hamlet explains:

> The king doth wake tonight and takes his rouse,
> Keeps wassail, and the swaggering up-spring reels;
> And, as he drains his draughts of Rhenish down,
> The kettledrum and trumpet thus bray out
> The triumph of his pledge.

When dealing with this passage, Dumas and Meurice had begun with Shakespeare, but then moved away in their search for rhyme:

> A force de flambeaux, de coupes, et de bruit,
> Le roi veut défier le silence et la nuit.
> Il fait sonner, joyeux, la fanfare de cuivre,
> Pour proclamer qu'il est le maître – et qu'il est ivre,
> Et pour porter, parmi les rires éhontés,
> Le défi de ses toasts jusqu'aux cieux irrités.

Schwob and Morand remained close to Shakespeare throughout: *Le roi soupe, ce soir, et mène ripailles, avec noces et caroles fanfaronnes. Et comme il vide des verres de vin du Rhin, il fait braire à trompettes et timbales son triomphe chaque fois qu'il trinque.*

  This was, as Henri de Régnier observed, 'at the same time literal and literary'.[45] In performance it acquired a strange, Byzantine resonance. Bernhardt's Hamlet reversed the gender-inversion that had been cus-tomary in the Elizabethan theatre. A mature female impersonated an adolescent male, pitching the drama in a remote and troubled key.

Whenever she spoke or moved, androgyny filled the stage with multiple ambiguity. 'The least word', wrote de Régnier, 'acquires on her tongue a double and mysterious sense.'[46] The time was out of joint in Elsinore not least because sexual identities had become intermediate and indeterminate. In this it reflected another aspect of contemporary Paris. Bernhardt's chalky-faced, tousled-haired sexual ambivalence was more subtle but no less emblematic than that of Yvette Guilbert, the flat-chested, raven-voiced doyenne of the *cafés-concerts*, whose notorious song *Madame Arthur* was entrancing homosexual audiences in the cabarets of Montmartre. Both belonged to a culture that had made of the hermaphrodite an erotic mascot: the culture that had spawned Rachilde's *Monsieur Vénus*, Péladan's *Le Vice suprême*, and the recondite lecheries of Proust's vast reminiscence of the City of the Plain. But the Schwob-Morand *Hamlet* was more than a peculiar period-piece. It was a portent of things to come. In 1932 it replaced the Dumas-Meurice version at the Comédie-Française, and remained there until the 1960s. It hastened, without a doubt, the death of the alexandrine. Once Shakespeare had passed into prose or *vers libre*, classical versification rapidly fell out of use, despite a few efforts (notably by Henri Pichette) to revive it. The rhyming alexandrine, recognised for 250 years as the signature of Frenchness, became obsolete, and the French theatre discovered at last that there was life after the death of Racine.

6

His Hour upon the Stage

The gradual 'restoration' of *Hamlet*, its transformation from something home-grown into something recognisably exotic, clearly indicated that the old 'fable décente et regulière' was retreating from the French theatre. Yet racialist ideas about Latinity and Frenchness were at this time assuming a gospel authority in ideological thinking and preaching. The more tolerant audiences became of authentic Shakespeare, the more stridently intellectuals proclaimed that he could never appeal to the authentic French.

Jules Lemaître, critic of the *Journal des Débats* and later a member of the Ligue de la Patrie Française, remained adamant that the *Hamlet* on show at the Comédie-Française in 1886 was alien to French eyes and ears. 'We are the French of today', he protested, 'and not Anglo-Saxons of three hundred years ago.' The Dumas-Meurice translation in its latest version persuaded him that Voltaire had been right. Shakespeare was a 'sauvage ivre', whose works were suitable for the French stage only when adapted and 'corrected'.[1] Twenty years later the idea of a racial divide between Shakespeare and the French was restated by Emile Faguet. Assessing the prospects of unprocessed Shakespeare in France, he ruled out any genuine rapprochement:

> I'm not saying it's a bad thing, I'm not saying it's a good thing that Shakespeare played integrally should succeed integrally in front of a French public of 2000 people – an average public of course, not a first-night one. I'm saying that when this happens – if it happens – the French race will have changed absolutely; that it will – to put it bluntly – have been replaced by another race.[2]

It was an opinion that the scholar Fernand Baldensperger, after surveying the history of Shakespeare in France, was ready to endorse. He doubted, in 1910, that Shakespeare's plays would ever be fully accepted by French audiences or even by French readers. He reckoned that partisans of Shakespeare in the French theatre had always been, and would always be, more hopeful than successful.[3]

During the interwar decades it became obvious that the facts of recent cultural history were demanding a radical revision of such views. To the critic Pierre Lièrre, looking back from 1936, it was apparent that a profound change in attitudes to Shakespeare had been taking place during the previous half-century. 'Our relationship with Shakespeare', he wrote in the *Mercure de France*, 'has modified ... and we no longer want adaptations. We want something that is as near as possible to the original text.'[4] Objections against surrogates were now coming even from conservative quarters. In 1919 Paul Souday, literary critic of *Le Temps* and an ardent Voltairean, had made a stand for authenticity – in the major works at least. 'When it's a question of a work eminently Shakespearean – of *Hamlet, King Lear, Macbeth, Julius Caesar, Antony and Cleopatra, The Merchant of Venice, The Tempest* – I wish to be given the masterpiece itself, complete and unabridged.'[5] Such appeals had been made before, and had gone unheeded. But the evidence now seemed irrefutable that what Henry de Montherlant called 'l'esprit du Grand Siècle' was no longer the powerful censor it once had been. In the early 1920s de Montherlant noted a relaxation of 'the idea that an ideal translation is one in which everything that is strong must systematically be weakened, and everything that is strange must be made banal'.[6]

The avant-garde that made Paris the world's centre of modern art in the early years of the twentieth century had its counterpart in the theatre. Once again the city hosted and incubated dramaturgical ideas and talents from abroad. As German and English Romanticism had galvanised Parisian literature and drama in the 1820s and 1830s, so now the modernism of Ibsen, Strindberg, Stanislavsky, Craig, Reinhardt, and Granville-Barker sent tremors through the Parisian theatre and shook out its old fusty repertoire of classical tragedy, vaudeville comedy, boulevard melodrama, and Second Empire operetta. And it was Shakespeare – again as in the 1820s and 1830s – who gave the revitalising, reforming spirit a local habitation and a name. There was, however, a crucial difference between the Shakespearean manifestation of the early nineteenth century and that of a hundred years later. The Romantics had not so much discovered Shakespeare as invented him. They had not looked beyond the vast variegated surface of his work, and they had done no more than set him up as a sacred relic in the museum of literature. As Gaston Baty put it in 1921, 'Romanticism halted in ecstasy before the multicoloured entrance, and went no further'.[7] It had failed to make good Shakespeare's absence from the French theatre. The avant-garde of the early twentieth century therefore undertook to remedy the great lacuna. It set out to ransom Shakespeare from the written page and restore him to the theatre, where it was convinced he belonged.

The most prominent figures in this enterprise were André Antoine, Jacques Copeau, and Georges Pitoëff. All were inspired by the invigorating theories and practices that were giving the theatre in general – and Shakespeare in particular – a new birth in Germany, Russia, and England. Pitoëff was himself Russian – an emigré who settled first in Switzerland, then in France. All were actors – though not of the ilk of Talma, Lemaître, Sully, Bernhardt, and Rachel, those hugely inflated personalities who had dominated the French theatre in the nineteenth century and hijacked dramatic texts as vehicles for their own charisma. Antoine acted rarely and reluctantly. Copeau appeared mostly in films, in order to earn a living. Pitoëff often acted, in partnership with his wife Ludmilla, but he never lost his Russian accent and this limited his repertoire and his professional success. It was as members of the first generation of French directors (*metteurs en scène*) that these men made their mark. Pitoëff attributed to Antoine the introduction into France of German ideas about stage direction, and he recognised in Copeau the French equivalent of Danchenko and Stanislavsky, the pioneers who had transformed the Russian theatre in the early 1900s.[8] With Antoine, Copeau, and Pitoëff there arrived in the French theatre the overseeing, coordinating intelligence that gave to enacted drama the coherence and transcendence it had never had in the days of the superstars. From being a random collection of satellite performances loosely held together by a central *tour de force*, a play became a 'production' (*mise en scène*) in which all aspects of the theatrical event – interpretation, costumes, décor, lighting, movement, gesture – were determined by the director's interrogation of the text. 'By *mise en scène*', wrote Copeau,

> we mean the pattern in dramatic activity. It is the ensemble, made up of movements, gestures, postures; of faces, voices, and silences fitting together.

It is the totality of the scenic spectacle, issuing from a single mind, which conceives it, organises it, and harmonises it. The director invents and fixes between the characters that secret, invisible tie, that reciprocal sensibility, that mysterious mutuality without which a play, even when interpreted by excellent actors, loses the best part of its expressiveness.[9]

This way of putting on a play made the text fundamental – the text as inherited from the author, that is, and not as adventitiously reconstructed. Performance became a ritual of deference not to some code of social propriety or to thespian talent, but to the artistic conception of a writer. The director's job was not to make this conception conform with the theatre, but to make the theatre conform with the conception. He was a hierophant, without whose exegetical and liturgical skills an author's intentions could not be understood or realised. 'An author', explained Gaston Baty, 'can express only a part of his dream. The rest is not in the manuscript. It is the function of the director to restore to the work of the poet the part which became lost in the passage from dream to manuscript.'[10]

In the case of a foreign writer like Shakespeare the first essential of modern performance was therefore complete and accurate translation. Retrieving Shakespeare for the stage meant performing his work whole and unmodified. Rigorously committed to this principle, Antoine, Copeau, and Pitoëff used translations that had been either specially commissioned, or made – with expert assistance – by themselves. Both Copeau and Pitoëff translated as well as directed Shakespeare. But it is perhaps Baty's encounter with the Bard that best shows how fundamentally French ideas about stage translation were changing.

Baty was one of the leading theatrical directors of the 1920s and 1930s. He was a member, like Pitoëff, of the innovatory Cartel des Quatre, and in one sense his view of Shakespeare was that of the avant-garde. In so far as he declined to venerate Shakespeare as a purely literary and philosophical genius, he dissented from the traditional French response. Baty was firmly convinced that Shakespeare belonged not in the library nor in the study, but on the stage. Like Molière, Shakespeare used the actor's technique of self-effacement, and – again like Molière – he wrote as only a man of the theatre could. In another sense, however, Baty was orthodox in his view. He reckoned that the stageworthiness of Shakespeare's texts was marred by disorder and excess. When he studied *Hamlet*, in preparation for his production of the play at the théâtre de l'Avenue in 1928, he decided that the essential, truly theatrical scenario was smothered by what he called a 'texte de remplissage'. This text was 'swollen with metaphors, bristling with preciosity, at once tumultuous and contorted'. What is noteworthy is that he contrived to provide himself with a more congenial version of the play without infringing the now virtually sacrosanct principles of authenticity and integrality. Another edition of the drama was available, that of the first quarto of 1603, which was much shorter and simpler than either the second quarto of 1604 or the folio text of 1623. It was, according to Baty, 'a constantly moving drama, without obscurities, without any slackening of the action', constructed according to 'une logique absolue'. It was, he might almost have said, 'une fable décente et régulière'. He therefore chose this version (translated by Théodore Lascaris) for his production of the play, arguing that he was thereby assisting, not hindering, the campaign for authentic Shakespeare. The first quarto was, he said, Shakespeare's own recension of his tragedy. The second quarto (on which the folio text was based) was an amplified adaptation. It was the work of some secondary figure who had been commissioned to turn the play into a vehicle for 'that scourge of the dramatic art of every age', the star actor – who in this case was obviously Burbage. Furthermore, this 'Burbage *Hamlet*' was a literary product. It had been concocted by a writer (Derby perhaps, or possibly Rutland or Oxford) whose tumid style was more modish that dramaturgic. So, Baty insisted, by discarding this version of the play he was not only giving *Hamlet* back to Shakespeare, he was also giving Shakespeare back to the theatre.[11]

This thesis attracted people like Baty because it vindicated their reluctance to accept Shakespeare whole; it humoured their nagging itch to reinvent him by separating the 'beauties' in the works from the 'faults' and attributing the latter not to Shakespeare but to the spirit of his age. Yet the terms of Baty's argument were different from those used by the Voltaireans. When Baty selected the one *Hamlet* and rejected the other, he did so not in the name of *goût* or *bienséance*, but in the name of authenticity. The argument was specious. The first quarto is clearly a defective, pirated text, and there is nothing in the second quarto that suggests multiple authorship. But its very speciousness is evidence of new priorities. It confirms that the French theatre was now less concerned about separating what was civilised from what was barbaric, and more concerned about separating what was genuine from what was apocryphal.

The cult of the text, the whole text, and nothing but the text was initiated by André Antoine, a director who had made his name by founding the Théâtre Libre and introducing into France the work of Ibsen, Strindberg, Hauptmann, and Tourgenev. Antoine hated what he called 'la manie des adaptations de Shakespeare'. When he acquired the lease of the théâtre des Menus-Plaisirs, on the boulevard de Strasbourg, he therefore decided that the time had come for him to present to Paris Shakespeare 'complete and unabridged, without the mutilations, the adaptation, and the transposing' that had so shamefully disfigured 'le grand Will' in France during the previous one and a half centuries.[12] What he had seen of the work of the German director von Possart, in Munich, had persuaded him that this was both technically feasible and artistically desirable. One of the reasons why Shakespeare's dramas in their original form were regarded as unactable was because they required more changes of scenery than a modern theatre could provide within the normal duration of a performance. Possart had overcome this problem by playing intermediate scenes front stage, before a proscenium curtain, while the set was being changed behind. Struck by the possibilities opened up by this novel procedure, Antoine decided to present *King Lear* fully staged and virtually uncut at his Montmartre playhouse – now renamed the théâtre Antoine. So it was that in 1904, three hundred years after it had been written, Shakespeare's tragedy finally arrived in Paris, with the director himself in the title role. 'For the first time in France,' wrote Antoine, 'it was possible to have a true sense of Shakespearean drama, with its sequence of pictures unfolding without interruption, in the rhythm of the work and within the usual duration of a French play.'[13]

The performance began at nine o'clock and Antoine was able to ensure that it was over before midnight by adopting von Possart's method of scene shifting, by allowing only two brief intervals, and by using a text which, though it retained the essential meanings of Shakespeare's, sacrificed most of the poetry. The translators were the sailor-novelist Pierre Loti and Emile Vedel, a fellow writer and naval officer. Their chief aims had been a spiritual rather than a literal exactness, and a clarity that preserved the archaic timbre of the original.[14] In practice this meant that they avoided substantial cuts – only about 150 lines were actually omitted – but made full use of the sort of shrinkage that could be obtained by paraphrasing and trimming. In his first soliloquy, Shakespeare's Edmund says:

> Wherefore should I
> Stand in the plague of custom and permit
> The curiosity of nations to deprive me
> For that I am some twelve or fourteen moonshines
> Lag of a brother?

In Loti's and Vedel's version he says: *Pour quelle raison irais-je me soumettre à la coutume qui me forclôt de l'héritage paternel?* – which is brief, but prosaic; and what is prosaic has a habit of becoming banal. Says Kent at the height of the storm: 'The tyranny of the open night's too rough / For nature to endure' – which is very thinly rendered by *Il n'est pas possible de rester plus longtemps dehors.* Yet in comparison with what had hitherto been heard on the French stage this was an integral *Lear*, and it fulfilled its purpose by being a theatrical rather than a literary event. Crowds flocked to see it, and Antoine revived it the following year. The production ran for a total of seventy performances, which was impressive even by commercial standards at that time.

Antoine continued to sponsor authentic Shakespeare from 1906 until 1913, when he was director of the Odéon. He mounted four further productions, for which he commissioned prose translations from Louis de Gramont (*Julius Caesar*, and *Romeo and Juliet*), Paul Sonniès (*Coriolan*), and, once more, Emile Vedel (*Troïlus et Cressida*). *Troilus*, presented in 1912, was a daring choice, since it was completely unknown and there was an obvious risk that it would fail for being undesirably classical rather than desirably *shakespearien*. There was little scope for epic ostentation with a play whose static dialogue was relieved only by some chaotic skirmishing. *Troilus and Cressida*, like traditional French tragedy, consisted mainly of speeches and conversations. These were woven into a uniquely Shakespearean verbal fabric, but Vedel was not up to transposing its brocaded richness into French. His text, though cogent and speakable, was impoverished and underpowered. Consequently it obscured the play's essential irony – the irony that links magnificent talk with paltry deeds. Magnificent talk is the calx of love, politics, and philosophy in Shakespeare's bleak epitome of the human condition. His Greeks and Trojans discourse splendidly and act despicably. Vedel's Greeks and Trojans are as short of fine language as they are of heroism and magnanimity. 'When the planets', says Shakespeare's Ulysses,

> In evil mixture to disorder wander,
> What plagues, and what portents, what mutiny,
> What raging of the sea, shaking of the earth,
> Commotion in the winds, frights, changes, horrors,
> Divert and crack, rend and deracinate,
> The unity and married calm of states
> Quite from their fixture!

The French Ulysses is laconic – too pressed for time, it would seem, to talk about time in the discursive way that Shakespeare's does: *Mais si les planètes se mettaient à errer pêle-mêle, songez aux désastres, aux révolutions et aux cataclysmes qui en résulteraient!* Eloquence as the thief of time and integrity is missing from this translation, which does not move far beyond the limits of parody and burlesque. Pugnacious, vainglorious Ajax declaring himself humble ('I do hate a proud man as I do hate the engendering of toads') becomes shrill and limp-wristed'(*Je trouve cette espèce-là odieuse, si vous voulez que je vous dise mon sentiment*). But there is no talk of Achilles as 'effeminate', and Patroclus is transformed from his 'male varlet' and 'masculine whore' into his *bonne à tout faire* ('maid of all work'). What sounded vicious, lecherous, has been made to sound comic. In effect, the play was reduced to a sophisticated prototype of the sort of Homeric pastiche made wildly popular during the Second Empire by Meilhac and Halévy, who wrote the libretto for Offenbach's operetta *La Belle Hélène*.[15] Nevertheless its appearance on the stage of the Odéon made theatrical history. *Troilus and Cressida* had hitherto never, so far as the records showed, been performed anywhere. In England it had been seen only in a heavily reworked version by Dryden, and this had disappeared from view in the 1730s. It says much for Antoine's vision and dedication that he recognised and finally brought to light this neglected masterpiece. It says even more for Shakespeare's international reputation that the first performance of one of his major plays should have been in Paris, in French.

Throughout his life Antoine remained sharply critical of any relapse into old bad habits. He demanded integrality even for Shakespeare's lightweight pieces. When *The Merry Wives of Windsor* was performed in a freely modified version at the Odéon in 1922, he felt that both he and Shakespeare were being betrayed. He talked about the mutilation of immortal masterpieces and rebuked those who would purify Shakespeare in order to protect the dainty French public. Then in 1936 the actor and playwright Jean Sarment drew his fire for having been too loose in his translation of *Much Ado About Nothing*, performed at the théâtre de la Madeleine: 'They are still hacking their way through the gigantic forests that are the works of Shakespeare, still combing the hair of the *sauvage ivre*.'[16]

Sadly, one of the culprits in this latter instance was Jacques Copeau, who counted himself among Antoine's dedicated disciples. At this time financial pressures were forcing Copeau to direct and to act in versions of Shakespeare's comedies (*Rosalinde*, 1934; *Beaucoup de bruit pour rien*, 1936) that did not satisfy his puritanical standards of authenticity. His great ambition was, and had always been, to escape from 'vulgar histrionic and commercial pressures' in order to concentrate on the essentials of theatre – words and actors.[17] Initially a critic, he took up directing in order to fight 'shoddy works and shoddy habits', and to bring to the stage a sense of literary morality.[18] His idealism was focused on Shakespeare, the whole of whose work he dreamt of presenting integrally and unadorned. Elaborate and illusionistic staging he spurned, as a distraction from its dramatic and poetic self-sufficiency. By the 1930s the dreaming had long since ended, and he was consoling himself by translating Shakespeare in collaboration with his partner, the actress Suzanne Bing. But in the earlier years of his career there had been a brief, exhilarating moment of achievement and hope. In 1914 he had been responsible for a production of *Twelfth Night* which became one of the landmarks of Parisian theatre history and a major event in the French encounter with Shakespeare. *La Nuit des rois* featured in the inaugural season of the Vieux-Colombier, a small auditorium tucked away on the Left Bank in the quarter of Saint-Sulpice. It attracted national and even international attention to this one-time meeting hall of the Athéné Saint-Germain, converted into an experimental theatre by the enterprise of Copeau and two of his colleagues from the *Nouvelle Revue Française*,

Jean Schlumberger and Gaston Gallimard. Houses were full, and so many people had to be turned away that the production was revived after the First World War. In all, over two hundred performances were given. This 'little miracle', as Copeau called it, was owing in large measure to the translator, Théodore Lascaris, who continually revised his text during rehearsals, so as to bring it closer to the actors' understanding and requirements. The result vindicated triumphantly Copeau's conviction that Shakespearean comedy – always reckoned more difficult to market than the tragedies in France – could be brought on to the stage.[19] When the production opened, in May 1914, the Comédie-Française was presenting its revival of Jean Richepin's version of *Macbeth*, first staged unsuccessfully by Sarah Bernhardt thirty years before. Its rhyming alexandrines and Romantic stage effects were made to seem even more old-fashioned by Copeau's Shakespeare. It was after seeing *La Nuit des rois* that Jacques Bainville delivered his damning verdict on Richepin's 'caricature'. It was, he said, 'une honte pour la Comédie-Française', and he advised those in search of Shakespeare to abandon the Salle Richelieu and make their way across the Seine to the Vieux-Colombier.[20]

The famous little theatre was forced to close in 1924, its finances and its spirit irreparably damaged by the failure of an officially inspired attempt to reconstitute it as the French Theatre in New York during the war. However, its Shakespearean mission was resumed by Georges Pitoëff, who had founded his own company in Geneva in 1918 and moved to Paris in 1922. He mounted *Measure for Measure*, *Hamlet*, and *Macbeth* in Switzerland, and the first two of these productions he later revived in France. In Paris he also presented *Romeo and Juliet*, at the théâtre des Mathurins in 1937. Of the three directors most closely associated with Shakespeare in these years, Pitoëff was perhaps the most exacting in his insistence on integral translation. He distanced himself from those who would 'adapt these works to current taste by transforming them, by mutilating them'. The right approach was to 'bring out their modern, their eternal resonance, while respecting their integrality'.[21] Public and critical opinion in Geneva proved unready for his unbowdlerised, uncompromising Shakespeare. In 1921 his production of Guy de Portalès' translation of *Measure for Measure* was halted by the official censors, who thus added to the pressures that finally drove him to Paris. The only French *Macbeth* that he found sufficiently scrupulous for his purpose was the accurate but unimaginative translation by the academic Alexandre Beljame. For *Romeo and Juliet* he collaborated with the poet Pierre-Jean Jouve on a made-to-measure translation which replicated Shakespeare's alternation of prose and verse. Jouve devised a *vers libre* which ebbed and flowed with the currents of Shakespeare's lyricism, and he managed to duplicate Shakespeare's imagery almost word for word without causing thrombosis in the delicate textures of French diction:

> Tu veux partir? Ce n'est pas près d'être le jour.
> C'était le rossignol et non pas l'alouette
> Qui a percé le fond craintif de ton oreille;
> Il chante la nuit sur ce grenadier;
> Crois-moi, amour, c'était le rossignol ... *

It was a slightly strange, but mystical and haunting text, which was less than fully successful in performance only because Pitoëff, now fifty-three and still hampered by Slavonic vowels, made an unimpressive Romeo. He died two years later, somewhat consoled for the disappointing outcome of his approach to another major writer, André Gide. In Geneva he had presented the Schwob-Morand translation of *Hamlet*, and he planned to revive this production in Paris in 1922. Schob's widow, however, withheld permission, and Gide was therefore asked if he would provide a new translation.[22] Gide agreed, but then abandoned the project after completing the first act. So it was not until 1927, when permission to use Schwob's text was finally granted, that Pitoëff's *Hamlet* reached Paris. Characteristically, the cuts made by Sarah Bernhardt had been restored, and the marathon text was performed in its entirety.

Gide's involvement with Shakespeare has a special significance, both as a notable surrender to the spirit of the age, and as the last major protest against it. His two translations, like Gide himself, are curious hybrids. They were a response to the current demand for a close equivalent of Shakespeare on the French stage; but they were also an old-fashioned attempt to subtract Shakespeare from the theatre and to

---

* Wilt thou be gone? It is not yet near day / It was the nightingale, and not the lark,/ That pierc'd the fearful hollow of thine ear;/ Nightly she sings on yon pomegranate-tree:/ Believe me, love, it was the nightingale.

gallicise him, to make him less offensive to the standards represented by
'French taste'. Gide was a scrupulous translator; but his profoundest
interests were less theatrical than literary, and he could never really shift
the bias of his sympathies. For the sake of *Hamlet*, however, he made a
truce with the theatre and with himself. The result was a translation in
French prose that captured most of the meaning and much of the
sonority of Shakespeare's verse.

Gide wrote plays himself, and he counted amongst his friends some
of the most eminent French theatrical figures – including Copeau and
Pitoëff. Yet he was never fully at home in their world. He never had a
playwright's rapport with either actors or audiences. 'Gide', said Copeau
in 1928, 'n'aime pas le théâtre.' The theatre was, according to Gide, 'un
art essentiellement impur', which could not lead because it was bound
to follow the public – 'compter avec lui et sur lui'. Consequently it could
never break free from a traditional and hackneyed depiction of human
psychology.[23] But a stronger reason for his aversion was that he was too
much in love with language ever to feel entirely comfortable with
speech. Gide was a reader's writer, and a writer's reader. He judged a
text with his mind's ear, and it was to the mind's ear that he appealed
in his own work as an author. The currencies in which he dealt were the
silent rhythms and harmonies of the printed page, which he would
vocalise by reading aloud. Gide was averse to drama as performance,
because other voices interfered with his aural imagination. It was impossible for him to 'hear' a text when he was listening to an actor. When
he read Shakespeare (*Othello* and the histories especially) he was transported by admiration. On the rare occasions when he saw Shakespeare
performed, he was either bored or hostile. Shakespeare then became for
him what he had been for Voltaire – the vulgarian, the prostituted
genius who pandered to the debased sensibility of the theatre-going
public. In December 1946 he passed a very unhappy evening at the
théâtre des Champs Elysées, where the Old Vic company was performing *King Lear* with Laurence Olivier in the title role. 'No sooner settled
in our box,' he recorded in his journal, 'or shortly after the curtain went
up, I began to feel a crushing boredom – of a rather special type, furthermore, such as I hardly ever experience except in the theatre.' His
powers of judgement paralysed by the histrionic mediation of the text,
he relapsed into violent diatribe. The play was 'exécrable' and 'absurde'.

'It's not human, it's *enormous*; Hugo himself never conceived anything more gigantically artificial, more false.' It reminded him of the clichés and the claptrap, the greasepaint and the buskin, of Romantic melodrama: 'constant antitheses; random actions and impulses with, every now and then, just a glimmer of real human emotion ... hecatomb where the mad and the wicked are mixed together in death.'[24] This was the play that he had judged 'magnificent' when he had read it in 1922.[25] Drama as performance brought out the worst in Gide. It stirred his deepest antipathies. So all the while he was translating for the theatre, he was resisting its special exigencies. He judged his work by how it 'sounded' not on the stage, but on the page.

Ida Rubinstein, after having trained as a dancer under Fokine with the Ballets Russes in St Petersburg, pursued a second career as an actress in Paris. In 1917 she invited Gide to translate *Antony and Cleopatra*, and his version was given five performances at the Paris Opéra in 1920, with Rubinstein herself as the serpent of old Nile. Gide, however, had lost interest as soon as the translating was finished and rehearsals began. 'Performance bores me', he wrote. He complained that the actors were unresponsive to 'the beauty of the words'. They flattened his carefully modulated prose with the monotony of their delivery. 'Once more I'm forced to conclude that it's impossible to make a work of art out of a play.'[26] It was as a literary event that the enterprise continued to engage his attention. He saw a first edition of his text through the press in 1920, and fifteen years later began revising it for publication in the prestigious Pléiade edition of the complete works of Shakespeare. It was only now that he turned his attention to the Italian episodes of the play, since these had been omitted from the stage version.[27] The new text was staged by Jean-Louis Barrault at the Comédie-Française in 1945; but this was not a theatrical commission. Gide's additional labour was designed to preserve his reputation outside the theatre, not within it.

Many people thought of Gide as a Huguenot. This was partly because he looked like a Protestant pastor (the ascetic, hairless head; the dark cape; the fragile, unadorned hands). It was partly, too, because he was forever engaged, with his conscience and his Bible, in a struggle against the flesh. But it was mainly because he often rebelled against the Catholic-classical mentality – against its dogma, its Cartesian absolutes and invariables. He saw the sin in classicism: the idolatry and the threat to truth that attended the pursuit of formal perfection. 'Academic form', he wrote, 'conventional beauty, etc., are often responsible, in psychology, for monstrous error. There are certain contours which only mendacity can fill.' He perceived, too, that the deductive method of Cartesianism had favoured a generalising tendency in French thought and French literature. The individual was often lost to view among archetypes and abstractions.[28] All these are familiar Protestant preoccupations, and towards the end of his life, in the aftermath of the Second World War, Gide reaffirmed his Protestant convictions. Shocked and disillusioned by a victory that had, in France, replaced the political tyranny of the Right by the intellectual tyranny of the Left, he decided that, of the two evils that Valéry had famously diagnosed in the human condition, excess of order was worse than excess of disorder. 'The world will be saved – if it can be saved – only by the insubordinate.'[29]

Yet temperamentally Gide was at odds with his intellectual self. He confessed to a horror of Calvin and all he stood for.[30] He was as obedient as the most orthodox of Catholics to the dispensations of authority and tradition. Furthermore his mythology of Revelation was far more Catholic than Protestant. For Gide, haunted by a vision of Beauty that had been vouchsafed once and for all, there could be no discoveries in art – only rediscoveries, and the jealous conservation of inherited superlatives. In modern music he recognised the victory of Pandemonium: a regression from the exquisite legacy of harmony and melody to the cacophony of barbarism.[31] Modern literature had been corrupted by the intrusive, hubristic self, the agent of linguistic onanism and 'volupté'.[32] Re-reading Kleist in 1942, he realised how deeply he detested 'le spasmodique' in literature, and he recalled Hamlet's injunction to the players: 'For in the very torrent, tempest, and as I may say, whirlwind of your passion, you must acquire and beget a temperance that may give it smoothness.'[33] Yet it was Shakespeare who had debased the theatre, by democratising it: 'At first only nobles, titled people, were allowed to appear on the stage; then came the bourgeoisie; then the plebs. The stage once invaded, it was soon indistinguishable from the street.'[34] Gide defined classicism as 'the triumph of order and proportion over interior romanticism'. One of its supreme achievements was the purged and purified language of Racine, in which passion was latent rather than explicit. It was therefore Racine, the Jansenist who had surveyed the tumult of life from the summit of art, who claimed his enduring and unqualified devotion. 'I admire Shakespeare enormously', he wrote, 'but Racine inspires me with an emotion that Shakespeare never gives me – the emotion that comes from perfection.'[35]

Gide was a conspicuous writer who had extensive contacts in the theatre. He also had experience – though no very great success – as a playwright. So it was in no way surprising that Ida Rubinstein and Georges Pitoëff should have sought his services as a translator of Shakespeare. But it was surprising, given the current insistence on authenticity and his own classical predilections, that Gide should have accepted these commissions. The decision to remove the Italian interludes from *Antony and Cleopatra* (made for scenic reasons; not even Antoine's method would avail for the constant changes of location) had left the drama with a shape that Gide felt better able to handle. It had become much less Baroque when it lost its world-ranging restlessness. Nevertheless, its highly charged carnality remained, and Gide failed to convince the cognoscenti that he had come to terms with this. He produced a translation that they judged too reticent, too cerebral and hard-edged. Jacques Copeau said, 'Gide's translation, like others, is deficient in that it explains much more than it translates or transposes'; and he found that the 'astonishing propriety of the language' ('l'étonnante propriété de la langue') often chilled the poetry.[36] When the fuller version was performed in 1945, Louis Jouvet confirmed that the translation was 'very fine, but exclusively literary and undramatic'. His verdict was that it read well, but that it was not suitable for spoken delivery.[37] Gide's text is untheatrical essentially because it is uniform. There are no great moments. Shakespeare's variations of emotional pitch, the tightening and slackening of dramatic tension, are replaced by a pallid harmony, a homogeneous limpidity. Furthermore the sentinel of *goût* has reappeared, prohibiting access to certain notes and accents. When the mortally poisoned Cleoptra bids farewell to her dying attendants, she uses the sort of conventional, decorous rhetoric that had been the mainstay of eighteenth-century tragedy. Shakespeare's lines are:

> Come then, and take the last warmth of my lips.
> Farewell, kind Charmian, Iras a long farewell.
> Have I the aspic on my lips? Dost fall?
> If thou and nature can so gently part,

> The stroke of death is as a lover's pinch,
> Which hurts, and is desired.

Gide's version (1938) is:

Cueillez la dernière chaleur de mes lèvres. Adieu, mes douces, Charmian, Iras; un long adieu. L'aspic est-il donc sur mes lèvres? Morte? Quoi, le nœud si facilement se défait? Ah! vraiment ton étreinte, ô Mort, est pareille à celle d'un amant; elle blesse mais on la désire.

Here a strained and obscure euphemism (*le nœud si facilement se défait*) replaces a transparent, valedictory, one; exclamation (*Ah! ô Mort!*) is used to elevate the diction; and an elusive paraphrase carries echoes of the old 'fable décente et régulière'. The word *étreinte* ('hug', 'embrace') does not translate 'pinch'. It is a chaste substitute which silences the erotic resonance of Shakespeare's word. It also loses sight of the asp, which causes death by puncturing, not by embracing.

Shortcomings such as these were predictable; and it was even more predictable that in tackling *Hamlet* Gide should soon find himself baffled and frustrated to the point of paralysis. He agreed to Pitoëff's suggestion in April 1922, while still in the flush of pro-Shakespearean ardour caused by a re-reading of *Othello*; but it was not long before he was fretting about 'une difficulté infernale'. He found himself torn by conflicting loyalties. He acknowledged the need for a 'faithful' translation; yet he discovered in Shakespeare's text asperities that would not adapt to 'good' French – the only French he felt able to write. He was exasperated by 'redundancy', 'false and precious imagery', 'stamping', 'absurd images', 'lame metaphors', 'sophistry', 'repetition'. Only by leaving Shakespeare far behind, he decided, could he avoid massacring his own language. In a letter to Pitoëff, he explained his dilemma: 'How is it possible, without betraying Shakespeare, without departing from him, to formulate a French text that is clear, easily understood straight away, ... sonorous, and whose imagery is not too shocking for the logical French mind?' It was in the middle of July 1922, when he had finished the first act (which he said cost him more trouble than the whole of *Antony and Cleopatra*), that he decided to abandon the project. He could no longer cope with 'this extreme intelligence [which] has not been reabsorbed into the matter of art'.[38] Later, like Gaston Baty, he vindicated his dissatisfaction with the full text of the play by arguing that it was adulterated Shakespeare. 'To me it seemed inadmissible to recognise here only the great Will.'[39]

However, this was not a final renunciation. Despite his protestations of paralysis and defeat, the decision of 1922 was no unconditional surrender to his classical and anti-theatrical prejudices. At this time, in fact, Gide was more than ever aware of his need to overcome them. He was becoming conscious of his obsession with fine writing ('bien écrire') as a drag on his artistic achievement. 'It is against fine writing', he admitted, 'that I must most of all struggle. My style is hampered by a certain hankering for balance, by indulgence in eurhythm.' He decided that he must aim for less polish and more breaks and accents ('moins de polissure; plus de cassure et d'accent').[40] The more compelling reason for the decision of 1922 is to be found in the temporary disruption of his private life by certain complications – complications which the translating of *Hamlet* would have compounded unbearably. Twenty years later, when the Second World War had swamped these personal preoccupations in an overwhelming sense of public calamity, he recovered his thirst for Shakespeare, and finished his translation.

In the summer of 1922 Gide, a fifty-three-year-old homosexual who was conveniently and platonically married to one of his cousins, suddenly found himself emotionally besieged by two women. One had achieved a sexual relationship with him. The other passionately wanted to. He learnt that Elisabeth, the young daughter of his close friends the Belgian painter Theo van Rysselberghe and his wife Maria, was pregnant by him, and the prospect of parenthood seems to have awoken a compelling need to rediscover and reaffirm his homosexuality. This need inspired him to write his notoriously frank autobiography (*Si le grain ne meurt*, 1926) and his most ambitious novel (*Les Faux-Monnayeurs*, 1926). *Hamlet* would not only have distracted him from these urgent explorations of his own identity; it would also have entangled him far more closely than he could bear with Dorothy Bussy, who lived with her husband, the painter Simon Bussy, at Rocquebrune in southern France. Dorothy, the sister of Lytton Strachey, had established a strong claim on Gide's attention and gratitude by translating his work into English and assisting his translation of *Antony and Cleopatra*. When she heard of his intention to tackle *Hamlet*, she pressed for a more intimate collaboration. 'If you are going to begin the translation of *Hamlet*,' she wrote to him (in French) early in July 1922, 'couldn't we go somewhere for two or three days – anywhere – to work on it together?'[41] She loved Gide with the sort of half-repressed, frenetic, tortured, now mute, now importunate love that only unrequited infatuation can generate. Gide could never have responded to sexuality that was female, middle-aged, and obsessive; and in 1922 he was less than able to tolerate it. He knew that if he persevered with the translation he would depend on Dorothy's linguistic skill and knowledge of Shakespeare. Yet the thought of her proximity dismayed him; so it may well be that he put *Hamlet* aside in order to discourage her expectations. During his last illness, Gide told Roger Martin du Gard that Dorothy terrified him; that he had armed himself against her love; and Martin du Gard testified that he had avoided her, fled from her advances, in order to spare her the anguish of outright rejection.[42] It was only when the Second World War had driven him into exile in North Africa, and Dorothy was a safely remote correspondent, that he ventured to take up *Hamlet* once more.

During the intervening years the project had never been completely absent from his mind. He felt the allure of a major challenge, and on reflection he judged himself uniquely qualified to surmount the obstacles in the way of Hamlet's entry into France. 'I'm extremely satisfied with my partial translation,' he wrote in 1928, 'and immodestly reckon that it's excellent, the only one which does not betray poetically an atrociously difficult style.'[43] He claimed a special insight into Shakespeare's mind, an ability to travel back along the channels of his language to the embryonic thought: 'It's not just the meaning that needs to be given; it's important to translate not words but phrases, and to express thoughts and emotions as fully as the author would have done had he written directly into French.'[44] In 1930 he published the completed fragment in order to test opinion and stake his pre-emptive claim to the play as a whole. Work was resumed on the project in 1932, but then again abandoned, and it was another decade before the urge to finish his translation repossessed him.

By now Pitoëff was dead; but on the eve of his embarkation for exile in Tunisia, Gide met Jean-Louis Barrault in Marseilles. Overwhelmed by a 'sympathie violente' for this young, enterprising, and immensely talented actor and director, he agreed at once when Barrault asked him to complete the translation of *Hamlet* with a view to a Paris production immediately after the war. This time there was no turning back. By the Mediterranean, at the small fishing village of Sidi-Bou-Said, in the light and heat of the North African summer, Gide at last kept his tryst with the sable-suited prince of Denmark. He began work in June 1942 and continued for over three months at the rate of six to eight hours a day, now discovering in the 'difficultés infernales' which he had once pushed aside as unworthy of his time and intellect an irresistible claim on the best that he could offer of both. 'What labour!' he wrote to Dorothy,

> I'm bringing to it all my intelligence, all my virtues and my gifts. Never yet have I undertaken anything so difficult ... I am passionately dedicated to this work; I labour at it for hours at a stretch, as long and as keenly as my declining strength will allow ... I'm spending an enormous amount of time on it ... thinking of you.

He was sustained by the conviction, which grew stronger as his work progressed, that his version was superior to all its predecessors by virtue of its 'exactitude poétique'. All previous translators had committed the cardinal fault – that of 'sacrificing lyricism, movement of phrases, textual beauty, for pedantic exactness of meaning'. Dorothy proved invaluable in his struggles with an idiom that he described as 'more abstruse, more intricate and full of ambiguity, traps, and pitfalls' than any other he knew. Her elucidation of obscurities, and her comments on the draft passed on to her by the typist at Nice, saved him from inadequacy and error. But there was a price to pay. Emboldened by her sudden importance, she risked (writing, as always, in French) an amorous confession: 'I suddenly feel overcome by violent affection ... Last night, unable to sleep, I desperately wanted to see you, to savour the melancholy autumn with "my brow resting on your knee"; to live thus for an instant; to die thus – reconciled, forgiven.' She never dropped the final formality. She dared not use *tutoiement*, the intimate form of address, in her letters to Gide, and sometimes she revolted against the cruelty of her position. She would then accuse him of insensitivity, of not reading what she wrote, of not using her correct address; of undervaluing her suggestions and corrections. Gide strove to avert a crisis by sounding firm but not unkind:

> Do understand that I need more than ever to be aware of your friendship, and that this is hardly the time to write to me in that diabolical 'pathetic

female' way, which seems to cast doubt on what ought to be *taken for granted* and which causes me more distress that you seem to realise.[45]

Gide's prolonged involvement with *Hamlet* reveals that he never surrendered to his antipathies, and never quite overcame them. He returned to Paris after the liberation and allowed himself to be drawn into the preparations for Barrault's production of his translation, which opened at the théâtre Marigny in November 1946. At rehearsals he demonstrated to the actors how certain passages should be spoken; but he was unhappy with Barrault's idiosyncratic delivery of Hamlet's monologues and found his interpretation of the role generally too physical, too exteriorised.[46] So his old sense of disappointment returned, and his concerns refocused on the extra-theatrical fortunes of his text. After publishing a bilingual edition in New York in 1944, Gide had compiled for posterity an archive of all his drafts and working notes, in order to assist its survival as an object of literary study. He regretted that he was unable to do for *Hamlet* what he had done for *Les Faux-Monnayeurs*, by publishing a journal of his labour.[47] In 1959, when Gide was dead, the Pléiade edition of Shakespeare was reissued with his translation of *Hamlet* substituted for François-Victor Hugo's. So his work achieved the apotheosis he most desired – that of the printed page.

Nevertheless, his experiences as a translator had caused a change in the nature of his appreciation of Shakespeare. He shifted from the traditional French view that Shakespeare was a poor dramatist and a great philosopher. It became clear to Gide that Shakespeare's profundity was inseparable from the stage; that he was wise not because he was apocalyptic, but because he was quintessentially dramatic.[48] And it seems that this discovery enhanced in some subtle yet perceptible way the theatricality of Gide's translation, because its success in performance was remarkable. Five years before he died, Gide scored his first and only theatrical triumph. He basked in media attention and critical acclaim. The Parisian press praised the fidelity, the lyricism, the dramatic cogency of his text. Some reviewers hailed it as definitive. *Hamlet*, it seemed, had finally arrived on the French stage, and French audiences had been vouchsafed an epiphany.[49]

A few critics found the translation too 'Gidean'. Julien Green judged that it was less than ideal because a 'poverty of colour' ('indigence des couleurs') detracted from the undeniable beauty of its style. Yves

Bonnefoy, who published his own free-verse translation in 1957, said that Gide was elegant whereas Shakespeare was strong, and that he had set up 'un théâtre de marionnettes, littéraire, faux et affecté'. Fifty years after its publication, Philippe Sollers found it quaintly prudish and academic.[50] So the note of disapproval has somewhat tarnished its reputation, and it is not difficult to understand why. As with *Antoine et Cléopâtre*, the smoothing, desiccating influence of taste and correctness is evident. Indecencies are coyly evaded. Hamlet's 'country matters', for example, becomes *manières de rustre*. The dynamics of Shakespeare's diction are scaled down. 'Haste me to know't', cries Hamlet, imploring the ghost of his father to reveal the facts of his murder, 'that I with wings as swift / As meditation or the thoughts of love / May sweep to my revenge.' *En hâte apprends-le-moi*, says Gide's Hamlet, *et prompt comme l'aile de la méditation, prompt comme une pensée d'amour, je vole à ma vengeance* – which substitutes a gentle image of winged ascent for Shakespeare's vigorous invocation of descending retribution. Shakespeare's tautology is discreetly removed. 'What may this mean,' asks Hamlet of the ghost,

> That thou, dead corse, again in complete steel
> Revisit'st thus the glimpses of the moon,
> Making night hideous ...?

'Dead corpse', 'again revisit' – Gide could not bring himself to replicate such pleonasm; so his Hamlet says: *Que signifie, cadavre bardé de fer, ton retour sous les rayons douteux de la lune? Tu emplis de hideur la nuit ...* What is concrete in the original often becomes abstract in the translation. Thus Hamlet's diatribe against the world – 'an unweeded garden / That grows to seed; things rank and gross in nature / Possess it merely' – Gide renders as *jardin où l'ivraie monte en grain, et qu'envahissent la puanteur et la vulgarité*. This is still, then, edulcorated, processed Shakespeare. But it is Shakespeare nonetheless, both in its range of meanings and in its poetic tonality. A distance remains between Gide's and the English text; but it is immeasurably smaller than the distance that separates Gide from Ducis or even from Meurice-Dumas.

Gide died in 1951, and within a generation was a diminished eminence. His fiction had begun to look small-scale and dated, the memory of his notorious lapses (he had judged Proust's masterpiece unworthy of publication; he had held aloof from the Resistance) lingered. During his lifetime, he had been an institution: founder and doyen of the prestigious *Nouvelle Revue Française*; international celebrity; winner of the Nobel Prize. It had therefore been easy to think of him as a power for the recovery of Shakespeare, to see his translations as an authoritative endorsement on Shakespeare's passport to the theatre and to classic status in France. Now, it was easier to think of Shakespeare as a power for the recovery of Gide. For Shakespeare had tapped resources in Gide that were still appealing in the postmodern age. Gide the translator of *Antony and Cleopatra* and of *Hamlet* recalled Gide the crosser of boundaries and mixer of genres; the subverter of dogmas and conclusions; the connoisseur of exotic places and pagan heresies; above all, the writer who used irony, satire, parody, and pastiche to destabilise French fiction and bring it to the point where logic collapses and reality begins.

7

The Trumpets of Fortinbras

The slow and chequered conversion of France to Shakespeare was the other French Revolution. To investigate why it happened is to encounter much more than just the fads and fashions of theatrical and literary Paris. It signified changes in habits of thought and attitudes to life every bit as widespread and profound as those that decreed the abolition of the Old Régime. Shakespeare's fortunes in France are related to an overturning of long-current assumptions and valuations; to the becoming obsolete of what had been modern, and the becoming modern of what had been obsolete. From late in the nineteenth century, the gulf stream of optimism and confidence that had sustained the temperate climate of European opinion, comforting its doubts and moderating its storms, was ebbing. The promise of a happy ending to the sad story of life, a promise bequeathed by Christianity and then renewed by the Enlightenment, was sounding ever more false and deluded. Scepticism was corroding religious and secular faith, and hope of an equitable final reckoning was lying amongst the litter of outdated guarantees.

Throughout Europe and the West not just educated élites, but people remote from intellectual concerns, were now afflicted by worldly events in a way hitherto unrecorded. All ages had known the summer and winter of good times and bad; but never yet had the shift to the darker side of a solstice in human affairs coincided with so complete a dereliction of traditional consolations. A crisis of religious doubt, followed by the collapse of reassuring science, left Europe without a philosophy to alleviate a new and excruciating spasm of its pain. 'In a universe suddenly deprived of illusions and lights,' wrote Albert Camus in 1942, 'man feels himself to be a stranger. There is no way out for this exile, because he has no memories of a lost home, and no hope of a promised land.'[1] Prophecies of progress once strident and clear – those of Hegel, Goethe, Comte, Michelet – suddenly sounded faint and barely comprehensible, like voices from an ancient phonograph. Forces deaf to prayer and to reason evoked an awareness not of evil but of something beyond it: a primeval darkness where no light could penetrate and all sense of value failed. In order to cope with modern experience, another language had to be invented: a language that revived forgotten words, like 'Armageddon' and 'holocaust', and made new ones, like 'genocide'. And with it there came a need for an art and a literature that were not compromised by the old illusions.

In France this need was especially acute, because nowhere else was the disarray, the disillusion, so complete. The French had signed and delivered testimonials for Catholicism and 'les Lumières'. They had staked everything on their truth. They therefore had little truly tragic literature; and in the moment of realisation that the world was, after all, tragic, they finally discovered in Shakespeare an author made not obsolete but modern by the passage of years.

It had taken two centuries for Shakespeare to be recognised in France as an authentic tragedian. Critical authority had long denied that his dramas were in any legitimate sense tragedies. Tragedy could have no truck with anything so misshapen and midnight-pigmented. According to enlightened understanding, the only form of *tragédie* was that described by Aristotle in his *Poetics*. It denoted action that was admirable, complete, and full of grandeur. It aroused pity and fear, by depicting the suffering of distinguished and worthy people. The best tragedies, Aristotle maintained, featured a change from good fortune to bad; but tragedy did not necessarily end in disaster. These were the terms in which Racine wrote of the genre in the preface to *Britannicus* (1669). 'Blood and death', he explained, 'are not indispensable in a tragedy. It is enough that the action be resounding; that the characters be heroic; that the passions be excited; and that everything partake of that majestic sadness which creates all the pleasure of tragedy.' The *Dictionnaire* of the Académie Française (1694) was more succinctly Aristotelian. 'Tragédie' it defined as 'une action grande et sérieuse entre personnes illustres'. Tragedy, that is to say, drew on mythology and history. Its stories were not invented but retold, and audiences did not discover, they recognised, its protagonists. It was the mythological-historical dignity of these protagonists that made the 'tristesse' of tragedy 'majestueuse'. In his long discussion of *tragédie* in *Eléments de littérature*

(1787), Marmontel, likewise, deferred to Aristotle. The tragic emotions were terror and pity. Horror had no place in the tragic repertoire. 'If the image [of misfortune] is too realistic, and the play too horrible, the spirit is repelled.' And repulsion was inappropriate, because the function of the tragedian was 'to imitate morals and at the same time correct them, by means of action that serves as an example'. Theatrical illusion, therefore, must never be complete. It was in order to mitigate it that tragedy used elevated, artificial diction.[2]

Marmontel did not, for obvious reasons, mention Shakespeare. Shakespeare's dramas were clearly not tragedies when judged by such criteria. They were relics, replete with horror and often lapsing from what was 'grande et serieuse' into what was mundane and trivial. It was Voltaire's refrain that they had lost the power to arouse pity and fear in an age of taste and politeness, and his refrain was still audible two centuries later. 'Opinions have not changed since Voltaire', wrote Jean-Louis Barrault in 1947. 'In the name of taste, Shakespeare is reproached for triviality; in the name of the rules, for long-windedness and implausibility. The paramount maxim of the French is still that art separates what nature has confounded.' French audiences were still refusing to take Shakespeare seriously. 'His bloody dénouements remain objects of our mockery. With every performance of *Hamlet* we have the devil's own job to master the public and stop them laughing at the sight of the final carnage.'[3] A critic discussing Charles Dullin's *Lear*, presented at the théâtre Sarah Bernhardt in 1945, detected an unbridgeable gap between Shakespeare and the modern sophisticated audience:

> The excesses and hecatombs of the Elizabethan theatre are barely acceptable to the twentieth-century public, who are apt to complain of over-acting when performers are merely being faithful to the spirit of an old text. Nowadays Shakespeare can be swallowed only when allowance is made for the conventions of a theatre whose greatness is not in question, but which belongs irrevocably to the past.[4]

Folklore, however, contradicted critical authority. Folklore said that Shakespeare was resisted in France not because he was not tragic, but because he was. He made the French uncomfortable because he dealt with those aspects of the human condition that they were unable or unwilling to confront. The French averted their gaze from what was desolate and painful. Their geniality, their dislike of the minor mode, was proverbial, both among themselves and among foreigners. 'The French look for the pleasant side of life', wrote Rivarol in 1783; 'the English seem always to be witnessing a drama.'[5] Even someone as serious as Ernest Renan, whose *Life of Jesus* preached pious agnosticism to the Second Empire, came round at last to the view that Frenchness was levity and pleasure. He recognised in the hedonistic *insousiance* of the popular poet Béranger the characteristic voice of France. 'The Frenchman', he wrote, 'is joyous; his favourite phrases imply a feeling for the gaiety of life, and the idea that at bottom nothing is very serious.'[6] In 1941 Oscar Hammerstein translated the legend into a poignant lyric, set to music by Jerome Kern:

> The last time I saw Paris,
> Her heart was young and gay;
> I heard the laughter of her voice
> In every street café ...

The stereotype of the mercurial, carefree Frenchman, flitting between the table, the boudoir, and the coiffeur, was borrowed from folklore by serious opinion. It has long been a French view that French writing lacks a tragic dimension. Diderot reckoned that only people with a republican mentality, like the English, fully appreciated tragedy. Monarchical nations like France preferred comedy. This was because wit ('plaisanterie') was harsh ('dure') where everyone was equal. Wit was good-humoured, however, in hierarchical societies because, as Diderot put it, 'it has to strike upwards in order to become light'. Consequently, he explained, the French had comedies, whereas the English had only satires.[7] In lectures delivered at Columbia University in 1916 and 1917, Gustave Lanson daringly suggested that French *tragédie* was not, properly speaking, tragic: 'The tragic, in the strict sense of the word, is accidental and rare in French tragedy.'[8] This judgement signalled a retreat from the customary understanding of the terms 'tragedy' and 'the tragic'. They lost their Aristotelian pedigree. The tragic experience was henceforth widely understood to be not exclusive but inclusive. If the illustrious of myth and history were tragic it was not because they were illustrious but because they were human. Tragedy, rightly understood, indicated a tragic sense of life. This was present in Aeschylus, Sophocles, Euripides, and Shakespeare; but it was generally absent from literature in French. With the possible exception of Racine, the French had always been reluctant to admit this element into their art. 'What is tragedy?' asked Jean Giraudoux in 1941.

> It is the affirmation of a horrible link between humanity and a destiny greater than human destiny ... What is France? It is the affirmation of a human truth which has no connection with super-truths and super-lies. Tragedy presupposes the existence of horror as such, of an immanent menace and a densely populated stratosphere. France supposes that above her rises an expanse of air good to breathe. The higher one goes, the less dense. What is the tragic hero? He is a being peculiarly resigned to co-existence with the forms and monsters of fatality. What is the Frenchman? A member of the human race who finds it hard to be cordial to strangers, let alone to the strange.[9]

Lecturing in Athens in 1955, Camus took up Hegel's thesis that tragedy represented the conflict between two equally legitimate principles. In melodrama and drama, on the other hand, only one principle was legitimate. 'Putting it another way, tragedy is ambiguous, drama is simplistic.' The tragic formula was 'all are justifiable; no one is just'. For Camus, as for Lanson, tragedy was a rare visitor to civilisation, and it was rarest of all in France. There had been no tragic writing in French since Racine. Romanticism produced no tragedies – only dramas.[10] In Barthes' controversial essays on Racine (1963), the tragic repertoire is even more restricted. Barthes defined Racinian tragedy as an enclosed ritual of language and gesture, which precluded the 'impurity' of death and physical action. Tragic reality remained remote. It belonged to the unseen exterior, and reached the stage only in fragments, 'distilled as news, ennobled as narrative'. The hero could reach it only by dying.[11]

Aristotelian theory made the happy ending the exception, not the rule. French practice made it the rule rather than the exception. The convention of *vraisemblance* ordained the depiction of a well-ordered universe, with a clear distinction between innocence and guilt, and the public was intolerant of anything harsh or mortifying. Even in the time of Louis XIV tragedies were much less popular than tragi-comedies, which had non-historical subjects, complicated plots, and happy endings. In the eighteenth century the biggest box-office draws were comedies – especially comedies of manners, like *Le Mariage de Figaro* – and cheerful operas about the triumph of love.[12] Mindful of these constraints, dramatists generally ensured that the Greek myths (like the plays of Shakespeare) reached the stage shorn of much of their moral ambiguity and unjustified suffering. Corneille adjusted the stories of Medea (1634) and Oedipus (1659) to a cosmic scheme of divine justice and human responsibility. Miscreants like Medea are guilty because they are free. No destiny controls them. Happiness eludes them not because they are tragic, but because they choose crime and the wages of pride. The Theban legend Corneille embellished by omitting the blinding of Oedipus, supplying amorous intrigue, and contriving a regular dynastic succession. The light of legitimate kingship and edifying love banishes Sophoclean darkness. For his *Iphigénie en Aulide* (1674), Racine chose the less harrowing version of the Greek legend. Innocent Iphigénie is not sacrificed to the gods, and an added character called Eriphile confirms the rule of *vraisemblance* by committing suicide after betraying the heroine.

In their treatment of the Orpheus myth the French persistently evaded the tragic. The Greek story of Orpheus and Eurydice, as told by Virgil, Ovid, and Seneca, is dire and harrowing. It tells how Orpheus won back Eurydice from the realms of Death with the enchantment of his music, and then lost her again because he could not forbear to look at her during the ascent from Hades. Virgil added the sequel of his wanderings after his second bereavement. He narrated how the women of Thrace, frantic votaries of Bacchus, tore him to pieces, and how his severed head, still singing of Eurydice, was carried down the river Hebrus. In the French theatre this threnody of martyrdom and loss and too-eager desiring became first a parable about the power of love and art to overcome the chthonic forces, then a jolly *divertissement*, and finally a surrealist fairy-tale. Gluck's opera *Orphée et Eurydice*, first performed in Vienna in 1762 and revised for Paris in 1774, has a happy ending. After Eurydice's second death, Amour intervenes to prevent Orphée from committing suicide, and the work ends with a second resurrection and general rejoicing. Offenbach's operetta *Orphée aux enfers* ('Orpheus in the Underworld'), premièred in Paris in 1858, is a deliquescent, satirical confection skimmed from the frothy surface of the Second Empire. It parodies both the legend and Gluck, whose music it facetiously quotes. Jean Cocteau's *Orphée*, of 1926, revived the *pièce à machine*, wildly popular in the seventeenth century. The sombre colourings of the archaic original are overlaid by stage illusionism (levitation, walking through mirrors, a speaking severed head, a house rising into the sky), smart contemporary dialogue, and – a happy ending.

Tragedy was as conspicuously absent outside as inside the French theatre. When the term was no longer restricted to tales of the illustrious in myth and history, and it was conceded that ordinary life might have its tragedies too, a search began for the French tragic novel. Interest focused especially on the marquis de Sade, long regarded as a mere pornographer. It proved difficult, however, to present a world-view so simple and so misanthropic as something authentically tragic. Sade's imagination never left the dwellings of despair. It haunted latrines, sewers, torture-chambers, brothels, and *abattoirs*. It fed with flies on purulence and carnage. But it conceived no sense of suffering. Sade's characters are demonic: willing accomplices of fate both in the infliction and in the endurance of pain. Sade was, in a perverted sense, true to the conventions of his time. He never moved beyond *vraisemblance*. He simply turned it upside down. His universe is as well ordered, as morally unambiguous, as that of Ducis. *Justine* (1791) and *Juliette* (1797) are inverted melodrama. Hell is heaven, heaven is hell; vice is triumphant, virtue vanquished.

These schematic reductions of reality have no affinity with Greek and Shakespearean drama, which is tragic in that it exposes the disparity between reality and all visions of order deduced from reason and the human sense of right and wrong. Sophoclean and Shakespearean characters proclaim ruling providence to be wise and just; yet they are born into a world that is at odds with reason and justice, and they look in vain for a world elsewhere. More sinned against than sinning, they suffer anguish for which there is no obvious justification and no promise of recompense. The Greek characters engage with capricious gods, whose presence is known from oracles and prophecies. Shakespeare's endure existential solitude, confronting certain death yet uncertain how to act. Prophecy is either silent or ambiguous, and there is no fixed measure of innocence and guilt. In the Shakespearean theatre disaster has moved from the end to the antecedents of tragic action. Sophocles' protagonists approach a preordained catastrophe. In Shakespeare's tragedies the catastrophe has already happened when the drama begins. His protagonists inhabit an unravelling universe, oppressed by the burden of history ('accidental judgements, casual slaughters, and purposes mistook'), and by the peremptory commands of offended memory ('Do not forget!'; 'Remember me!'). Aware of their plight, they resist; but there is no hope of victory, because every battle won is also a battle lost. The fatality that governs their lives is the fatality of time, and time has cancelled all providential order. In Shakespeare's world the old Christian chronology, stretching from Creation to the Last Judgement, has been superseded by 'recorded time' – time charted in national history and individual consciousness.[13] This empirical time is 'envious and calumniating'. It divides our being into the no longer and the not yet; transforms our tomorrows into yesterdays, and hope into regret.

Giraudoux thought that the absence from French culture of the tragic sense had something to do with the French language. 'Lucid and precise in syntax as in vocabulary', this resisted translation into the 'non-human'.[14] But Camus identified the real reason when he linked the abeyance of tragedy in Europe to the advance of Christianity. He pointed out that the Christian religion, by plunging the whole universe in the divine order, destroyed the tension between opposing goods.[15] The ideas of providential injustice and cosmic chaos are essential to tragedy; tragedy therefore retreated when Catholicism erected its taboo against them. The French Catholic reproach against Shakespeare was precisely that he was tragic, and the influence of Catholicism in France explains why French literature was not. Catholicism was offended by a philosophy that forever withheld paradise. 'It is in vain', remonstrated Paul Claudel, 'that Shakespeare's heroes demand it of each other with all the resources of poetry, wisdom, and despair. It has vanished; it is lost; and it is in vain that the enchantment of Prospero will try to raise it from the ocean ...'[16] For this Catholic writer, Shakespeare's was a flawed portrait of humanity because it lacked 'that sacred light which illuminates everyone coming into the world':

> Shakespeare's world lacks ... what? The most important half – the sky, the third dimension, the vertical direction ... At the level of facts, and of the horizon, it's impossible to imagine plays richer, more intelligent, more entertaining, more dramatic, more illuminating, more suggestive. But when all's said and done, all these people go about their business under their own steam. They are never invited, or compelled, to rise above themselves, to surpass themselves.

When he saw the Old Vic production of *King Lear* at the théâtre des

Champs Elysées in November 1946, Claudel was dismayed by the void at the heart of the play:

> The Middle Ages are not long past, yet faith has almost as completely disappeared from the theatre of Shakespeare as if the Gospel had never been preached to humanity. Paradise is lost ... There is no longer even a gleam of Christianity to enlighten these desperate shadows.[17]

Surveying history and humanity from the high vantage point of his faith, Claudel the dramatist saw individual suffering not as tragic loss, but as the purchase of a superior happiness under God's providence. There is a stricken, minor-mode sonority in his *Partage de midi* (1906), an early play about European expatriates in the hot latitudes of the China Sea. A heavy, tragic atmosphere accumulates around illicit passion, thwarted religious vocation, and political turmoil. But this is characteristically dispelled by the author, who reunites his adulterous lovers beyond death, and launches them into a long final dialogue that is pitched somewhere between the eroticism of a Wagnerian *Liebestod* and the spirituality of Platonic-Catholic *agape.*

Time in Catholic teleology is not destructive but healing. Death is the threshold of prelapsarian beatitude. This catechism remained at the heart of intellectual and artistic France long after the decommissioning of Christianity. It was not demolished but reinforced by the Enlightenment, which constructed human history around the pillars of Nature, Reason, and Progress. A vision of deliverance from conflict and catastrophe checked and corrected the tragical list not just in the writing of eminent Catholic preachers and thinkers like Pascal, but in the great enterprise of secular intelligence as well. Classicism promised that suffering would end with the apotheosis of syntax. Marxism – extensively theorised, like Catholicism, in France – promised that it would end with the apotheosis of the proletariat.[18] Under this dispensation, a tragic view of life was heresy. The only way Racine could write a *tragédie* that was tragic was by revisiting a world as yet unredeemed by the mercy of Christ. *Phèdre* is tragic because it depicts a pagan universe in which the voice of repentance is unanswered by the voice of pardon. Sade the atheist remained steeped in the Catholicism he vilified. His novels are full of black masses, sacraments of evil, Satanic rituals, litanies of perversion. Blasphemy so violent bespeaks an overpowering sense of sacrilege and sin. The Decadent precipitates of Sadism betray the same inverted Catholicism, which in some notable cases reverted to orthodoxy.[19] This deeply rooted Catholic mentality made France barren territory for any philosophy of pessimism. In the 1880s and 1890s *schopenhaurisme* enjoyed a brief vogue in Parisian literary circles, but Schopenhauer himself was neither seriously studied nor fully understood. The resistance to *schopenhaurisme* was far more characteristic than the enthusiasm of a few young Decadents and Symbolists of the mood of intellectual France at this time. Joseph Reinach, essayist and politician, insisted that the Schopenhaurian *Weltanschauung* was profoundly unFrench. 'On the territory of France', he wrote, 'territory of progress in all its forms, pessimism will remain an exotic plant.'[20]

This pervasive Catholicity kept France comparatively free from tragic consciousness. But before the twentieth century was very far advanced, clear signs were accumulating that its consistency was thinning; its chemistry changing. Attitudes and ideas once deemed exotic in France were becoming endemic. Foreign heresies were disrupting settled habits of thought and breaching the Catholic taboo against fatalism and negation. Nietzsche's teaching subverted Christian assurances of salvation through passive suffering. God was dead and the human condition demanded a futile, and therefore heroic, defiance of tragic destiny.[21] Miguel de Unamuno, a Spanish writer, argued in *The Tragic Sense of Life* (1912) that consciousness was a disease. It is consumed by a longing that can never be satisfied – the longing for certain knowledge of immortality. We live in perpetual uncertainty, betrayed both by sentiment and by reason, since 'sentiment cannot turn consolation into truth, and reason cannot turn truth into consolation'. Our only resource is an existential act of will: 'We must feel and act as if an endless continuation of our earthly life were reserved for us after death.'[22] Between the wars, two French Catholic writers took up this theme of uncertainty and made it crucial to the theological mystery of humanity that is offered heaven yet remains in hell. The novels of François Mauriac and Georges Bernanos present the wide mournful hinterlands of France – Les Landes, Flanders, Picardy – as the epitome of a world obsessed by guilt and damnation. The characters are insecure, self-loathing, pathologically penitent; and it is never made clear that they die in the assurance of grace. Their plight is tragically ironic, since either joy has passed them by unrecognised, or they spurn it as a diabolical illusion. The grim substance of Bernanos' narratives (murder, rape, madness, lynching, suicide, self-torture), and the aching compassion in his narrating voice, evoke lives lived beyond the reach of religious consolation. He writes of country priests who, bereft of the peace they bestow, are more akin to tragic heroes than to Christian martyrs. They confer their gift with empty hands, and die spiritually as well as physically tormented: unsure, even in their crucifixion, that they are not accomplices of evil, lured to Calvary by Satan. Other writers worked not at the centre of the Catholic-classical-Marxist tradition, but at its margins, where it interacted with Nietzsche, existentialism, surrealism, and psychoanalysis. Authors like Breton, Aragon, Sartre, and Camus extended the French literary gamut into unfamiliar regions of heterodoxy and hybridity. 'THERE IS NO PARADISE OF ANY SORT!' shouted Louis Aragon, exasperated by the addiction of fashionable writers to themes of evasion, departure, travel, and suicide. There is no escape, said Aragon, no world elsewhere. Hope is an illusion, and the only way to cope with the catastrophe of life is by laughing at it. Humour alone, because it confronts reality, has the power to overcome it.[23] Aragon entitled a collection of some of his darkest poems, composed between 1927 and 1929, *La Grande gaieté*.

The Catholic taboo once infringed, French writers were free to revisit Greek mythology and treat its evocation of malignant destiny not as an archaic curiosity but as a timeless commentary on the human predicament. Jean Cocteau, in *La Machine infernale* (1934), retold the Theban trilogy of Sophocles, reinstating the horror that Corneille and Voltaire had removed, and removing the embellishments that they had added. Cocteau's was a stark parable of remorseless providence. 'See, spectator', the amplified voice of the author enjoined at the beginning of each performance, 'wound up tightly, so that the spring unwinds slowly throughout a human life, one of the most perfect machines constructed by the infernal gods for the mathematical annihilation of a mortal.' With *Electre*, produced in 1937, Jean Giraudoux introduced to the French stage the Greek legend of the children of Agamemnon, on whom the gods have entailed the atrocious duty of remembrance and revenge. The return of her brother Orestes banishes the silence, the amnesia, which are Electra's refuge from the past. Her illusion of happiness collapses when she reveals to Orestes that he is the son of 'a prostituted

queen and an assassinated king'. In *Eurydice* (1941) Jean Anouilh
stripped the Orpheus myth of its French fairy-tale felicity. His Orpheus
is a café musician; his Eurydice a provincial actress who is killed in a
road accident. They are reunited in the railway station where they first
met; but he loses her forever when he breaks the terms of her resurrection by looking at her before dawn, and dies heartbroken and
remorseful. Anouilh's *Antigone* (1942) depicts a tragic conflict of goods.
Antigone defies authority in order to bury the corpse of her criminal
brother; but her executioner, her uncle King Créon, commands sympathy as a weary ruler harassed by the cares of office and the ingratitude
of a rebel determined to be a martyr. This play brought to the French
stage the Sophoclean chorus, which reveals to the audience the illusion
of characters who believe themselves to be free and happiness to be an
option. The third of Anouilh's classical dramas, *Médée* (1946), restored
the Euripidean fatality that Corneille had carefully erased. Medea is the
instrument of the gods in their vendetta against human happiness.
Sartre was held back from tragic fatalism by his existentialist philosophy; but in his reworking of Aeschylus's *Oresteia* (*Les Mouches*, 1943) he
depicted the tragic implications of a liberty that is not chosen. The gods
cannot compel obedience. They confront men and women who are free.
Those who reject them, however, are driven into exile and tormented by
the Erinyes, the black flies of remorse. Sartre saw in Orestes the archetypal existentialist hero, who creates his own destiny, defies the gods,
refuses to repent or to acknowledge guilt. Seeking the life that begins 'on
the other side of despair', he discovers that he is 'a stranger to
[him]self ... Out of nature, against nature, without excuse, without any
resources but [his] own'. Camus made ironical use of Greek mythology
in his essay *Le Mythe de Sisyphe* (1942). This shows how the pitiful plight
of modern man has been caricatured by existentialism, the philosophy
that 'denies the gods and lifts rocks'. Sisyphus is an existentialist who
compounds absurdity with absurdity. Although condemned by the gods
to a pointless and degrading punishment, he believes himself to be free
and to be performing his futile labour not for the gods but for himself.
'Thus, persuaded of the human origin of all that is human, blind and
desiring to see yet knowing that the night has no end, he is still at work'
– rolling his boulder up the hill, and requiring that we deem him
happy.[24]

Camus' *La Peste*, published in 1947, was a new departure in French fiction. Never before had a French novelist dealt so intrepidly and so relentlessly with the big tragic themes of time, exile, bereavement, and fatality. Set in Oran in French Algeria during an epidemic of bubonic plague, the novel is not a reworking of Greek tragedy. Nevertheless it makes a crucial reconnection with Greek myth, by using Gluck's *Orphée et Eurydice* as a vehicle of tragic irony. The purloined, sugar-coated legend, presented by a visiting opera company while the city is under quarantine, is repossessed by the Greeks when the singer in the role of Orphée, infected by the bacillus, collapses on the stage. He dies hideously before the audience, and the performance, cut short by horror and chaos, becomes an emblem of Taste overcome by the reality it had sought to camouflage. With this novel Camus exposed the falsity of the culture of Taste and Reason. 'We mustn't prevent nice people from sleeping', comments Jean Tarrou, one of the central characters. 'That would be in bad taste, and taste, as everybody knows, means not insisting.' The narrator, Dr Rieux, taught by the Enlightenment to believe that there is no real vice but ignorance, is compelled to confront a world in which knowledge is the path to tragic consciousness. No victory is possible, and martyrdom is futile, because the plague that afflicts humanity remains as capricious in its remission as in its virulence. Truly enlightened, Rieux becomes 'l'homme moderne' – that is to say, 'l'homme tragique par excellence', who 'proclaims his revolt knowing that this revolt has limits, who demands liberty and is subject to necessity'. He is 'contradictory, torn apart, henceforth aware of the ambiguity of humanity and of its history'.[25]

It is remarkable how the Catholic inhibition against tragedy should have relaxed after three hundred years, and how French literature suddenly became suffused with a tragic sense of life. The most obvious explanation is in the exceptional circumstances under which French writers worked during the first half of the twentieth century. Diderot had long before suggested that there was symbiosis between powerful literature and violent history:

> Poetry demands something enormous, barbaric, and savage ... It is when the fury of civil war or of fanaticism arms men with daggers, and blood flows in a great tide over the earth, that the laurels of Apollo quicken and become verdant. When shall we witness the birth of poets? It will be after times of

disaster and great misfortune, when exhausted peoples begin to breathe. Imaginations shaken by terrible sights will then portray things unknown.[26]

From the later nineteenth century, the terribleness of modern times was heavily traded as an explanation for the characteristic features of modern creativity. Bourget and Taine, writing in the 1880s, regarded the Franco-Prussian War as a physical and psychological lesion that had weakened French resistance to spiritual disease. It accounted for the morbid obsession with self and sensation that was now so evident in French literature and art. In the aftermath of the trauma of 1870–71, French effort had become focused on what Taine called 'the shameless ostentation of ignoble preferences, vicious preoccupations, leprosies, and intimate soiling'.[27] Looking back from 1947, Sartre described how writers of his generation had suddenly, in the 1930s, become aware that they were participants in history and not merely witnesses to its 'final convulsion' ('dernier bouleversement'). 'From 1930', he explained, 'the world crisis, the advent of Nazism, the events in China, the Spanish Civil War, opened our eyes ... Suddenly, unexpectedly, we found ourselves situated ... Historicity surged back over us.' During the Occupation, torture as a daily fact of life had destroyed the legacy of Catholic-Enlightenment ideology. It had become clear that evil cannot be redeemed or conquered; that it is a metaphysical absolute, 'fruit of a free and sovereign will'; that there persists amidst the relativity of history 'the great polar night of the inhuman and of unknowing'. A whole literature had therefore become obsolete – the literature of 'the temperate regions', which dealt in 'modest virtues' and 'average situations'. French writers, 'abruptly reintegrated in history', were compelled to create 'a literature of historicity'.[28]

Sartre identified the work of Camus as an example of such literature, because it was obvious that Camus was profoundly influenced by political and social actuality. *La Peste* is full of direct allusions to the Europe of its time. The novel operates, furthermore, as a double metaphor, in which the plague is the Nazi occupation of France, and the Nazi occupation of France is the plague entailed on humanity. Sartre's own work is likewise highly topical, fully engaged with the philosophical issues and moral dilemmas raised by political and social events. Wartime experience was also clearly evident in the postwar response to Shakespeare. It was only a minority who were still claiming, in the 1940s and 1950s, that

Shakespearean tragedy was obsolete. Most critics now recognised in this drama the sort of literature that modern times demanded – what Sartre called 'la littérature des grandes circonstances'. After seeing *Antoine et Cléopâtre*, Mauriac noted how 'terriblement actuel' Shakespeare was now,

> when, to adopt the distinction made by Péguy, we are living not in a 'period' of history (that is to say, a time of transition devoid of essential events), but in an 'epoch' , which imposes a shape on human destiny and, perhaps, fixes it for centuries. Shakespeare is a poet and dramatist not of periods but of epochs. There is not a word of his drama ... that does not relate to one of our agonies as survivors struggling on the surface of a Europe three-quarters destroyed, in this glacial May of 1945.[29]

Jean-Louis Barrault took up the idea of Shakespeare our contemporary in a lecture at the Edinburgh Festival in 1948. 'In these times', he said,

> Shakespeare seems more topical to us than does Molière; he is more in touch with us. Shakespeare lived in the midst of murder, revolution, and catastrophe; one might say that he lived, like us, 'between two ages' ... Shakespeare, at this moment in time, is for us more *modern* than Molière.[30]

Georges Neveux, who translated *Othello* for the production at the Comédie-Française in 1950, wrote of the modernity of Iago's methods of torment. 'Judges, torturers, police, have striven to degrade their victims. Since 1940, destroying a character has become a science, an art, almost a pleasure.'[31]

History, then, must feature in any explanation of the collapse of the Catholic taboo against Shakespeare and the tragic view of life. Yet it is not the whole explanation. Jean Anouilh disclaimed 'historicity', and denied that there were any topical allusions in *Antigone*. Perhaps he was parrying accusations, made by the clandestine press, that his play was favourable to the collaborating French government at Vichy.[32] Even so, it is clear from other evidence that tragic public circumstances do not necessarily generate tragic art. The French Revolution produced no literature of catastrophe; nor did it fundamentally alter French responses to Shakespeare.[33] The disasters of the early twentieth century did both these things – but only because they acted in combination with a catalyst: an intellectual revolution that overturned traditional science and demolished belief in progress and happiness. Because this revolution was scientific, its effects were especially harrowing in France. French thinkers had always relied for their peace of mind on empirical science. They had never invested seriously in metaphysics.

At first it had not mattered that natural science was contradicting scripture. Those initial contradictions could be resolved by exegetical subtlety. By retreating from biblical literalism into allegory and poetic truth, it could be argued that science told the scriptural story in a different language. The crisis of belief that racked so many Christians – both Catholic and Protestant – in the nineteenth century owed much less to geology and palaeontology than to biblical scholarship. It was internal evidence that exposed the fallibility of scripture. Ernest Renan lost his Catholic faith long before he encountered modern science. Later, however, the contradictions began to matter. From the end of the nineteenth century science was not just speaking a different language; it was telling a different story. It withdrew its endorsement of the Christian promise, and translated the message of the earth and the stars as a new and Godless apocalypse.

The old science had aroused no premonition of tragedy. It had encouraged jubilance and hope. It had made possible belief both in Reason and in immortality. Armed with the book of science and the human sense of right and wrong, the enlightened intelligence had contemplated the earth and the stars and concluded that all was well. The Newtonian cosmos was a witness to divine justice and divine artistry. God was still the supreme designer and benevolent legislator, and man was still in God's image. The scientific poets and preachers of the nineteenth century were confident that, as he deciphered the Creator's secrets, man would himself attain to divinity. Tennyson and Herbert Spencer in England, Renan and Comte in France, envisaged humanity as the summation of a great symphony of being, which transcended time, flux, and suffering. Comte – widely heeded on both sides of the Channel – taught that a 'positive' age, following the 'theological' and the 'metaphysical', would be the final and glorious phase of history. This scientific utopianism was essential to the 'Naturalist' fiction of the 1870s and the 1880s. Zola's novels portray the awfulness of an existence that is governed by the iron laws of heredity and environment; but, like the positivistic science to which they so often refer, they are fundamentally anti-tragic. Zola the clinical investigator of life's leprosy was also an evangelist. He believed in the transfiguring power of the Christian-humanist remedies that he preached in his last three novels (or 'gospels', as he called them): Fecundity, Work, and Truth. Renan, too, was a positivistic visionary. He regarded science as divine: a revelation that would solve the riddle of the universe and confirm man's hopes of apotheosis. Man would himself become God as God realised himself through man. In prospect were light, justice, harmony, and the transformation of transitory into eternal life.[34]

Very different, much grimmer, was the strain of meditation inspired by science at the end of the nineteenth century. By now science had broken its collaboration with Christianity, and ended its triumphant anthem. Its story was no longer Catholic and positive, but Shakespearean and tragic. Catastrophe, it said, is not something the world is moving from, but something it is moving to. There is no escape from perdition, because not only disorder, but order too, is catastrophic. Victory is not possible, because the beauty of a world in conflict and the beauty of a world in repose both herald the return of Ancient Night.

Following Darwin, science gave up the idea that nature is just. Truth, according to Darwin, was beautiful, but it was not good. Its kingdom was not God's, nor even Satan's, but somewhere beyond the moral law that God had made and Satan had violated. Darwin's beautiful universe was not heavenly but terrible, and man was not its possessor, but its possession. By removing the hand of God from the exquisiteness of nature, Darwin severed science from teleology. Design and justice gave way to random survival and gratuitous extinction. The fossil record became a vast necrology, telling of countless species created for no reason and destroyed without cause. It was a witness to indifference and waste; to battles won that had been battles lost.

Zoology depicted terrible strife. Physics depicted terrible calm. The Second Law of Thermodynamics was as fatal as the law of Natural Selection to the dream of grace. Rudolf Clausius, in his reformulation of the Second Law (1865), demonstrated that harmony and stasis in the cosmic scheme signified not life and form, but inertia and chaos. Life and form were sustained by energy: by the transfer of heat between bodies of unequal temperatures. Yet the universe was tending towards thermal equilibrium. The laws of thermodynamics decreed that to move from disorder to order, from conflict to calm, from mutability to stability, was not to break the entail of catastrophe, but to close the circle of male-diction. A new word, 'entropy', came into intellectual language, doom-laden and dreadful. As defined by Clausius, entropy was a meas-ure of the energy that was not available to do work and sustain complexity and variability. According to his restatement of the Second Law, entropy increases within a closed thermodynamic system, since all spontaneous transfers of heat move in one direction (from hot bodies to cold) and are not reversible. The solar system is such a system; so its entropy is increasing as it approaches thermal equilibrium. When every-thing it contains is at the same temperature, maximum entropy will obtain and all energy will fail. Mutability and evolution will cease, and the lukewarm world will remain forever uniform and inert. Henri Bergson conveyed this chaotic prospect with a simile of death-in-life:

> The instability to which we owe the richness and diversity of the changes occurring in our solar system will, little by little, give way to the relative sta-bility of elementary oscillations, each of which will repeat itself indefinitely. Just like a man who would keep his strength, but would devote it less and less to actions, and would end up by using it all to keep his lungs breathing and his heart beating.[35]

Leading intellectuals were fully alert to the implications of the new thermodynamics. 'For a soul avid for life', wrote Unamuno, 'it is the closest to nothingness that can be imagined. Under this dispensation, the soul yearns for a continuation of the conflict between reason and desire; for purgatory rather than paradise.'[36] Herbert Spencer aban-doned his theory of cosmic progress, whereby homogeneity gave way to heterogeneity. Nietzsche overturned Weimar classicism and all its nos-talgic vision of Hellenic stasis and harmony. In writings that were themselves increasingly convulsive, fragmented, and dissonant, he insisted that the greatest achievements of Greek art and thought were born not of serenity but of dialectical ferment. More generally, a response to thermodynamic theory was observable in the waves of emo-tional unease and intellectual dissent called up by the levelling, homogenising processes of modern history – democracy, socialism, feminism, tourism, miscegenation.

In France, Darwin, like Shakespeare, initially met the resistance of incomprehension and fear. He was widely recognised as a genius who would permanently change the fundamentals of thought. But a world in which might overcame right was especially fearful in a country that had been defeated by Prussian militarism. One French intellectual observed that if Darwin was correct, then 'everything which exists is without purpose, and the universe is, and can only be, an immense and profound despair'.[37]

The leaders of educated opinion in France were so accustomed to associating beauty and equilibrium with design and value that they hesitated to follow Darwin's quantum leap from teleology to chance. Shocked by a theory that divorced organic perfection from all aesthetic and moral consciousness, they continued to insist that they were inseparable. But their *rappel à l'ordre* was itself now ominous, because Elysium, too, was an incubus. Contemplating the transition from war to peace in 1919, Paul Valéry wrote that it was 'more obscure, more dangerous, than the transition from peace to war'. He predicted that homogenising tendencies – the spread of social equality, the diffusion of knowledge – must mean the end of Europe's privilege. In order to reverse galloping entropy, in order to repeat the miracle of Cana and change water back into wine, he demanded a suspension of holistic ideologies, and a reconsecration of the destabilising individual.[38] Victor Segalen, in the *Essai sur l'exotisme* that he left unfinished at his death in 1919, postulated diversity as the source of all vitality. He urged the preservation of 'the lively and curious reaction of strong individuality against an objectivity whose difference it perceives and tastes'. There was a need for an aesthetics of diversity, based on the law of exoticism and the cult of the Other. It was in connection with such thinking that racialism became so widespread in France, and anarchism was preached – and practised – as an antidote to the decadent homogeneity of bourgeois art and life.[39]

Trapped between two tragic visions, the French intelligentsia turned to Bergson. They devoured his books, flocked to his lectures. Darwin had replaced a world governed by design with a world governed by chance. In *L'Evolution créatrice* (1907), the book that made him famous, Bergson envisaged a world governed neither by design nor by chance, but by a mysterious life-force, the *élan vital*. Adaptation, argued Bergson, was a matter not of chance but of orthogenesis. It signified creation, not mechanical elimination and replication. The universe is not made, it is being made, by a supreme will that communicates itself through heredity and diversifies as its original impulse reverberates through time. Nothing is accidental or haphazard, because absence of order is neither conceivable nor possible. All reality is order, of one sort or another. No rule of chance, then, in Bergson's universe – but no rule of entropy, either. Thermodynamics said that we are caught up in a process of degradation, of running down. The laws of physics decree that a weight must fall. But the *élan* is a will to rise. It is an effort to ascend the slope that matter descends. Hence it reveals the possibility, the necessity even, of a reality that inverts material laws and creates itself through destruction.[40]

Bergson was phenomenally popular before the First World War; but neither science nor religion was on his side. By the 1930s, when geneticists were explaining inheritance and geologists were increasing their estimation of the age of the earth, scientific reservations about Darwin's theory collapsed and Bergson was left looking desperate and implausible. Prominent intellectuals – including Durkheim and Julien Benda – attacked him as a shoddy and opportunistic thinker, and their censure, coupled with that of the Church, sapped his reputation.[41] In the inter-war years empiricism returned, and literature began to accommodate its tragic theme.

In a memorable passage in his first and very influential book, *The Birth of Tragedy* (1872), Nietzsche had explained how the world was suffering for its Socratic beliefs. Socrates had taught that reason is the path to knowledge; that knowledge is the means to virtue; and that only the virtuous are happy. Yet science was now approaching those outer limits of knowledge where optimism must collapse:

> When the inquirer, having pushed to the circumference, realises how logic in that place curls about itself and bites its own tail, he is struck with a new kind of perception, which requires, to make it tolerable, the remedy of art ... If we look about us today ... we shall see how the insatiable zest for knowledge prefigured in Socrates has been transformed into tragic resignation and the need for art.

But Socratism was doubly culpable, because not only had it enhanced the tragic consciousness; it had also demolished the tragic art that solaced it. Socrates had destroyed tragedy by banishing Dionysus, the god of music, dance, and orgiastic abandon, and making Apollo paramount

– Apollo, the patron of well-tempered serenity and individuation. At first Nietzsche maintained that the lost Greek synthesis was being recovered by Wagner, whose music-dramas recreated the electric tension between Dionysian power and Apollonian form. Later, however, he changed his mind. He decided that the Wagnerian *Gesamtkunstwerk* was the least Greek of all forms of art. It was Romantic self-enhancement owing nothing to the Dionysian dithyramb, which submerged the self in communal ecstasy. For the older Nietzsche, modern art remained bereft of Dionysus. In thrall still to Socrates, it manifested 'declining strength, approaching senility, somatic exhaustion'.[42]

What, then, would the new art be like? Nietzsche was sure only that it would be more like Shakespeare's than like Wagner's. For Shakespeare was Dionysian. He was fearless in the face of the fearful and the questionable. He came from 'a restless, vigorous age … half drunk and stupefied by its excess of blood and energy'. He embraced and converted into art a world suffused with pity and terror. He made truth aesthetic, and therefore bearable.[43] French writers, likewise, now regarded Shakespeare as an authentic tragedian who spoke for all ages, including their own. 'We civilisations', wrote Valéry in 1919, 'now know that we are mortal'; and he recognised in Hamlet the archetypal bearer of that oppressive knowledge. Hamlet is heir to all the controversies and achievements of devastated Europe; weary with all its learning and unable either to renounce or to resume its tremendous effort. From the emblematic terrace of Elsinore, 'which extends from Basle to Cologne, and touches the sands of Nieuport, the marches of the Somme, the chalk of Champagne, and the granite of Alsace', he looks down upon millions of ghosts. Taking up the skulls of the eminent dead, he meditates on their hopes betrayed, and sways between the two abysses of order and disorder.[44] This piece of Shakespearean bravura, published first in English in the *Athenaeum*, made a great impression. Its image of a shattered civilisation being retrieved as incoherent fragments by a feverish effort of the collective memory was versified by T. S. Eliot in *The Wasteland*. In France it helped to fix the idea of Shakespeare as the voice of a culture dismembered and disconsolate. To many of the intellectuals who were victims and witnesses of the 1930s and 1940s, Shakespeare became a habitual, even a sacramental resource. His imagination was not only big enough to encompass 'Buchenwald … Auschwitz … the retreat

from Dunkirk ... Hiroshima ... dictators strung up by their feet ...
lampshades made of human skin'; it had by some feat of prophetic
insight prefigured them.[45]

Shakespearean strains and keynotes became frequent in French writing at this time. The opening scene of Cocteau's *La Machine infernale* –
sentries on the ramparts of Thebes are accosted by the ghost of a dead
king – is borrowed from *Hamlet*, and registers the link established by
Freud between Oedipus and Shakespeare's hero. Giraudoux reverted to
the rich, highly imagistic language of Shakespearean drama, and introduced to the French stage the long Shakespearean monologue and the
wise Shakespearean fool. Anouilh's Antigone has an obvious kinship
with Shakespeare's Juliet. The performance of *Orphée et Eurydice* in *La
Peste* recalls the Shakespearean play within a play. And Shakespeare is a
presiding presence in *Le Crève-cœur* ('Heartbreak'), a collection of verse
by Louis Aragon which became a mascot text of the Resistance after a
first, tiny edition was suppressed in 1941. Tapping the current of poetic
language that ran 'like a secret stream' through the *chansons, plaintes,*
and *cantiques* of pre-classical France, Aragon revisited Shakespearean
tragedy and history.[46] The allusions and enigmas of *Hamlet* are reflected
in the broken surface of 'Romance du temps qu'il fait' ('Romance of the
Weather Now'). Elsinore, a place of death and affliction, haunted by
spectral monarchs and mad Ophelias, is no longer an archaism, but a
template of the modern world:

> Notre monde atroce démarque
> Le royaume de Danemark ... *

'Richard II Quarante' ('Richard II Forty'), written in October 1940, after
France had capitulated and German troops had moved into the Occupied Zone, is constructed around two lines from *Richard II*:

> You may my glories and my state depose
> But not my griefs; still am I king of those.

In a simple epicedeum for his martyred country, the poet identified
himself with Shakespeare's dispossessed and inconsolable sovereign:

> Et je ressemble à ce monarque

* Our atrocious world imitates / The kingdom of Denmark.

> Plus malheureux que le malheur
> Qui restait roi de ses douleurs. *

'All unhappiness', said Pascal, 'comes from the fact that a man can-not sit still in a room.'[47] In France, Shakespeare had always been resisted, as the Baroque had been resisted, in the name of a higher order: an order founded on Reason, and measured by a Cartesian clock which regularly counts the hours and years between the beginning of things and their end. Here Baroque art had been much less extravagant, much less restless, than it had been in Italy, Germany, and England. It had remained a dignified dance to the music of Cartesian time. For over two hundred years the French cherished the belief that beatitude is in still-ness and decorum; that salvation is Beauty proclaiming

> Je hais le mouvement qui déplace les lignes
> Et jamais je ne pleure et jamais je ne ris.†[48]

Bergson argued that Descartes had falsified time, by linking it to the idea of space. Descartes had thought of time as extension, whereas it is actu-ally experienced, said Bergson, as duration: as a sequence, that is, not of disparate but of interrelated moments. Yet Bergson's time, though het-erogeneous, remained harmonious. Though it was not perceived uniformly, like the beats of a clock, it still cohered, like the notes of a melody or the features of a face.[49] It was not Baroque. It was therefore at odds with the modern spirit. Pascal had observed that 'our nature is in movement'; that 'entire repose is death';[50] and when reason itself confirmed that the stillness of the happy ending is more deathly than the flux of the Baroque, French opinion moved strongly against classi-cism and all the rules and sedatives with which it had tried to tranquillise the rowdiness of art. The French then rejected syntax and structures and happy endings, and opened their minds and their stage to the unruly pulse of Shakespeare's hours and years.

Shakespeare's writing teems with images of time, because his charac-ters are always inventing and reinventing it. Deconstructed by their

---

* And I resemble that monarch / More unfortunate than Misfortune / Who remained king of his griefs.
† I hate the movement which displaces the lines / And never do I weep, never do I laugh.

metaphors, similes, and analogies, it loses objectivity and unity. In their experience time has no music; and there is a music that does not keep time. They are vexed, like Richard II, by a universe without coherence and synchrony. The world is not rhythmic; it obeys no metronome. The broken music of life makes wise men mad, because it tells not of the clock, not of time kept, but of time wasted, and wasting. And yet, supreme benediction of Baroque genius, Shakespeare's was a wisdom that that fractured music could not make mad. He both recorded and transcended the tragic absurdity of life because somehow, writing amidst the delirium of life's theatre, he contrived, in the words of a modern French scholar, 'to give form and intelligibility to the hazards of existence'.[51]

The Shakespearean Baroque, defying contours and postponing resolution, acquired a special validity at a time when thought and music had discovered their essential resource beyond dogma and tonality. What could now be more modern than an author who reached out ever further through outlandish keys and registers, always deferring a verdict and resisting a final cadence? And what could be more needful than writing which, though dealing in agnostic and chromatic uncertainties, bore incontrovertible witness, with the fact of its own existence, against disorder and neurosis? Like Mallarmé, Aragon discovered in the ending of *Hamlet* a paradigm for an age when answers mattered less than questions. For Shakespeare's is an ending that is not an ending: not a conclusion, but an interrogation. It is a threshold, open still to possibility, to something unseen, unheard, over the page, off the stage. In Aragon's poem, the princely figure, tragically isolated, does not hear the trumpets of Fortinbras; but they are pealing out triumphantly nevertheless:

> Elle dit n'ouvre plus tes bras
> Et lui reste sourd aux fanfares
> Dont la nuit pourtant se timbra
> O trompettes de Fortinbras. *

---

* She said embrace no more / And he remains deaf to the fanfares / Which struck through the night nonetheless / O trumpets of Fortinbras.

8

Waiting for Shakespeare

By the middle of the twentieth century Shakespeare in France had been disentangled from the ideology of race. Pioneering theatre directors like Antoine, Copeau, and Pitoëff, with André Gide as a converted accomplice, had ensured that the old 'fable décente et régulière', in which Shakespeare was reconstituted for 'French' taste and 'French' sensibility, finally disappeared from the stage. The sequel was a voyage of exploration and discovery. Not just the theatrical world of Paris, but that of the provinces too, succumbed to a Shakespeare mania. Between 1940 and 1960, twenty of Shakespeare's plays were performed in France, and several of these (*King John*, *All's Well That Ends Well*, *Richard II*, *Henry IV*, *Cymbeline*, and *Pericles*) had never before been seen there. The future that came to pass, however, was not the future that the pioneers had envisaged. Their way of thinking and their way of treating Shakespeare soon fell out of fashion. They came to be regarded as too reverential; too literary; too exclusive. They were accused of having lost sight of the wider public from whom Shakespeare was reckoned to have come and for whom he was reckoned to have written. It was, increasingly, as a 'popular' author that Shakespeare was discovered and promoted in France after the First World War. Prominent theatrical figures made it their mission to give him – and the classics generally – back to the people; to restitute the legacy that had been usurped by intellectuals and the privileged. The director Michel Saint-Denis, Copeau's nephew and one-time secretary of the Vieux-Colombier, insisted in 1933 that Shakespeare was first and foremost a popular dramatist and that it was therefore important that 'the French spectator find himself in the presence of a show, and not of a text overloaded with commentaries'.[1] This new preoccupation meant that Shakespeare became disentangled from the ideology of race only to become entangled with the ideology of class. Just as he had been essential to the Romantic rebellion against classicism, and to the avant-garde rebellion against Romanticism, so now he became essential to the radical rebellion against the avant-garde.

It was an eighteenth-century idea that Shakespeare as a theatrical experience had less to do with poetry, which was the attribute of tragedy, than with 'action, spectacle, mouvement [et] variété', which were the attributes of opera. This notion derived partly from classical rigorism, which discounted the tragic status of blank verse, and partly from the historical coincidence whereby Shakespeare was discovered at the time when opera was gratifying audiences with sights and sounds unknown to the tragic theatre. From his first entry on to the French stage, Shakespeare was adapted to the scale and visual register of opera. The word 'opera' occurred frequently in critical appraisals of performances of his work.

Although the early stage versions were versified and regularised, 'Shakespearean' exoticism was from the beginning recovered through pictorial supplementation. This included ballet, pantomime, and supernatural effects. Such operatic treatment was favoured by logistics – by the sheer size of the prestigious Parisian theatres. The four houses occupied by the Comédie-Française since 1689 have all had a seating capacity of about 2000, and the other main theatres have been of similar dimensions. The théâtre de la Porte-Saint-Martin had 1500 seats and a cavernous stage. The théâtre des Nations, which became the théâtre Sarah Bernhardt in 1899, had a capacity of 1700 and a stage in proportion.[2] Furthermore they were equipped with stage machinery and technical resources that became ever more sophisticated after the introduction of electricity. Shakespeare's work seemed ideally suited to all this space and apparatus, since it was replete with ancient, medieval, and modern pageantry, battles, crowds, supernatural phenomena, and musical and choreographic interludes. The presentation of his plays therefore became ever more extravagant and monumental. They were amplified to fill enormous stages, entertain large audiences, and show off versatile machinery and clever lighting. When André Antoine became director of the Odéon in 1906, he was warned by a previous director, Paul Porel, that it was 'a chasm where every nuance [was] lost'. At the Odéon, he said, 'you're always expecting a battleship to pass by in a play with two characters'. It was suitable only for 'important plays ... presented with large-scale, realistic scenery' – and Shakespeare's *Julius Caesar* came at once to mind.[3] To Paris theatre audiences and theatre managers Shakespeare signified massive *décor* and epic spectacle. You never said 'Shakespearean' when you meant intimate, lyrical, or *sotto voce.*

No record survives of the *décor* for the first of the adaptations, Ducis' *Hamlet*, performed at the Comédie-Française in 1769. Ducis' *Lear*, however, presented in the court theatre at Versailles in 1783, is known to have been staged with elaborate, realistic sets and a full range of pyrotechnics to imitate the storm. The *Mémoires Secrètes* reported that the first two acts were played with scenery depicting a fortified castle. In the third act the stage portrayed 'a forest bristling with rocks; in the background, a cavern with an old oak beside it; it is night; a fearful storm is brewing ... lightning flashes and thunder rumbles.'[4] For Ducis' *Macbeth* at the Comédie-Française in 1784 evocative gothic scenery was provided and music was used to create an appropriate mood. This production also featured the first appearance on the French stage of a Shakespearean ghost. In Ducis' *Hamlet* the ghost had been visible to the prince alone. In *Macbeth* there was no Banquo, but murdered Duncan reappeared and shook his gory locks both at Macbeth and at the audience. Thereafter ghosts were an essential element in the Shakespearean package, and they became more and more spectral with advances in stage lighting. By the time the Dumas-Meurice *Hamlet* was revived at the Comédie-Française in 1886, electricity had replaced gas, and the supernatural effect was especially ingenious. It was not, however, without its drawbacks, as the critic of *Le Figaro* discovered. 'The ghost', he wrote,

> is generally seen only within the thickness of the masonry itself, which is made transparent by means of metallic gauzes. The system is very clever, but it requires the stage to be very dark because the least light would make this species of magic lantern invisible. On the other hand, when, in the third *tableau*, Hamlet is swallowed up by the night as he follows the ghost, the effect is very striking.[5]

In Sarah Bernhardt's *Hamlet* the pictures of the two kings referred to by the prince in his dialogue with his mother were full-length wall portraits. When the ghost of Hamlet's father reappeared, he did so within the frame of his own portrait, as the light changed and the painted surface became transparent.[6]

Lavish scenery became a hallmark of Shakespeare at the Comédie-Française. For de Vigny's *More de Venise* (1829), seven ponderous *décors* of painstaking, documentary realism were designed by Pierre-Luc Ciceri, prompting *Le Constitutionel* to comment: 'The play is mounted with a luxury that rivals the Opéra.' The audience were dazzled by a series of sumptuous stage pictures – the interior of the Ducal Palace in Venice, with the senate in session; the landing-stage in Cyprus with a stormy sea and passing ships in the background; Othello's audience chamber; Desdemona's boudoir. 'This time', wrote the critic of *Le Figaro*,

> M. Ciceri has surpassed himself. It is not scenery which we see before us; there is nothing to suggest the theatre in these compositions, which are beautifully in period, and which have, it would seem, been discovered among the monuments of the middle ages.[7]

When the Dumas-Meurice *Hamlet* was premièred at the théâtre Historique in 1847, the text was structured as seven *tableaux* requiring four *décors*. When the revised version was presented at the Comédie-Française in 1886, it comprised thirteen *tableaux* and required nine *décors*. Six of these *décors* were full-scale, three-dimensional sets. The remaining three were shallow sets, positioned front-stage. They enabled the action to continue while the stagehands were at work behind. Even so, four long intervals were needed in order to give sufficient time for all this freight of painted wood and canvas to be shifted and shunted. Over 32,000 francs were spent on scenery; a further 45,000 on costumes, weapons, footwear, and headwear. The director of the Comédie, Jules Clarétie, justified this exorbitance by arguing that theatrical art was currently required to offer 'as much to the eye as to the mind'.[8] When it revived Richepin's translation of *Macbeth* in 1914, the Comédie remained true to this *décoromanie*. Costumes were expensively and accurately feudal, and the stage depicted blasted heath, vaulted chambers, castle park, and gloomy cavern with bubbling cauldron and all the usual paraphernalia of witchcraft. This visual overload, coupled with the stentorian delivery of Paul Mounet in the principal rôle, caused one bewildered spectator to comment: 'It was like being at the opera. I couldn't understand a thing.'[9] But the other state theatre, the Odéon, was not to be outdone. During the administration of Paul Porel

(1885–94) Shakespearean spectacle was its speciality. In 1886, when Paul Meurice's version of *Hamlet* was playing at the Comédie, his translation of *A Midsummer Night's Dream* was filling the stage of the Odéon with fairy-tale opulence. Jules Lemaître wrote of 'eye-catching décor ... fantastic and unreal lighting ... precious fabrics ... gold and jewels on the silks of the costumes'. The production included a female *corps de ballet* dancing to Mendelssohn's music, which was performed by orchestra, soloists, and chorus.[10] This was the first of seven Shakespearean events designed to take advantage of the Odéon's huge stage and show off the skill of its electricians and *machinistes*.

Even Porel's extravaganzas were pale beside the feast of Shakespearean colour, light, and sound that was offered to war-weary Parisians in 1917 and 1918. Enemy zeppelins were looming in the sky, cyclopean artillery was pounding in the distance, food and fuel were in perilously short supply, but at the théâtre Antoine audiences wallowed in glamour and sensuality. Firmin Gémier's productions of *Le Marchand de Venise* and *Antoine et Cléopâtre* laid under contribution not only the opera, the circus, and the Ballets Russes, but the music hall as well. With the footlights removed, and the stage connected by ramps to the auditorium, the actors made exits and entrances through the audience, in the manner of variety artistes. This was Shakespeare lavish and daring as never before. For *Le Marchand de Venise* two hundred costumes were copied by Emile Bertin from paintings by Carpaccio and Veronese. *Antoine et Cléopâtre* featured twenty-five *tableaux*, three orchestras, and an orgy that caught the headlines and made French theatrical history. Colette reported that she had been 'stunned by light, colour, dancing, martial clamour'; and she warned the public to expect, at the end of the second act, 'the first orgy to merit the name of orgy'. She described how

> a single cry went up from the house as the curtain rose revealing the carpet of women covering the rostra, all motionless yet palpitating like beautiful reptiles ... At a sign from the orchestra all rise up and hurl themselves into a mêlée whose brutality remains harmonious and disciplined by dance. The audience were uplifted by wholesome delight – delight like that of the oozing vine-harvest, of the heaped-up grain, a delight such as that claimed by the sight of the riches of the earth.[11]

There is a special significance in Gémier's Shakespearean enterprise, because it set the first agenda for a popular theatre in France. The pressures of the Great War had encouraged an understanding of Shakespeare that forsook the ideology of race. The traditional idea of an Anglo-Saxon author requiring to be gallicised was now challenged by the notion of a common heritage requiring to be defended. These performances at the théâtre Antoine were sponsored by the Société Shakespeare, which Gémier had set up in order to foster cultural bonding between the allies. Shakespeare's had become the voice of beleaguered Civilisation; his achievement one of its precious trophies. He must therefore be made widely known and appreciated in France. 'Our main object', said Gémier, 'is to make our public fond of Shakespeare.' After the war, his ambition to democratise the legacy of world drama led him to found the first, short-lived, Théâtre National Populaire (TNP).

Gémier wanted to recover drama as community festival, as the 'religion laïque' that had been celebrated by the Greeks and the Elizabethans. He believed that directors should pull in the crowd by staging spectacular events. Little theatres stifled inspiration. They engendered 'little authors and little works'. For Gémier the ideal performing space was a huge venue like the Cirque d'hiver or the Trocadéro. He scorned those who were timid or dull under the pretext of being faithful. Words were essential, but not sufficient. Great authors, he said, 'are not merely poets but also masters of ceremonies at festivals for the eye'. He therefore drew freely on the related arts – circus, ballet, opera, mime, architecture, painting – in order to give full realisation to images that he had 'deduced' from the text. This was the way to recreating the total theatrical experience.[12]

Gémier's brand of big, bravura Shakespeare remained a feature of mainstream serious theatre in France down to the 1950s. Gaston Baty and Jean-Louis Barrault both inherited much of Gémier's ideology and temperament, and their productions were similarly bold and eclectic. Baty linked his pursuit of total theatre to the campaign for authentic Shakespeare. He argued that the Elizabethan stage had not been a naked platform on which the words did all the work, but a crucible of all the arts: a fusion of costume, music, dance, mime, and speech. The modern director's task was to redeem the damage inflicted by Romantic stagecraft, which had abused 'décor, costumes, et accessoires', and turned them into an encumbrance. By retrieving the lost synthesis, the modern director would be able to 'rethéâtraliser le théâtre'.[13] In practice this meant that Baty presented Shakespeare much as Gémier had done. His production of *La Mégère apprivoisée* at the théâtre Montparnasse in 1941 actually replicated, with modifications, a *mise en scène* that Gémier had devised for the Société Shakespeare in 1919. His *Macbeth*, mounted the following year, featured a baronial castle that rose from the earth and vanished into the mist.[14] Barrault's Shakespeare was likewise strongly visual. For Gide's translation of *Antony and Cleopatra*, revived at the Comédie-Française in 1945, he commissioned seven *décors* from Jean Hugo, and the stage became a kaleidoscope of changing images as the play made its rapid flights from continent to continent. In all there were twenty-three changes of scene, and the embellishment was extended to mimed battles and an orgy on Pompey's galley that recalled Gémier's notorious precedent. In 1960, when Barrault was director of the Odéon (now called the Théâtre de France), a replica of the Teatro Olimpico at Vicenza was constructed for Yves Bonnefoy's translation of *Julius Caesar*, and the costumes were copied from pictures by Mantegna. This sort of pictorial Shakespeare was seen frequently at the two state theatres in Paris in the 1950s. *Othello* (translated by Georges Neveux and directed by Jean Meyer) was staged at the Salle Richelieu in 1950 with complex mobile scenery. 'Walls', reported Robert Kemp in *Le Monde*, 'fold back, descend into the depths, fly up into the sky. Some buildings seem to dissolve; others solidify on the spot.' The following year the forest of Arden, assembled almost leaf by leaf, was one of eighteen *décors* designed by François Ganeau for Jacques Charon's production at the Odéon of *Comme il vous plaira*, translated by Jules Supervielle. In 1952 the architecture of medieval Verona was brought to the same stage by Georges Wakhevitch, for Jean Sarment's version of *Romeo and Juliet*, directed by Julien Bertheau.[15]

Gémier, Baty, and Barrault enjoyed great prestige and authority; yet not even their brilliant talents could overcome a persistent current of ideological and critical resistance. The belief was widespread that their sort of treatment was right neither for Shakespeare nor for the people. The claim that it would bring the two together was challenged by both the connoisseurs of Shakespeare and the advocates of democratic theatre.

The operatic presentation of drama in general and of Shakespeare in particular had been attracting critical disapproval for generations. Again and again the objection had been heard that elaborate and costly stage effects were at best an irrelevance and at worst a distraction. Even Voltaire, who relished the opera, had reckoned that its intrusion into the tragic stage was going too far. Hearing of Ducis' *Hamlet* in 1769, he complained that the 'action' and 'pantomime' were overdone. 'I wanted to liven up the theatre a bit by introducing more action, and now everything is action and pantomime ... We are falling head over heels into exaggeration and the *gigantesque*.'[16] The correspondent of the *Mémoires Secrètes* protested against the pyrotechnic literalism in Ducis' *Lear*:

> As for the hail, the lightning, and the thunder – all these natural calamities are excellent in an opera, and ridiculous in a tragedy, where storms must occur not in the atmosphere but in the hearts of the characters and, as an after-effect, in those of the audience.[17]

The complaint was often made that *décoromanie* smothered the text and destroyed its coherence by multiplying interruptions. Scene-shifting in de Vigny's *More de Venise* occupied so much time that even after cuts were made the performance lasted more than four hours.[18] In the 1860s Alfred Mézières argued that the 'multiplicité des décors et l'habileté du machiniste' were diminishing instead of increasing the dramatic impact of Shakespeare on the stage. When the eye was sated, the mind was hindered.[19] Francisque Sarcey, reviewing the Dumas-Meurice *Hamlet* in 1886, grumbled about money being squandered on details that no one even noticed: 'I'll never be persuaded that a dramatic work needs all these additives ... Everything, even commonsense, is being sacrificed to this craze for stage effects.'[20] In 1913 the critic Maurice Sponck repeated the standard indictment against operatic Shakespeare at the Comédie-Française:

> Ingenious technicians ... have not merely the disadvantage of being very expensive, they are even more culpable in that they distract the attention. The text of a great writer is sufficient in itself ... Luxury of *décor* and *toilette* is a barbaric amusement, and it has already been rightly said that the theatre perishes by spectacle.[21]

Gémier's riposte, that the theatre lived by spectacle, remained very controversial. His critics insisted that his showy stagings of Shakespeare obscured rather than illuminated the plays. François Mauriac accused him of stifling the poetry with exhibitionism.[22] Jacques-Emile Blanche said that the Gémier *Antoine et Cléopâtre* reminded him of the operas of Richard Strauss and 'des festivals pour millionnaires'. He deplored the interpolated orgy, which was 'at the antipodes of the Shakespearean aesthetic'. He feared that it would cause sensualists among the audience 'to forget what they had better remember about one of Shakespeare's most amazing tragedies'.[23] Colette discovered that the coming and going of actors through the auditorium actually weakened the sense of involvement, since it divided rather than concentrated the spectator's attention. It confirmed that, even with the footlights removed, there was no access to life and reality from the counterfeit world of the opera stage. When Mark Antony strode through the orchestra stalls crying *en Egypt! en Egypt!* he was no longer the legendary paramour who had kissed away kingdoms, but an actor in heavy make-up and fake armour heading for the exit to the boulevard de Strasbourg.[24] Gide judged the production 'une horreur', but found himself involved in something very similar when his own translation of Shakespeare's play was given its first staging at the Paris Opera. Ida Rubinstein set out to mimic and to surpass Gémier. As Cleopatra, she moved across a stage decked with sumptuous sets and milling with tumultuous crowds, and when she retired from view to change into another of Jacques Dresa's renditions of Egyptian *haute couture*, the orchestra portrayed military engagements and the naval battle of Actium. Stravinsky had withdrawn from the production when he learnt that it would not be in modern dress, but the composer Florent Schmitt had obliged with a full score. The last thing anyone was aware of was the play itself. The Palais Garnier was so enormous, and the stage was so busy with oriental pageantry, that Gide, watching the first performance from a box, could hardly hear what the actors were saying – and what he did hear he could not recognise as the words he had written. Marcel Proust, in Princess Soutzo's *loge*, gave up pretending to take it all seriously. He spent the evening chatting to his friends and quizzing the audience. Roger Martin du Gard came away complaining that Shakespeare had been reduced to 'une lamentable exhibition de music hall'.[25]

No one who was present at these performances in 1920 ever again saw such a meretricious treatment of Shakespeare; but Baty was often accused of directorial self-indulgence, and the Shakespearean productions at the two subsidised theatres in the 1950s provoked a lot of disparagement. There were scathing references in the press to 'Venice and Cyprus in cut-out pasteboard', 'displays of conjuring', 'superfluous frippery', '*trompe–l'oeil*', and so on. Ostentatious literalism now seemed obsolete as a mode of serious theatre. The whole drift of modernism, which was towards expressionism and abstraction in art, was against it; and the cinema, with its greater command of panoramic spectacle and photo-documentary realism, made it seem redundant. Film was especially significant with regard to Shakespeare – not because it proved a suitable medium for the performance of his plays, but because it assisted a better appreciation of their rhythm and structure. In the age of the cinema it became clear that far from being carved with a hatchet, as French detractors used to claim, they prefigured in a remarkable way cinematic techniques such as the close-up, montage, and the free manipulation of space and time. Gémier had once conceded that it might be possible to play Shakespeare without scenery. An opinion more in keeping with modern thinking was that it was impossible to play him with it.[26]

From an ideological point of view the operatic style of production fell out of favour following the general radicalisation of art and intellect after the Second World War. These expensive stage confections, like the upholstered and gilded playhouses in which they were displayed, were disparaged as so much cosseting for a spiritually atrophied, conspicuously consuming middle class. This shift to the Left was made vividly obvious by the tribulations of Jean-Louis Barrault. In 1959, following several triumphant overseas tours which included performances of Gide's *Hamlet* in New York and Tokyo, Barrault's troupe was singled out for special recognition by the recently established government of Charles de Gaulle. André Malraux, minister for cultural affairs, installed it as resident company in the newly refurbished Odéon-Théâtre de France. By accepting this official favour, and agreeing to serve as director, Barrault seemed to be demonstrating a symbiosis between his sort of theatre and the political mentality of the Gaullist Right. He therefore found himself doubly impugned by the Parisian intelligentsia. Their acrimony and critical sniping made him feel like the victim of a mafia: 'The intellectuals, through their writings and a certain intimidating mode of behaviour, shape opinion ... For my part, since I had begun "before the war", I was not "their sort". I had existed before them, so I ought not to exist.' Their response to his Shakespearean productions was especially harsh. With regard to the *Julius Caesar* of his inaugural season, Barrault admitted that he had made 'serious errors' of artistic judgement; but he reckoned that the *Henry VI* of 1967 was some of his best work. He made his own adaptation, compressing Shakespeare's trilogy into a single play of four hours' duration, and staged it in the Gémier manner, with period costumes, lavish sets, music, mime, and dispersal of the actors among the audience. The critical attacks left him shocked and dazed – but they were not the worst that intellectual Paris had reserved for him. The full measure of its hostility became apparent only in May the following year, when France and the French government were traumatised by the most serious civil insurgence that the country had known since the Commune of 1871. The Odéon, identified by the Comité d'Action Révolutionnaire as an emblem of 'la culture bourgeoise', was selected by student extremists for occupation and symbolic desecration. It was invaded by two and a half thousand demonstrators, and this number increased to about ten thousand as the crisis intensified and the forces of order made it their priority to defend other, more important buildings. Barrault, ignored by a paralysed and pusillanimous government, was forced to abandon his theatre to a mob bent on destruction and defilement. The property store, workshops, and wardrobe were broken open and ransacked. The velvet stage curtain was slashed and sullied. The auditorium was wrecked and littered ankle-deep with a debris of costumes, footware, wigs, weaponry, furniture, mirrors, light bulbs, refuse, and excrement. The air became fetid and unbreathable.[27] Later in the year, when the troubles were over, the Odéon was cleaned, redecorated, and brought back into use; but Barrault lost his job as director. He was dismissed for having dared to question the wisdom of Malraux.

In his reminiscences Barrault compared 1968 to 1789, and his own misfortunes were indeed those of a public figure made a scapegoat for the sins of an *ancien régime*. When the Odéon was sacked and its stock-in-trade destroyed, a tradition was overturned that had long been stigmatised as privileged and élitist. But probably the tradition was moribund in any case. It was discredited even within the theatre itself (Barrault recognised many actors and actresses among the invaders), and the need for change, for a new start, had already been recognised and answered. An alternative theatre was in place. It was the work of directors who had taken over the populist ideology and steered it away from Paris and opera. They had hitched it to an ungarnished, unpretending mode of production that was derived partly from Antoine, Copeau, and Pitoëff, and partly from Brecht.

Antoine, Copeau, and Pitoëff had not only brought Shakespeare out of the library and on to the stage, they had also delivered him from the sybarites. Antoine was an experimental and eclectic director. His 1906 *Jules César* was lavish and archaeologically exact, yet he had already breached the tradition of pictorial literalism by playing intermediate scenes of *Le Roi Lear* without scenery. For his production of *Coriolanus* in 1912 he eliminated scene-shifting by using a single set. This revealed in the text what Copeau called 'a cohesion, a grandeur, that had not been fully perceived, before it was performed, even by those who knew it well'.[28] Copeau took the idea a step further at the Vieux-Colombier by constructing a permanent stage architecture of tiered levels and a gallery over an alcove. The proscenium arch he in effect abolished by extending the acting area into the auditorium. It was a stage, he said, 'at the same time rudimentary in resources, and rich in aesthetic possibility, like the Greek or the Elizabethan stage'.[29] Here he presented Shakespeare and Molière without scenery, creating visual variation by the use of draperies and lighting. 'We decongested the dramatic arena and denuded the stage', he wrote. 'Such a rigorous purge of all scenic superfluity liberated the poetry of Molière and Shakespeare.'[30] Even the critic René Doumic, who hated *Twelfth Night*, had to agree. 'Here', he wrote, 'you have to like the plays for themselves.'[31] Pitoëff adopted single sets for all his Shakespearean productions. He experimented with semi-abstract configurations of lines and planes in order to reclaim the stage for the actors and the words. 'I demand', he said of the actor speaking the famous monologue of Hamlet, 'that he be alone in the middle of the stage, with no help, no support, deprived of all assistance. I want him to be strong enough to carry without faltering the heavy burden of the genius of Shakespeare.'[32] Minimalism won many converts in the 1930s, and even the state theatres stripped down their Shakespeare. In 1932 the Comédie-Française mounted its first *Hamlet* in twenty years, and signified its break with the past by dropping the Dumas-Meurice version with its heavy cargo of *décor*, props, and Romantic associations. The Schwob-Morand text was chosen and the stage decoration reduced to draperies and a few movable accessories – an apse, a gothic postern, a fragment of wall. The same year *King Lear*, in a new translation by Charles Méré, was performed at the Odéon with no scenery except a few backdrops and some mobile screens. Louis Gillet noted how the dramatic cogency and narrative thrust of the plays was restored: 'We had forgotten that *Hamlet* is before all else a play, a sort of melodrama, even a detective story ... a blockbuster of a novel'.[33]

It was direct, uncluttered, spartan Shakespeare that the promoters of democratic theatre took to the people in postwar France. The young director Jean Vilar believed, like Copeau, that true dramatic art travelled light. He rejected as obsolete the ornamental, operatic stagecraft of Gémier, Baty, and Barrault. In 1946 he declared that he was fighting against 'rethéâtralisation', 'spectacle pour le spectacle', 'décoromanie', 'l'art primaire de l'éclairage', 'la pataphysique parisienne du costume'. Such things had become aberrant at a time of cultural revaluation and spiritual fundamentalism:

> It seems to me that a people compelled by the war to rediscover not merely the basic needs of existence but also, perhaps, a more vivid sense of existence, will require of us something other than dressiness and superfinery – something other than, let the word be repeated, a show.

He aimed to provide theatre that was unsophisticated, straightforward, and accessible to all ('aux effets simples, sans intentions, familier à tous') and to attract an audience that was dedicated rather than casual and chic. In order to signify an ethos of reform and rebirth, he chose Shakespearean texts as yet unperformed in France, and he chose a venue very different and very far from the theatres of Paris. His first Shakespearean venture was *Richard II*, mounted in the open air at Avignon in 1947. The stage was a simple platform, eighteen metres by ten, set up in the *cour d'honneur* of the Palace of the Popes. This was the inaugural production of the first Avignon festival. For the fourth festival, in 1950, Vilar chose both parts of *Henry IV*, condensed and performed as a single work. The plays, translated by Jean Curtis, were performed 'disencumbered of all the mechanical contraptions of both the open-air and the indoor theatre'.[34] The success of the Avignon festivals was immense. It led to a revival, under state sponsorship, of the Théâtre National Populaire (TNP), with Vilar as director. It made Shakespeare's Richard II, played initially by Vilar himself and subsequently by Gérard Philipe, admired in France as one of the virtuoso rôles of world drama. The play was revived in Paris at the théâtre des Champs-Elysées in October 1947, and then again at Avignon in 1952. From there it was transferred once more to Paris, where the TNP occupied the Palais de Chaillot. At Avignon in 1954 Vilar directed *Macbeth* to great acclaim, and this production too was later revived at the Chaillot.

Shakespeare was carried to the wider French public by the festival movement, which played an important rôle in postwar France as a means to decentralising and democratising the arts. In addition to the productions at Avignon, there were *Julius Caesars* in the arenas at Nîmes (1950) and Arles (1954); a *Richard III* at Perpignan (1951); a *King John* at Angers (1952); a *Cymbeline* at Quimper (1952); a *Coriolanus* at Nîmes (1955); an *Othello* at Toulon (1956).

The aesthetic austerity associated with Avignon and the TNP was abetted by the general trend of intellectual politics. Since the 1930s European intellectuals across the political spectrum had been opposing the general ethos of materialism and corruption that was associated with industrialised and commercialised leisure. The protest from the Right, articulated in Britain by T. S. Eliot, F. R. Leavis, and other critics, focused on the threat to Culture and the legacy of excellence that it patronised. Intellectuals on the Left were preoccupied by the erosion of working-class consciousness and the consequent weakening of the impetus to revolution and renewal. It seemed that under the pressures of advertising and the mass-media the proletariat were being assimilated to the bourgeoisie in a common orgy of consumerism. By the 1960s there was talk among Continental Marxists of a 'bourgeois entropy' portending social and cultural homogeneity with no dynamic for change.[35] Such concerns were voiced, most notably, by Antonio Gramsci, founder-member and chief ideologue of the Italian Communist Party. Writing in prison in the 1930s, Gramsci had revised the Marxist critique of capitalism by extending its reference from economic to cultural oppression. He argued that the development of a national popular consciousness was being thwarted in Italy by entertainment and literature that mass-reproduced the taste and ideology of a cosmopolitan élite. He proposed a cultural strategy that would undermine the hegemony of the dominant class by radicalising education, the press, and the performing arts. At the same time in Germany, Bertolt Brecht was attacking the theatre as the 'merchandise' of a depraved and parasitic class, and developing in practice as well as in theory a dramatic art that would counteract the inertia of bourgeois sensibility.

In France this radical current of protest ensured that Shakespeare – like other great writers – was polemicised as he was popularised. Once excluded from the public stage on grounds of race, he was now admitted on grounds of class. The Anglo-Saxon dramatist who offended French taste had become an *engagé* artist who assisted the proletarian struggle. In 1957 the twenty-six-year-old director Roger Planchon, who had forsaken Paris for the Théâtre de la Cité at Villeurbanne, a working-class suburb of Lyon, presented both parts of *Henry IV* as the chronicle of a society in seismic convulsion. Planchon's view was that the plays were the work of an author instinctively drawn to such Marxist themes as class conflict, economic oppression, and redemption through communism. 'The characters', he wrote, 'are never treated as distinct selves, but always as caught up in great historical collisions, and ... individual destinies are always indissolubly linked to the wider collective destiny.' Vilar, too, had defined theatre as the arena of social conflicts and public crises. Unlike the novel, it dealt with history, not with psychology and the inner life. Ideological continuity was therefore assured when Planchon's company inherited the designation Théâtre National Populaire on Vilar's death in 1971 – though Planchon's stagecraft was polemical to an extent that Vilar's never was. Planchon owed much to Brecht. Like Brecht, he added mime in order to elicit desired meanings from the text (notably the sufferings and humiliation of the soldiers and common people) and, again like Brecht, he used projected commentaries in order to prompt appropriate audience responses.[36]

So the price of popularisation, in this instance at least, was the loss of Shakespeare's impartiality: that absence from his own creations that had so impressed earlier generations. More generally popularisation meant that the playwright took precedence over the poet. Copeau and Pitoëff had looked for lyricism both in the translations that they used and in the theatrical effects they created. By performing finely tuned texts in small theatres (the Vieux-Colombier had only 365 seats) they ensured that Shakespeare in French was never prosaic. Pitoëff had been at pains to satisfy the 'educated ear'. Theatre, he said in 1925, had become 'a subtle art, and full of nuance'. He talked of 'a theatre of intelligence [and] suggestiveness', in which the actor would find it impossible to use the old techniques. These would now seem 'childish and clumsy' ('enfantins et grossiers').[37] But subtlety, nuance, and suggestiveness were what many critics found missing in Shakespeare as purveyed by the democratic theatre.

Logistics, again, were in part responsible. In France the notion of popular theatre was tinged with megalomania. It was inspired by a yearning for the theatre of ancient Greece, with its multitudinous audiences and mighty arenas. The *cour d'honneur* at Avignon had seating for 3000 people. The amphitheatres at Arles and Nîmes accommodated tens of thousands. Even the indoor theatre of the Théâtre National Populaire, the Palais de Chaillot, had 2500 seats. Vilar disdained to use amplification; but Jean Renoir resorted to it for *Julius Caesar* at Arles in 1954, and the audience endured the schizophrenic experience of hearing the words come not from the actors they were watching but from loudspeakers under their seats. Such conditions made subtlety, nuance, and suggestiveness impossible. Shakespeare had to be Greek, Aeschylean, epic. He had to conform to what Vilar called 'le cérémonial tragique'. Vilar's productions relied heavily on the dynamics of action – on what the critic Marc Beigbeder identified as the 'Shakespearean' qualities of rapidity and simultaneity. When Shakespeare was less 'Shakespearean', Vilar's success was less well assured. *Henry IV*, with its domestic themes of paternal anxiety, princely debauchery, and rustic tranquillity, failed, in Beigbeder's view, to project beyond the stage at Avignon.[38]

But there were other reasons, too, for the suppression of Shakespeare's lyrical voice. Western culture generally, and theatrical culture especially, were less and less at ease with poetry. Nurtured on anthropology, sociology, and Marx, the modern serious theatre cancelled the inherited taxonomy of totem and taboo. It was not just that it validated, for purposes of art, the old abominations – carnage, dissonance, scurrility. So much had already been done by Romanticism and its Decadent derivatives. It was rather that it invalidated much of the hallowed apparatus of drama – eloquence, sympathy, psychology, illusion. Brecht devised the non-Aristotelian play, by discarding mimesis and catharsis, and he argued that poetry should be kept out of the theatre. Poetry hindered understanding (*Verstand*) and encouraged an obstructive empathy (*Einfühlung*) among both audiences and actors. In France the reversal of values was truculently expounded by Antonin Artaud, a theorist and one-time actor who, like D. H. Lawrence, had heard the call of the blood and the drumbeat of primitive ritual. Artaud attacked the 'masterpiece' (*chef-d'œuvre*) – the work of art that came down from the past loaded with psychology and noble language. These, he said, were objects of bourgeois idolatry and popular indifference. In the 1930s Artaud proclaimed the Theatre of Cruelty, which by replacing words with semiotics and violent, convulsive action would demolish sensibility, reawaken the dormant imagination, and reassert man's position between dream and reality.[39]

Beigbeder perceived echoes of this iconoclasm even at the Comédie-Française. Reviewing Jean Sarment's translation of *Romeo and Juliet*, premièred in 1952, he noted that what had once been called *grossièreté* was now acknowledged to be *simplicité*, but that the *simplicité* was 'narrowly confined in prose, so that it [might] not be realised that this most popular of dramatists [was] at the same time the most poetic. Let the academics soak up his poetry in the library! The general public must be allowed to know only the script-writer.'[40] The advocates of democratic theatre were uncomfortable, and often hostile, in the presence of 'literary' phenomena, since these were the attributes not of a community but of a class. Nothing isolated Copeau more than his habit of referring to an author as 'le poète' and to a text as 'le poème'. There developed a conviction that poetic Shakespeare, the Shakespeare of fine language, could be neither truly theatrical nor truly popular. Speaking of Claudel, the author who had laboured to revive French poetic drama, Vilar asked: 'Is he of our time? Is he of our future?'[41] Poetic translations of Shakespeare – whether in verse, like Jouve's, or lyrical prose, like Gide's and Maurice Maeterlinck's – were seldom performed.[42]

Shakespeare was not so roughly handled by those who would make him popular as he had once been by those who would make him French. There was no retreat, in principle at least, from authenticity. Nevertheless, those who knew the texts sometimes had difficulty in recognising what they heard in the productions of Gémier and Planchon. Edmond

Jaloux reproached Gémier for using translations (by Lucien Népoty) which coarsened the originals:

> Le Marchand de Venise was at times a hotch-potch where little remained of the original play. To superimpose on such a work humour of the 'boulevard' type, to add entire scenes, and to make it finish with Shylock pursuing his daughter Jessica crying Chrétienne! Chrétienne! [Christian! Christian!] is to go over the limit. Likewise, some of the finest passages of Antony and Cleopatra were omitted for no apparent reason.[43]

Georges de la Fourchardière, who translated The Taming of the Shrew for Gémier, asserted that unassisted Shakespeare could never appeal to the general public. Shakespeare was often tedious ('embêtant') and it was the efforts of tinkerers ('tripatouilleurs') that had brought about his remarkable success.[44] Planchon admitted that he confronted a problem in the highly wrought diction of Shakespeare's kings and princes, since this had nothing to do with language as communication. 'There is a difficulty for us, who are looking for critical realism, in that we have to subtract that poetic "aura" which magnifies the characters but threatens to obscure them.' Somehow he had to cancel the 'sublimity' without destroying the 'poem'. He contrived to do this by requiring the actors to play against the lyrical flights of the text. At Villeurbanne King Henry IV delivered his opening speech, about embarking on a crusade, while eating a heavy meal. This obliged him to swallow as many words as mouthfuls of food, and eloquence was conveniently dissolved in gastric juice.[45]

After 1968 all this populism was berated as fraud. Modernism was eclipsed by postmodernism, and the new theatrical avant-garde denounced the Avignon festival as a cultural supermarket. Marxism was dismissed as a modernist 'master-narrative', untrue and coercive. Postmodernism demanded an end to critical foreclosure, to reverence founded on reputation and dogma. It talked of deconstructing the classics and remaking them: penetrating their mythological mystery, dispersing their spectral aura. It carried a mass of its own intellectual baggage and it swamped the theatre once more with ornamentation – this time of a linguistic, esoteric, purely cerebral kind. The event overflowed from the stage to the page. 'We are not philosophical enough', insisted the avant-garde director Georges Lavaudant in 1977. 'The spectacle is too much considered as something for and in itself, not significantly tied to a history of forms. We need a real debate of ideas.'[46] For Daniel Mesguich, another young director, Shakespeare was not a great bard but 'the greatest theoretician'. When he staged *Hamlet* at Grenoble in 1977 he used it as a vehicle for abstruse theories about *mise en scène* as writing ('écriture'); about theatre as the difference between writing and speech; about theatrical language as semiotics; about actors reciting texts but playing themselves. In effect this meant that he presented both the story in the play, and the story of the play – which had its own attendant ghosts. His production was a collage, an accumulation and a disintegration, in which two actors played each of the principal rôles, and Shakespeare's text shared the stage with the recollections and interrogations of a crowd of directors, actors, critics, and translators, both living and dead.[47] Mesguich and his translator (Michel Vittoz) read *Hamlet* and thought of Mallarmé, Freud, Gide, Brecht, Lacan, Barthes, Derrida, and twentieth-century feminists. They believed that this retinue was inseparable from the text, and that it precluded innocence. It is no longer possible, they contended, to see a classic like *Hamlet* for the first time. We have been made old and sophisticated by surrogate experience. The classics do not come to us as they were left by their authors; they cannot be 'restored', disencumbered, and vacuum-packed. When it encountered *Hamlet*, the contemporary intelligence encountered not Shakespeare but many Shakespeares, dispersed into a spectrum by the refracting medium of history. Picking up the work's references to spirits, mirrors, plays within plays and stages within stages, they plied ambiguity and multiplicity, exposing the impossibility of Hamlet's desire 'to be'. Just as there is no single *Hamlet*, so there is no single prince of Denmark either. There is an infinity of *Hamlets* (plays within plays), and Hamlet is not only both himself and his own ghost, he is also both a character and an actor, passing restlessly back and forth between fiction and reality. Teasing, challenging, provoking, frustrating, and bewildering in its refusal to decide, to interpret, to clinch, to say 'this is this and not that', *Shakespeare's Hamlet* was nothing if not theatre for 'the educated ear'.

But the question that loomed largest in the postmodern debate about the theatre was whether authors and texts were not now extinct. In 1977 Julia Kristeva, *Wunderkind* of La Nouvelle Critique, argued that the textual theatre was displaced because in the modern crisis of religion, state, and family, no narrative could make it possible for audiences and actors to recognise themselves in the same author.[48] It appears that the theatrical text was suspect for the same reason that the master-narrative was suspect. It was totalitarian and repressive. It signified the theatre of subjugation. Authors reduced actors to surrogates, and audiences to spectators. The postmodern condition required a theatre of spontaneity and improvisation, which would reunite art with life and enable actors and audiences to reclaim their freedom in conjugation. Experimental efforts to create such a theatre were failures.[49] They did not invalidate, they verified, the bleak vision of Samuel Beckett. In *En attendant Godot* (1952) and *Fin de parti* (1957) Beckett had expounded the pitiful plight of dramatic characters in the absence of the Author. Without authorial intervention, they can neither make sense of their lives nor resolve the absurdity of their language. Ultimately the refusal, or inability, of the master-author to appear decrees the abolition of the theatre itself. In Beckett's *Breath* (1969), which lasts for thirty seconds, there are no characters, no dialogue, no set. There is merely an empty stage and a sound of breathing – an aspiration in both senses of the word. It is a sigh; and it is a desire, desperate but unable, to pass from nothingness into being. Without a storyteller, there is no story; without a story, no cosmos.

So – paradoxically, given its aversion to endings and resolutions; characteristically, given its acceptance of paradox – the postmodern debate ended the ambiguity that had always dogged French attitudes to Shakespeare. For as long as the critical response had been shaped by a literary 'discourse' or 'language game' whose key terms were 'genius', 'barbarian', 'taste', and 'race', there had been equally strong reasons for both taking him and leaving him. But with the decommissioning of the old master-narrative of Enlightenment, this discourse lost its legitimacy, and opinion could no longer be so evenly divided. The major reasons for leaving him (he was barbaric, he was Anglo-Saxon) became obsolete, and the need for him seemed all the more urgent when postmodernism failed to redeem its promise of an alternative, autonomous theatre. Samuel Beckett always said that he did not know who Godot was. Somewhere amid the vertiginous circlings, contortions, retreats, somersaults, and lateral leaps of postmodern skirmishing, there appears to be a logic suggesting that he was Shakespeare.

9

The Metamorphosis of Envy

In the winter of 1773–74, fashionable London was discussing a new picture in the High Renaissance manner, on view at the Royal Academy. It was by Sir Joshua Reynolds, and it was called *The Triumph of Truth*. The foreground was occupied by a magisterial figure in the robes of an Oxford doctor of civil law. In the background hovered the angel of Truth, holding aloft the scales of justice and flaying three diabolical adversaries. There was some mystery about this flight of Reynolds's mature fancy. It was not clear, exactly, what Truth was chastising. Was it vice, or madness? Or both? Reynolds had obviously had in mind Palma Giovane's (or, as he thought, Tintoretto's) *The Expulsion of Heresy*; but his title was unspecific and the demons in his allegory were variously and vaguely supposed to be Prejudice, Envy, Scepticism, Error, Falsehood, Infidelity, Sophistry, and Folly. Rumour had it that two of them portrayed Gibbon and Hume. However, their faces were obscured and Sir Joshua, when questioned, was evasive and discreet. Only two things were emphatically clear. The dominant figure draped in Oxonian scarlet was Dr James Beattie, professor of moral philosophy at Marischal College, Aberdeen, and author of *An Essay on the Immutability of Truth*. Equally certainly, the fiend cowering abjectly under the thrust of the triumphant angel's arm was Voltaire, heretic and traducer of Shakespeare. Reynolds had copied the features from a medal, and everybody recognised them. 'She is treading [*sic*] on a head', wrote Mrs Montagu to Mrs Vesey, 'very like to Mr Voltaire's.' So apparent, in fact, was Reynolds's intention to vilify Voltaire that Oliver Goldsmith was indignant. He reprimanded the artist for perpetrating a crass insult:

> It very ill becomes a man of your eminence and character to debase so high a genius as Voltaire before so mean a writer as Beattie. Beattie and his book will be forgotten in ten years, while Voltaire's fame will last forever. Take care it does not perpetuate this picture to the shame of such a man as you.[1]

Goldsmith was one of a few English admirers of Voltaire. Reynolds's picture was one of many English diatribes against him. Only a very small number of foreign writers have ever been so well known in Britain as Voltaire, and none, probably, has ever been so deeply and so persistently despised. Several of Voltaire's plays were translated into English and successfully performed on the London stage. *Zaïre*, translated as *Zara*, appeared at Drury Lane in 1736. In the 1760s and 1770s five of his works were produced by Garrick at Drury Lane, and another two were in the repertoire at Covent Garden. His historical books were read and admired by the educated British public, and when *Candide* appeared in English it had an enormous sale. But as Voltaire's fame and influence increased, as Europe began to buzz with his renown, so he became the Frenchman the British loved to hate. Many who had known him in London in the 1720s recalled him with dislike. Accusations of treachery, dishonesty, and sycophancy had even then begun to spoil his friendships. During the remainder of his life the homage paid to him in Britain was far outweighed by mistrust and detestation. 'No one knows', Thomas Gray once said, 'what mischief that man will do.' When, at the age of eighty-four, Voltaire died from a self-administered overdose of medicinal opium, the British press exulted, and denigrated his memory.

> Voltaire, who poisoned all mankind,
> His death to poison owes

gloated the *Universal Magazine*. An obituary in the *Gentleman's Magazine* talked of 'the malice of a monkey, the cunning of a fox, the traiterous disposition of a cat'. Others called him 'wicked', 'the Devil incarnate', and 'the anti-Christ'. Coleridge said his judgement was no better than that of a monkey. He was 'that wretched sciolist whom Frenchmen, to their shame, have honoured before their elder and better worthies'. William Blake derided his mockery:

> Mock on, mock on – Voltaire, Rousseau!
> Mock on, mock on – 'tis all in vain!
> You throw the sand against the wind,
> And the wind blows it back again.[2]

John Morley, writing in 1872, was appalled by the 'rank vocabulary of malice and hate' that the British had always reserved for this remarkable man. He reckoned that 'the noisome fringe of the history of opinion [had] received many of its most fulminant terms from critics of Voltaire'.[3] A vendetta had been flickering and smouldering for more than a century.

Voltaire was as controversial in Britain as Shakespeare was in France. He had his advocates, even his worshippers. To Byron, he was 'that great and unequalled genius', 'the universal Voltaire', 'the greatest genius of France'.[4] He was appreciated for his crusade against fanaticism and hypocrisy, and the British public responded generously to his appeal for funds to help the family of Jean Calas, the victim of a judicial system corrupted by clerical bigotry. But for all his altruism and all his brilliance, Voltaire was intolerable. He was offensively modern in his scepticism, and offensively outmoded in his manners. The social habits and style of speech he picked up in London remained with him all his life. The English élite, on the other hand, became polished and polite. The male culture of the club, the cockpit, and the coffee house was tamed by the feminine régime of the tea table and the chapel. When Voltaire was in England it was customary, as Daniel Defoe put it, to fart before the justice and talk bawdy before the queen. The evangelical generations behaved better. They did not swear, or break the sabbath, and they were pious even in their agnosticism. Voltaire had seemed coarse to the contemporaries of Pope. To those of Jane Austen he was disgusting. Wordsworth called the French 'a most frivolous people' for having honoured him in his decrepitude .[5] Thomas Carlyle, who venerated toughness and strength of character, spoke for the Victorians when he condemned the French admiration of Voltaire ('the withered pontiff of Encyclopaedism') as the most 'dim and perverted' form of hero worship.[6] His charisma was sinister, because it meant that even the devout and the worthy found him irresistible. Lord Chesterfield was dazzled by his intellect and his energy. Edward Young wrote of his disturbing allure:

> Your works in our divided minds
>   Repugnant passions raise,
> Confound us with a double stroke,
>   We shudder while we praise;
>
> A curious web as finely wrought
>   As genius can inspire,

From a black bag of poison spun,
With horror we admire.[7]

There was copious evidence of this insidious fascination in the constant stream of British visitors who made their way year after year to
Ferney. When Voltaire retired from the world, the world came to
Voltaire, chiefly in the form of wealthy young Britons passing through
Geneva at the beginning of their Grand Tour. 'For fourteen years', wrote
Voltaire testily from Ferney in 1768, 'I've been the inn-keeper of Europe,
and I'm tired of this profession. I've been "at home" to some three or
four hundred English.' He was one of the sights of the Continent. No
account of the Grand Tour was complete without a description of
Voltaire in the life – though hardly in the flesh, for of flesh, as his visitors never failed to observe, there was now hardly a vestige on that
mummified anatomy. He resisted their importunity. He would send to
tell them that he was ill; that he was dying; that he was dead. Still they
insisted on coming – to see him bedridden; to watch him expire; to
inspect his corpse. Most caught no more than a glimpse of the legendary
figure, as it wandered in the gardens or tottered through the drawing
room to dinner, bestowing a royal wave or a greeting in English as it
passed. Some, like Gibbon, were invited to Voltaire's private theatricals
and saw him act in his own plays, declaiming heroically in breastplate
and *perruque*. A few, like Boswell, enjoyed the privilege of his hospital-
ity. Knowing that they all wanted to be shocked by his talk about
Shakespeare and the Saints, he would oblige by profaning both, and add
a few *risqué* anecdotes and apophthegms for good measure. It was his
custom, he said, to receive English visitors with 'minimum fuss, a bit of
squabbling about Shakespeare, and a few general remarks'. Once an
intrepid guest ventured to defend the Bard. Shakespeare had his faults,
he protested, but he was natural. The sage transfixed him with a gor-
gonic glare. 'By your leave, Monsieur,' came the lethal riposte, 'my arse
is natural, but I still wear trousers.' Often he would speak in English,
garnishing his patter with archaic oaths and Shakespearean quotations,
remembered from his London days. News of these encounters caused
hypertension in British family circles. 'He has ruined the principles of
half our young people', declared Mrs Montagu.[8]

In England, Voltaire became the Other, just as Shakespeare became
the Other in France. An age avid for racial stereotypes and paradigms

turned him into the type of Frenchness, just as it transformed Shakespeare into the quintessential Anglo-Saxon. 'He is the realised ideal of every one of them', wrote Carlyle of Voltaire and the French, 'the thing they are all wanting to be; of all Frenchmen the most French.'[9] And nothing was more French that Voltaire's views on Shakespeare. When he talked about Shakespeare, the British heard the voice of France, and for a very long time his criticism poisoned their feelings both about him and about his nation. As Shakespeare's popularity in Britain rose, Voltaire's sank, and gallophobia intensified. Voltaire's objections obscured other French reactions, including the other reaction of Voltaire himself. It was forgotten that he had expressed admiration, as well as contempt. 'They tear me to pieces in London', he once complained to a British visitor, 'as an enemy of Shakespeare; I am, it is true, shocked and repelled by his absurdities, but I am no less struck by his beauties.' He claimed to possess an edition of Shakespeare in which he had marked, with his own hand, a multitude of fine things.[10] Because the British constructed the 'French view' of Shakespeare from Voltaire's strictures, it was widely assumed that Shakespeare had no admirers in France. In the 1920s a British scholar, compiling a calendar of European responses to Shakespeare, confessed that he was surprised when he turned up a laudatory essay by Lamartine, published in 1865. 'It has been so commonly thought', he explained, 'that the French do not appreciate Shakespeare.'[11]

This naïve reaction indicates a growing awareness that the popular idea of Shakespeare as a sort of litmus, divulging difference and contrast, was fundamentally flawed. The truth was beginning to dawn that the Anglo-French encounters at the centre of the Shakespearean event had been as much about consensus as about conflict. Not only were there French people who admired Shakespeare; there were also Britons who had deep misgivings about him and about the phenomenon that in France was called 'la superstition shakespearienne'. Voltaire and the French critics who echoed him were, when they judged Shakespeare, only giving back what they had borrowed. They were speaking a critical language that had its origins not in some peculiarly French perception, but in a common mentality compounded of esteem, misgiving, wonder, and despair. When Shakespeare went to France, he did not travel light. He carried a heavy luggage of assessments and assumptions which, like his texts, were translated into French. They ranged between the poles of critical opinion, and they were readily assimilated in France because there was a recognisable French strain in their genealogy. Critics like Rapin and Boileau had been closely heeded in Restoration Britain – by Dryden, most notably. So the Voltairean response to Shakespeare was neither eccentric nor vernacular. It did not belong exclusively to Voltaire, nor even to the French. It was a common currency, minted from widely distributed perceptions of loss and gain, and widely shared anxieties about art, society, and the burden of the past . Shakespeare was canonised as the National Poet, with a statue in Westminster Abbey (1741) and a shrine at Stratford (1769). Nevertheless British references to him still often sounded like Voltaire's. Wordsworth once said in a fit of peevishness that he too could write like Shakespeare if he had a mind to. George Bernard Shaw maintained that if he had been born in the era of blank verse he would have 'given Shakespeare a harder run for his money than all the other Elizabethans put together'.[12] The severest castigators of the cult of Shakespeare were British, not French. Criticism rebuking itself for having conjured up a reputation it could not bridle spoke more often than not in English.

Until the discovery of the Renaissance, the idea of Shakespeare as an untutored genius, promiscuously mixing the best of himself with the worst of his age, was more or less universal. Long before Voltaire set foot in England, talk of faults and beauties, of beauty without art, was commonplace; the image of jewels in a dungheap was a cliché. Dryden judged *Troilus and Cressida* 'a heap of rubbish under which many excellent thoughts lay wholly buried'. To Nahum Tate, *King Lear* was 'a heap of jewels unstrung and unpolished'. Nicholas Rowe, whose edition of Shakespeare appeared in 1709, wrote of 'a great many beauties ... in a heap of rubbish', and excused Shakespeare for his lapses by pointing out that he had lived 'in an age of almost universal licence and ignorance'.[13] Pope, in his own edition of Shakespeare (1725), distinguished between the faults and the beauties by using marginal stars and signals, and attributed the dross to the debauched taste of Elizabethan audiences. This was the wisdom that Voltaire imbibed when he came to London, and the refrain continued after he had left. Oliver Goldsmith admired 'as they deserve' the best things in Shakespeare, but wished that much of his work were forgotten: 'A man blind of one eye should always be painted in profile.'[14] Adam Smith and David Hume agreed. Smith's view was that Shakespeare had written good scenes but not one good play. Hume wrote of beauty disfigured by blemishes and deduced that 'great fertile genius' was in itself insufficient and even dangerous for art.[15] Samuel Johnson, in the preface to his edition of Shakespeare's plays, recycled the 'barbaric age' thesis and refurbished the old trope about jewels: 'Shakespeare opens a mine which contains gold and diamonds in inexhaustible plenty, though clouded by incrustation, debased by impurities, and mingled with a mass of meaner minerals.'[16] Lord Kames, in his *Elements of Criticism* (1771), explained that Shakespeare's blemishes were more apparent than his beauties because these lay too deep for common perception.[17] In 1772 George Steevens, editor of Shakespeare and theatre critic, detected 'many pearls among the rubbish' of the last two acts of *Hamlet.*[18] Voltaire went to his grave, and still the Voltairean chant went on. To Hugh Blair, professor of rhetoric at Edinburgh, Shakespeare was 'genius shooting wild; deficient in just taste and altogether unassisted by knowledge or art'. He was disfigured by faults attributable to 'the grossness of the age in which he lived'.[19] In the new century Carlyle returned to the theme. There were 'sunbursts of splendour' in Shakespeare, but 'the surrounding matter' was not radiant. Shakespeare, alas, 'had to write for the Globe playhouse; his great soul had to crush itself as it could into that and no other mould'.[20] The nineteenth century passed into the twentieth, and Lytton Strachey ploughed the same furrow, now a chasm, yet deeper. Shakespeare's reputation was assured by 'the triumph of a few exceptions'. His 'lesser works' (which included *Troilus and Cressida*) betrayed the malignant influence of the theatre of his time.[21]

British critics were not reticent about Shakespeare's 'faults'. Sometimes they were more Voltairean than Voltaire. In *The Tragedies of the Last Age* (1678) and *A Short View of Tragedy* (1692), Thomas Rymer had deployed a battery of mockery, sarcasm, acerbity, and derision that made no concession to 'sublimity' or 'beauty'. He was especially scathing about the improbabilities, absurdities, and trashy dialogue of *Othello* ('a bloody farce without salt or savour'). Dryden reckoned that Shakespeare often wrote worse than 'the dullest writer of our own or any preceding age'. His work, he complained, 'is so pestered with figurative expressions that it is as affected as it is obscure'. Addison deplored Shakespeare's obscure metaphors and forced expressions. Pope said that as Shakespeare had 'certainly written better' than any other, so he had 'perhaps written worse'. Johnson detected 'faults sufficient to obscure and overwhelm any other merit'. Horace Walpole perceived 'faults enough to glut the critics'. Matthew Arnold accused Shakespeare of lapsing often into writing that was 'detestable'. Strachey arraigned him for 'looseness of structure ... vagueness of purpose ... dulness, insipidity ... bad taste ... flatness and folly ... impotent conclusions ... the grossest indecency and the feeblest puns'.[22]

Voltaire and his successors propagated in France the message that Shakespeare in his received form was unfit for performance on the modern stage. However, this notion was nowhere more firmly established than in Britain. Both before and during Voltaire's lifetime the London theatre was setting precedents for the adaptations and appropriations that later appeared in Paris. 'We English laugh at Dumas when he alters *Hamlet*', wrote George Henry Lewes in 1849, 'and at M. Deschamps when he alters *Macbeth* ... but we should remember that Cibber had done the same with *Richard III* and that Garrick ... had practised still bolder experiments.'[23] Before Shakespeare had even been heard of in Paris it was generally admitted in London that his diction was too turbid and his stagecraft too ramshackle for modern taste. Elizabethan English did not merely sound old-fashioned to the Restoration ear; it also sounded disturbing – too unpleasantly reminiscent of the religious 'enthusiasm' that had recently been stifling cultural life and reaping political whirlwinds. The modern sensibility demanded precise, crystalline language. Thomas Sprat, in his *History of the Royal Society* (1667) applauded the resolution of the society 'to reject all amplifications, digressions, and swellings of style; to return back to the primitive purity and shortness' that had once brought the English tongue 'as near the mathematical plainness' as was possible.[24] Early adapters, including Dryden (*Troilus and Cressida*), Davenant (*Macbeth*), and Otway (*Romeo and Juliet*), modernised Shakespeare's idiom by correcting the grammar, simplifying the imagery, deleting archaisms such as the second-person singular form of verbs and pronouns ('thou', 'thine', 'thee'), substituting 'elevated' for 'low' terminology. Davenant's Lady Macbeth did not say 'knife', 'blanket', and 'dunnest smoke', but 'steel', 'curtains', and 'smoke as black as hell'. Others, such as Cibber (*Richard III*), Granville (*The Jew of Venice*), Tate (*King Lear, Coriolanus*), and Garrick (*Romeo and Juliet, Macbeth, Hamlet*), compressed, purified, tidied up, and even contrived happy endings, but disguised their intervention by using pastiche Elizabethan English.[25] Several of these acting versions had a very long life, and in their final avatars turned up in Paris in 1827–28. The English actors who are supposed to have given French audiences their first taste of real Shakespeare in fact served up something less than that. They played *Romeo and Juliet* in Garrick's version, which cut more than half the text and used Otway's modifications to the last scene. For *Lear* they restored Shakespeare's ending, but followed Tate by retaining his love intrigue between Edgar and Cordelia and eliminating the Fool. *Richard III* was given in Cibber's version of 1700, which incorporated characters and speeches from the other history plays and added a few touches by Cibber himself. *Othello, Hamlet, The Merchant of Venice*, and *Macbeth* were all heavily cut – in the last instance so as to make room for the witches' chorus and ballet composed by Matthew Locke for Davenant's adaptation of 1664. These garbled texts left knowledgeable French critics disappointed. 'It was Shakespeare, good or bad, that we wanted', wrote Charles Magnin in *Le Globe*. 'It's a sorry thing to suppress striking beauties, like the scene of the willow song in *Othello*, and to add false gems such as the love of Cordelia for Edgar in *King Lear*.'[26] When Macready returned to Paris with Helen Faucit in 1844, to play Shakespeare at the théâtre des Italiens, his *Macbeth* still featured Locke's dancing and singing witches.[27]

Given that the Voltairean response to Shakespeare was more or less universal, it needs to be explained why it was so notorious when it came from Voltaire himself. Why, if he was saying only what everyone was saying, were his comments about Shakespeare held so resentfully against him? The most obvious explanation is in his nationality. Opinions that were sagacious when expressed by Britons in English became insufferable when spoken by a Frenchman in French. There was a background of age-old animosity. Everyone thought of France as the national enemy. All of Britain's European wars from the 1680s until the beginning of the nineteenth century, as well as her major imperial conflict, were, or became, wars against France, and one of the legacies of the French Revolution was a hardening of old prejudice. The Catholic rival had been replaced by a godless one, with a nefarious record of atrocity and barbarism. British tourists were shocked by the evidence of French pillage when they returned to Italy during the peace of 1802–03. John Chetwode Eustace, author of the best-known British guidebook, told his many readers that 'the French ... in every invasion [had] been the scourge of Italy'. They had 'rivalled or rather surpassed the rapacity of the Goths and Vandals'. They were aggressive imperialists 'endeavouring to supplant the dialects of Greece and Italy in order to substitute the flippant jargon of France in their stead, and to replace the bullion of ancient wisdom by the tinsel of Gallic philosophism'.[28] This gallophobia was boosted by the revolutions and scandals that convulsed French public life in the nineteenth century. To the Victorian historian John Edward Bodley, the French were turbulent and vicious, less addicted to fraternity than to fratricide. Writing of the trauma of 1870–71, he pointed out that 'the Germans ... had not left so many French corpses at Gavelotte, or even at Sedan, as fell by French hands during the epilogue to their victories'. In comparison, how benign, how innocuous, were the memories of modern Britons! 'The oldest people we have ever known in our childhood had perhaps seen George III bathing at Weymouth, or watched a pressgang at work; while those of the next generation remembered the talk about Mr Perceval's murder, or heard the bells for Princess Charlotte's wedding.'[29]

A result of all this friction was a flux of British self-consciousness, a Union Jack patriotism braying *Rule Britannia!* and *God Save the King*. It anathematised France and Frenchness, and read into Voltaire's remarks about the British National Poet a sneer, an inflexion of contempt and insult. Voltaire was implying, it was said, that the British were too purblind, too dim-witted, to discover Shakespeare's shortcomings for themselves. Aaron Hill, who translated Voltaire's *Mérope* in 1743, objected to the 'presumptuous puffiness' in Voltaire's slighting references to English drama, painting, and music.[30] Elizabeth Montagu, in her essay on Shakespeare (1769), emphasised that the dramatist's flaws 'passed unquestioned' in Britain. No one disputed that he was guilty of 'nonsense', 'indecorum', and 'irregularities' – some of them unforgivable. But Voltaire was gross and presumptuous 'in pronouncing that, in a country where Sophocles and Euripides [were] as well understood as in any in Europe', dramatic poetry was no better appreciated than among the Chinese. 'Ridiculously', she protested, 'has our taste been represented.'[31] George Steevens, writing about *Hamlet* in 1772, admitted that the play contained 'fundamental blemishes'; but these had been 'felt by every Englishman of understanding even before Voltaire had [had] existence'. Voltaire's comments revealed nothing except his own relish for ridicule, falsehood, effrontery, and malice.[32]

It was not so much the matter, then, as the manner of Voltaire's critique that rankled with the British. His tone epitomised vicious Frenchness, and this was compounded by the French vice *par excellence* – envy, the deadly sin. All Frenchmen – it was understood – were envious of the British: of their empire, their constitution, their freedom, their commerce, and their prestige; and Voltaire – it was assumed – was especially envious, because he had discovered in Shakespeare a literary genius he could not match and a celebrity that exceeded his own. It was noticed that a couple of his plays (*Zaïre* and *Mahomet*) bore some resemblance to *Othello* and *Macbeth*, and the similarities were read as evidence of insidious envy. Colley Cibber, in the prologue he supplied for Aaron Hill's translation of *Zaïre* (*Zara*), drew attention to the familiarity of certain aspects of Voltaire's work:

> From rack'd Othello's rage he raised his style,
> And snatched the brand that lights his tragic pile.

In James Miller's prologue to the English version of *Mahomet* (*Mahomet the Imposter*, 1744), Voltaire was trounced as a literary marauder:

> Britons, these numbers to yourselves you owe;
> Voltaire had strength to shoot in Shakespeare's bow:
> Fame led him at his Hippocrene to drink,
> And taught to write with nature, as to think:
> With English freedom English wit he knew,
> And from the inexhausted stream profusely drew;
> Cherish the noble bard yourselves have made,
> Nor let the frauds of France steal all our trade.

It was almost impossible for British critics to think of Shakespeare without thinking of envy. Ben Jonson, in his dedicatory poem in the first folio, had desired to keep Shakespeare's apotheosis uncontaminated by this nastiness:

> To draw no envy, Shakespeare, on thy name,
> Am I thus ample to thy book and fame ...

Envy, nevertheless, insisted on lurking wherever Shakespeare was known and admired. It haunted the literary psychology, and dogged the footsteps of greatness.

> Envy will merit as its shade pursue,
> But like a shadow, proves the substance true

chanted Pope, in his *Essay on Criticism*. Envy was despicable because it led to calumny. 'I believe that those who dispraised his plays', said Margaret Cavendish, duchess of Newcastle, in 1664, 'dispraised them more out of envy than simplicity or ignorance.'[33] 'When most they rail', wrote Dryden of Shakespeare's critics, 'know then they envy most.' Envy also led to plagiarism, and plagiarism, once tolerated as part of the normal give-and-take of the literary economy, was criminalised in an age that made fetishes of property and originality. It became the larceny of an authorial underclass, impoverished, unscrupulous, and heavily penalised. Those caught helping themselves to other writers' ideas were pilloried and ridiculed – most notably by Sheridan. *The Critic* (1779), his comedy about theatrical life, features Sir Fretful Plagiary, a hack author (based on Richard Cumberland) who is 'as envious as an old maid verging on the desperation of six-and-thirty'. He filches his best lines and effects from Shakespeare, while sententiously deprecating envy ('there is not a passion so strongly rooted in the human heart').

In the case of Voltaire, envy was doubly reprehensible because it was both calumniating and plagiarising. Voltaire, it was said, purloined Shakespeare's ideas and then tried to camouflage his crime with caustic denigration. In 1747 the playwright Samuel Foote called him 'that insolent French panegyrist who first denies Shakespeare almost every dramatic excellence and then, in his next play, pilfers from him almost every capital scene'. Edward Burnley Greene, in his *Critical Essays* (1770), attributed Voltaire's 'exaggerated censures' to 'an invidious disposition, conscious of an incapacity to emulate the work it condemns'. George Steevens referred to Voltaire as 'a mighty felon' who had set fire to the house he had pillaged. James Beattie, whose rectitude Reynolds contrasted pictorially with Voltaire's turpitude, denounced him as 'a highwayman who ha[d] strong reasons afterwards to murder'.[34] Horace Walpole was convinced that his rancour was 'grounded upon his conscious inferiority'.[35] Voltaire was accused of fretful plagiary in Paris, too. After the publication of Le Tourneur's *Shakespeare*, Parisian gossip had it that he was furious because the extent of his plundering was now revealed.[36]

So the arraignment gathered weight, as generation after generation added its endorsement. Voltaire's treatment of Shakespeare seemed fixed in the British way of thinking as an outrageous act of piracy, an enduring testimony to French envy and malice.

But then, soon after the middle of the nineteenth century, the prevailing gallophobic mood began to change. British antipathy to Voltaire and to the cultural ethos that he represented diminished; appreciation and approval became respectable – even fashionable. Matthew Arnold singled out the France of Voltaire and Rousseau as a cradle of civilisation, comparable to the Italy of the Renaissance.[37] George Henry Lewes moved the discussion about Shakespeare and Voltaire to new ground. He argued that Voltaire's response was complex, and much more ideological than that of his detractors: 'He took his stand on certain definite principles ... and a man who judges from principles may be wrong, but he cannot justly be called superficial by those who judge from none.' Undoubtedly, Voltaire misunderstood Shakespeare; but Shakespeare would equally have misunderstood Voltaire, because Voltaire was right when he saw in Shakespeare the grandeur of a barbarian.[38] In 1872 John Morley published an encomiastic biography of Voltaire. Morley was an agnostic. When editor of the *Fortnightly Review* he printed 'god' with a lower-case initial. Nevertheless he helped to reconcile Voltaire to Victorian evangelical opinion, because he depicted him as an Old Testament scourge, unleashing divine vengeance on the iniquity of Catholic France. Voltaire, Morley insisted, was 'a stupendous power', and Voltaireism was 'one of the cardinal liberators of the growing race'. The rays from this 'burning and far-shining spirit' banished darkness and death.[39] Full rehabilitation came in the early part of the twentieth century, when the trend-setting literati of Bloomsbury rebelled against the Victorian obsession with Italy and embarked on a celebration of France and Frenchness. The habits and perceptions of British connoisseurs and collectors were changed by the enthusiasm of Roger Fry and Clive Bell for neglected French painters. Suddenly it was smart to appreciate Poussin, Claude, Watteau, Chardin, Ingres, Degas, Daumier, and Cézanne. Bell was a fervent admirer of the France of the eighteenth century – 'that adorable eighteenth century'. In his view it was a locus of 'high civilisation', comparable to fourth- and fifth-century Athens and Renaissance Italy, and Voltaire was one of its brightest ornaments. He was a leading light among 'amiable and courageous people', who contrived to combine 'the serious discussion of fundamental questions ... with good temper and humanity'.[40] The literature of classical France was made modish by Lytton Strachey, Edmund Gosse, and F. L. Lucas. Gosse, who wrote regularly for the *Sunday Times* as resident expert on French literature and French affairs, educated the British public in the exquisiteness of the culture of *le Grand Siècle*. 'However revolutionary it pleases us to be', he told his readers in 1918, 'we cannot get away from the perfection of the age of Bossuet, and Racine, and La Fontaine, and Fénelon.'[41]

A reaction against Romanticism was in full spate. Clive Bell wrote of 'the scum of Romanticism', of the 'monstrous lack of taste' that characterised French art of the Romantic era. Peter Quennell commented in the 1920s on the obsolescence of French Romantic language:

> No period, I suppose, of modern literature is at present further removed from our understanding than that of the first fifty years of the nineteenth century ... The daemonic energies of those men are like voiceless cyclones; we notice the havoc they have made ... but we cannot hear the accompanying tumult, and we cannot tell whence it blows.[42]

The critic Henri Peyre, who taught French to British students between the wars, was aware of the same sense of alienation. 'The best Anglo-Saxon students', he reported, 'find it much easier to feel and love the poetry of Racine than that of de Musset and Victor Hugo.'[43] The early fiction of Hugo and Dumas was phenomenally popular in English translation, but not so their drama. Theatre audiences were nauseated by its tumescent declamation and its exorbitance of orgy, adultery, incest, murder, and violence. It was, said Frances Trollope, 'a national disgrace', sordid and shoddy. It was full, said Lytton Strachey, of 'the stagiest clap-trap'.[44]

All this anti-Romantic sentiment stirred up a new and widespread preference for the French classical inheritance. Repelled by the 'highly rouged wanton' who, according to the *Foreign Quarterly Review*, was Victor Hugo's muse, the London public rallied to 'the pale and languid beauty' of Racine.[45] When the *grandes dames* of the French stage performed the classical repertoire, they had no more fervid admirers

THE METAMORPHOSIS OF ENVY

anywhere than among the British. The ageing Mlle Mars, still playing Molière's young heroines at the age of fifty-six, entranced Mrs Trollope.[46] Charlotte Brontë was transported by Rachel's *Phèdre*, which she saw in Brussels in the 1840s. Her epiphany became the 'Pythian inspiration' of Lucy Snow, heroine of *Villette*:

> Suffering had struck that stage empress, and she stood before her audience neither yielding to, nor enduring, nor, in finite measure, resenting it. She stood locked in a struggle, rigid in resistance. She stood, not dressed but draped in pale antique folds, long and regular like sculpture. A background and entourage and flooring of deepest crimson threw her out, white like alabaster – like silver: rather, be it said, like Death ... I had seen acting before, but never anything like this: never anything which astonished Hope and hushed Desire.

When the Comédie-Française visited London in 1879, Matthew Arnold (who also had vivid memories of Rachel) remarked: 'There is a new generation growing up among us ... a new generation which takes French poetry and drama as seriously as Greek.'[47] It was obvious to the veteran French critic Francisque Sarcey that this predilection was for classical poetry and drama. Accustomed to seeing Molière's *Le Misanthrope* played to respectful but unenthusiastic audiences in Paris, he was astonished by its reception in London: 'It's something unheard of ... incredible ... *Le Misanthrope* has made a prodigious impression.' All the more prodigious in that the reaction was patently not just the posturing of a bewildered foreign audience. 'They laughed in the right places, you heard little murmurs of satisfaction running through the stalls to the boxes.' Sarah Bernhardt, performing the second act of *Phèdre*, was rapturously applauded – even though, in Sarcey's opinion, she was distinctly off form that night.[48]

Anti-Romanticism assisted the rehabilitation of Voltaire because it rehabilitated Neoclassicism generally and because it provided a new French writer for the British to detest. They discovered that Victor Hugo's delinquency diminished and even transformed Voltaire's. Hugo's vanity made Voltaire's seem like maidenly modesty. Voltaire's language was minted bullion in comparison with Hugo's inflated paper money. Voltaire's intelligence looked superlative beside Hugo's commonplace mind. Swinburne alone among the Victorian reading élite remained dedicated to Hugo. The others were disenchanted by the humourless tedium of his fifty-eight volumes and the preposterous ostentation of his funeral. In the British view, the public honours paid to Voltaire were much less offensive than those paid to Hugo, for the reception of whose remains the Pantheon was specially deconsecrated.[49] Strachey summarised the general verdict. Hugo combined impressive technique with 'windy inflation of sentiment ... superficiality ... ridiculous petty egoism'.[50] Clearly, there were failings more culpable than Voltaire's, and if they were less stridently deprecated than Voltaire's had been this was because the air was now much less heavy with gallophobia. Bodley, writing in the 1890s, observed that 'for the first time since the Norman Conquest three generations [had] passed by without the armies of England and France meeting in battle array'. History had moved on, leaving behind the age-old enmity:

> The last of the veterans of Toulouse and Waterloo have passed away, and it seems certain that, for the first time since the invention of gunpowder, there is no man living who has fired a shot in warfare between the French and English nations ... The generation of writers now grown gray is the first which has had no opportunity to supply contemporary chronicles of French and English mutual slaughter.[51]

Anti-Romanticism and a spirit of *entente cordiale* combined, then, to detoxify Voltaire; and his reputation benefited too from some fundamental changes in critical thinking. These included a new understanding of literary indebtedness, and increasing dissent from the cult of Shakespeare. The term 'influence', imported from astrology, became dominant in the critical vocabulary, displacing envy and plagiarism from their close association with artistic borrowing. 'Influence' did not criminalise, and it was not caricatured. It was regarded as a natural and essential aspect of the literary process, and a huge effort of learned research was devoted to charting its currents and calibrating its subtleties. The result was an awareness of a different sort of fretfulness: the fretfulness of writers equally convinced that they must be original and that originality was impossible. This state of mind, it was realised, had long been present in Western literature as a nagging sense of belatedness, and in the 1970s it was famously defined as 'the anxiety of influence'.[52] By this time, too, Anglo-American criticism had begun to reclaim its freedom from the orthodoxy of Shakespearomania.

A spirit of demur, of protest, was disrupting the old critical premises and rituals.

From the time of Dryden, English poets and dramatists had been thinking of themselves as post-Shakespearean. Shakespeare's work had been looming larger and larger as the superlative legacy that no one could ignore. It induced in British writers a morbid self-consciousness, akin to the melancholy sense of tardiness and derivation that haunted French literature from La Bruyère to Verlaine ('Ah! Tout est bu! tout est mangé! Plus rien à dire!'). Shakespeare precluded innocence and innovation, because he had anticipated everything – including the experience of belatedness:

> If there be nothing new, but that which is
> Hath been before, how are our brains beguiled ...[53]

His rapacious genius soared to the sun, impoverishing remote generations and bathing their effort in a pallid reflected light. Shakespeare had cannibalised his predecessors and transformed his successors into latecomers, afterthoughts, inheritors, revisionists, an epilogue. 'It is almost a miracle', observed Dryden, 'that ... he that began dramatic poetry among us ... should by the force of his own genius perform so much, that in a manner he has left no praise for any who come after him.'[54] In his *Essay of Dramatic Poesy*, speaking as Neander, Dryden confronted the alternative that had been bequeathed to the modern age by Shakespeare and his contemporaries – 'either not to write at all, or to attempt some other way'. But what other way had been left open by that 'giant race before the flood'?[55] 'They *engross* our attention', wrote Edward Young in his *Conjectures on Original Composition*, '... they *prejudice* our judgement ... and they *intimidate* us with the splendour of their renown.'

To know Shakespeare was to imitate him, and imitation was bad because it perpetuated not the best but the worst in an outstanding author. Imitation explained the post-Shakespearean decline of the English theatre. 'We imitate him so ill', said Dryden, 'that we copy his failings only, and make a virtue of that in our writing which in his was an imperfection.'[56] Voltaire maintained that indiscriminate imitation had destroyed the modern English stage and inflated still further the kudos of Shakespeare:

> The merit of this author has been the ruin of the English theatre ... Most of

the bizarre and freakish ideas of this writer have after two hundred years acquired the right to pass for sublime; almost all modern authors have copied him; but what was successful in Shakespeare's work is a flop in theirs, and you can see why veneration for this old boy increases as the moderns are scorned. No one realises that he should not be imitated, and the indifferent success of his copiers means only that he is deemed inimitable.[57]

The truth was so apparent that it became a cliché. John Morley attributed the desolation of the Victorian stage to the influence of Shakespeare. 'We have preferred the methods of lawless genius, and we are left with rampant carelessness and no genius.'[58]

Shakespeare was an incubus not just because he disabled art. He disabled criticism too. Criticism found itself confounded by the legend it had itself created. Literary criticism as a distinctive genre dates from the seventeenth century, when the advocates of 'modern' poetry engaged in their famous quarrel with the 'ancients' in France. As practised by Dryden, its function was to distinguish between the merits and faults of the masterpieces of the past, in order to impede the transmission of error. 'All writers', wrote Dryden,

> have their imperfections and failings, but I may safely conclude in the general, that our improprieties are less frequent, and less gross, than theirs. One testimony of this is undeniable, that we are the first to have observed them; and certainly, to observe errors, is a great step to the correcting of them.[59]

With Samuel Johnson the prerogative of criticism was enlarged. It reached beyond hermeneutics and the customary academic territory of correctness and edification. It began to evaluate and re-evaluate; to deal in comparisons and classifications. From now on, criticism periodically changed its ground, so as to uncover authors that had been obscure, and to obscure authors that had been prominent. The topography of literature altered as the angle of critical vision shifted. Fashions came and went; reputations rose and fell; things marginal became central, and vice-versa. But in Shakespeare, criticism encountered something immutable, incomparable, unchallengeable, unclassifiable. Corners were turned, the viewpoint was changed, but he was still there: unmoved, undiminished, and inexplicable. His prestige eluded criticism's jurisdiction, and imposed a crushing embargo on its liberty and its mission.

Matthew Arnold defined the law of criticism's nature as 'a free play of mind on all subjects which it touches';[60] but when criticism touched Shakespeare, it found its nature transformed. Its will to criticise became an impulse to worship. Elucidation and discrimination gave way to mysticism and rhapsody – to what the Augustans had called 'enthusiasm'. 'We are all methodists with regard to Shakespeare', wrote a contributor to the *Town and Country Magazine* in 1773. 'We carry our enthusiasm so far that we entirely suspend our senses towards his absurdities.'[61] G. H. Lewes noted how critics lapsed into 'incoherent fervour' when they confronted his work. 'After taxing their ingenuity to discover merit in details which offend all unprejudiced minds, they proceed to condemn similar or lesser faults in other writers.' Sound judgement gave way either to metaphysical sophistry like de Barante's, or to vacuous rhetoric like Hugo's. 'It contains little thought and much grandiose nonsense', wrote Lewes of Hugo's essay.

> Thoughtful readers will turn impatiently away from its emptiness and bombast; critical students of Shakespeare will be amazed at its carelessness and ignorance ... With all due allowance for ... occasional felicities, we must still pronounce the work a melancholy mistake. Its swelling ambition irritates and wearies.[62]

Even Swinburne, assertively deviant as a poet, was critically mute face to face with Shakespeare. *The Winter's Tale*, he said, contained qualities 'all alike beyond all expression of praise'. The merits of *Troilus and Cressida* commanded 'forebearance from all attempt at critical definition or articulate recognition of their peculiar quality or their immanent presence'.[63] Small wonder, therefore, that a professor lecturing to the British Academy in 1959 talked about 'the tyranny of Shakespeare', and declared him to be 'a dead issue'.[64] In the 1970s an American scholar noted that twentieth-century responses were 'making explicit the tendency ... to resort to irrationalist and magical terminology in dealing with Shakespeare's hold on us'. Shakespeare was credited with 'a verbal power that makes mystics of us all'.[65]

Irate in its paralysis, criticism chafed at the Shakesperean superstition. 'Shakespeare nowadays', protested a Cambridge academic in 1972, 'is pretty well beyond criticism.' Because modern opinion assumed Shakespeare's perfection, 'all sorts of interesting questions' about him could not be asked. 'Our minds are not free; our attitudes are restricted to undifferentiated deference.' Critics, he insisted, must reclaim their 'freedom of action' by conceding the possibility of 'inequalities and unevennesses' in Shakespeare's plays. He then reclaimed his own freedom by re-opening the dossier on absurdity, incoherence, and inconsistency, and by chiding the silliness of critics who struggled to make sense of the silliness in Shakespeare.[66] In the 1980s radical criticism attacked academic criticism (including that calling itself 'New') for aiding and abetting the formation of a sinister 'Shakespeare myth', which legitimised and reinforced the hegemony of brutal capitalism. Assisted by the 'libidinal excess' of Shakespeare's language (implying 'mastery, violence, and manipulation'), literary critics had made the name 'Shake-speare' something 'merely metonymic of an entire politico-cultural formation', like the names 'Disney'and 'Rockerfeller'.[67] As the millennium neared its end, the remonstrance became appropriately chiliastic. 'By overestimating Shakespeare's importance and uniqueness', thundered a prominent expert in 1990, 'Shakespearean critics insult the truth'; and he went on to invoke Shakespeare's apotheosis as an astrophysical cataclysm:

> Shakespeare has become a black hole ... The light of other stars – other poets, other dramatists – is wrenched and bent as it passes by him on its way to us ... Before he became a black hole Shakespeare was a star – but never the only one in our galaxy ... He, too, was limited, confined by space and time and the boundaries of his own perception.[68]

Those Voltairean notes of exasperation and pugnacity, that Voltairean strain of heresy and scepticism, help to explain, perhaps, why Voltaire himself was now no longer the demon he once had been. He had become a victim of the modern crisis in criticism and art. Now that the old crimes had become misfortunes; now that envy and fretful plagiary had given way to the anxiety of influence, and critical enthusiasm was a symptom of disablement, he at last received his due from the English-speaking world. Both as a dramatist and as a critic Voltaire had known himself to be a latecomer, trammelled by an incomparable inheritance. In France it was perceived that he had been an uncomfortable disciple of tradition. A 'disturbing impression of insincerity' was received from his work; his theatre suggested 'ambiguity and anxiety'.[69] Voltaire was therefore a contemporary.

But the influence that aroused his anxiety, and transformed his will to criticise into an impulse to venerate, was not exerted by Shakespeare. It was now apparent that Voltaire had felt threatened and offended by Shakespeare. He had not been significantly envious of Shakespeare's achievement, and he had not been critically disabled by it. His experience was similar to, rather than identical with, that of English-speaking writers. The influence about which he was anxious, the past which he felt as a burden, were different from those that afflicted them. In the 1930s it was demonstrated authoritatively that Corneille and Racine were Voltaire's models for *Zaïre* and *Mahomet,* and that the details for which he was supposed to be indebted to Shakespeare were common in French seventeenth- and eighteenth-century drama and novels.[70] To Dryden, 'the giant race before the flood' had existed in the days of Shakespeare. To Voltaire, it had existed in the days of Dryden. It was when he thought about the Europe of Louis XIV that Voltaire felt elated and oppressed, and experienced the despair of the modern emulator. He suffered from the surfeit of greatness in that vanished eldorado. 'The time will never recur', he sadly observed, 'when a Rochefoucauld, author of the *Maxims,* coming from conversation with a Pascal or an Arnauld, goes to the theatre of a Corneille.' What was there left to do after this golden age, save cherish its memory and measure the meanness of the present?

> The track was difficult at the beginning of the century because nobody had yet trodden it; it is difficult today because it is beaten. The great men of the last century taught people how to think and to talk: they said what nobody knew. Those who succeed them can hardly do other than say what is known. And a sort of revulsion has been produced by the multitude of masterpieces.

He pondered the 'long sterility' that had followed this fecundity in literature and the arts, and attributed it to the exhaustion of poetic material. 'The subjects and embellishments suitable for poetry are much more limited than is supposed ... Those who come after ... find the quarry fully worked.' And this was especially true of the art that concerned him most, the art of the theatre. 'It must not be thought', he stressed, 'that the great tragic passions, and the great sentiments, can be infinitely varied in new and striking ways. Everything has its limit.'[71]

By the twentieth century Voltaire's conception of modern history was

obsolete. In his view Shakespeare had been hostage to insular barbarity
and the meridian of English culture had coincided with the splendid
refulgence in France. 'The English', wrote Voltaire, 'have made a greater
advance towards perfection in all fields since 1660 than in all the preceding centuries.'[72] When the Renaissance, of which he knew nothing,
became known and understood, it invalidated his historiography and
consigned to the museum his verdict on Shakespeare and Elizabethan
England. That verdict had been neither idiosyncratic nor national.
Voltaire never said anything about Shakespeare that had not already
been often said in English. On this topic as on others he was the con-
veyor of British opinion to the main arena of European debate. Yet
despite this internationality, and despite his rehabilitation as a universal
and contemporary figure, vexed by some of the most pressing concerns
and predicaments of literature in the modern world, everyone continued to think of him as quintessentially French. Carlyle's tag ('of all
Frenchmen the most French') had a long survival. Valéry, in a lecture at
the Sorbonne in 1944, defined Voltaire as 'specifically French, incon-
ceivable under any other sky'.[73] Ten years later, at the inauguration of
the Institut et Musée Voltaire in Geneva, its president, Theodore Besterman, declared that Voltaire was 'the most typically, most completely
French man' that had ever been known.[74] The conviction persisted that
in order to hear a Frenchman, you needed only to open a volume of
Voltaire; in order to visualise a Frenchman, only to look at that extraordinary bust by Houdon – one of the most familiar images in the gallery
of Western portraiture.

This is why Voltaire's response to Shakespeare is uniquely fascinating.
Theirs is an encounter on which the imagination loves to dwell – not
least because it never took place and never could have taken place, even
if they had not been kept apart by the accidents of space and time. Spiritually they were separated by Voltaire's restiveness. He knew little of
Shakespeare and he refused to find out more, seeking in self-imposed
innocence a refuge from what he feared to know, cherishing the fiction
of foreignness in order to purchase reassuring illusions. But his ignorance could not make him any the less aware of Shakespeare, and in that
awareness there germinated a legend of Frenchness, Englishness, race,
frontiers, difference, otherness, invasion, resistance – a whole mythology of cultural clash and cross-over. And because that mythology

became so powerful in France, by nurturing the ideology of exception to which the French élites retreated as universality ceased to be theirs, it is difficult to believe that if Voltaire had never sat in the audience at Drury Lane, had never dipped his pen in gall to indict Shakespeare and his panegyrists, things would still have been much the same. In the story of Shakespeare's journey to Paris, and indeed of the global apotheosis that followed his arrival, Voltaire therefore claims the first word, and the last.

Notes

The place of publication is Paris unless otherwise indicated.

Notes to Introduction

1. J.-J. Jusserand, *Shakespeare in France under the Old Régime*, Eng. trans. (London, 1899),170; M. Monaco, *Shakespeare on the French Stage in the Eighteenth Century* (1974), 4.
2. C.-M. Desgranges, *Geoffroy et la critique dramatique* (1897), 61. See also 'Originalité': *L'Encyclopédie* (1751–72).
3. A. Rivarol, 'De l'Universalité de la langue française' in *Maximes, Pensées, et Paradoxes*, ed. P.-H. Simon (1962), 111.
4. Paul de Saint-Victor, *Les Deux masques* (1884), iii, 14.
5. J.-J. Jusserand, *Histoire abrégée de la littérature anglaise*, 3e édn (1921), 132.
6. Cited in C. Latrelle, 'Un Episode de l'histoire de Shakespeare en France': *Revue d'Histoire de la Littérature de la France* (1916), 53–63.
7. André Suarès, *Poète tragique: portrait de Prospero* (1921), 41, 131, 230, 367, 370.
8. André Gide, *Journal 1889–1939* (1982), 239, 389, 764, 1120, 1328.
9. Voltaire, *Œuvres complètes* (1877–85), xiv, 156, 435.
10. P. Hazard, *La Crise de la conscience européenne*, nouvelle édn (1961), 415.
11. Henri Fluchère, 'Shakespeare in France 1900–1948': *Shakespeare Survey*, ii (1949), 115–25.

Notes to Chapter 1: Farewell the Tranquil Mind

1. See Georges Ascoli, *La Grande Bretagne devant l'opinion française au dix-septième siècle* (1930).
2. Antoine-François, abbé Prévost, *Mémoires et aventures d'un homme de qualité* in *Œuvres*, ed. P. Berthiaume and J. Sgard (Grenoble, 1978), i, 253.
3. Ibid., i, 254–55.

4. Voltaire, *Lettres philosophiques*, nouvelle édn (1964), 8e Lettre.

5. Prévost, *Mémoires*, i, 234, 252.

6. A. Ballantyne, *Voltaire's Visit to England*, new edn (London, 1919), 48–9.

7. Voltaire, *Lettres philosophiques*, 18e Lettre; *Discours de la tragédie* (1730) in *Oeuvres complètes*, ii, 316–18; *Dissertation sur la tragédie ancienne et moderne* (*Semiramis*, Préface, 1748) in ibid., iv, 501–3; *Essai sur les mœurs* (1756) in ibid, xii, 246–7; *Le Théâtre de Pierre Corneille* (Geneva, 1764), Commentaire, in T. Besterman (ed.), *Voltaire on Shakespeare* (*Studies on Voltaire and the Eighteenth Century*, liv, Geneva, 1967), 93–156.

8. Prévost, *Mémoires*, i, 241; G. R. Havens, 'The Abbé Prévost and Shakespeare': *Modern Philology*, xvii (Aug. 1919), 1–22.

9. F. A. Hedgcock, *David Garrick and his French Friends* (London, 1912), 109, 218–19.

10. The author of these articles was Louis de Jaucourt.

11. Denis Diderot, *Correspondance*, ed. G. Roth and J. Varloot (1955–70), xv, 38.

12. Besterman (ed.), *Voltaire on Shakespeare*, 62, 174, 177, 211–12.

13. Ibid., 180, 186–209.

14. See F. M. Grimm and J. H. Meister, *Correspondance Littéraire, Philosophique, et Critique*, ed. M. Tournaux (1877–82), xi, 298–99, 319, 382.

15. Voltaire, article on Lord Kames from the *Gazette Littéraire* in *Œuvres complètes*, xxv, 159–63. See also *Dissertation sur la tragédie*.

16. Voltaire, *Appel à toutes les nations* (1761) in *Œuvres*, xxiv, 192–211.

17. Voltaire, *Le Théâtre de Pierre Corneille* in Besterman (ed.), *Voltaire on Shakespeare*, 155.

18. J.-J. Le Franc de Pompignan, *Œuvres* (1784), iii, 451. See also P. van Tiegham, *La Découverte de Shakespeare sur le Continent* (1947); M. England, 'Garrick's Stratford Jubilee: Reactions in France and Germany': *Shakespeare Survey*, ix (1956), 90–100; S. Williams, *Shakespeare on the German Stage 1586–1914* (Cambridge, 1990).

19. J. L. Borgerhoff, *Le Théâtre anglais à Paris sous la Restauration* (1913), 159–64.

20. Alexandre Dumas, *Mes Mémoires*, ed. P. Josserand (1954), ii, 420.

21. Hector Berlioz, *Mémoires* (1969), i, 125.

22. Ibid., ii, 302. See also Hector Berlioz, *Correspondance générale*, ed. P. Citron (1972–2001), i–iv *passim*. The letter quoted is at i, 315.

23. J. B. Fort, 'François-Victor Hugo, traducteur de Shakespeare': *Etudes Anglaises*, xiii (av.–juin 1960), 105–15.

24. Borgerhoff, *Le Théâtre anglais*, 76, 78, 79, 112.

25. Ibid., 43.

26. J. Texte, *Jean-Jacques Rousseau and the Cosmopolitan Spirit in Literature*, Eng. trans. (London,1899), 262–71.

27. See Josephine Grieder, *Anglomania in France 1740–1789* (Geneva, 1985).

28. Desgranges, *Geoffroy*, 169, 320–23, 404; A. Lacroix, *Histoire de l'influence de Shakespeare sur le théâtre français* (Brussels, 1856), 235–39.

29. J. H. Thomas, *L'Angleterre dans l'œuvre de Victor Hugo* (1934), 140n.

30. Victor Hugo, *William Shakespeare*, nouvelle édn (n. d.), 71–2, 282.

Notes to Chapter 2: A Genius in the Kingdom of Taste

1. Rivarol, 'De l'Universalité de la langue française', 90–119; K. Swart, *The Sense of Decadence in Nineteenth-century France* (The Hague, 1964), 132; D. Pick, *Faces of Degeneration: A European Disorder* (Cambridge, 1989), 55, 95–8.

2. A.–F. Villemain, 'The Life and Genius of Shakespeare', Eng. trans. in Nathan Drake (ed.), *Memorials of Shakespeare* (1828), 204–51 [originally pub. in Villemain, *Mélanges historiques et littéraires*, 1827]; [J.-F. de Saint Lambert and D. Diderot], 'Génie': *l'Encyclopédie*; Marie de Vichy, marquise du Deffand, *Lettres à Horace Walpole*, ed. Mrs Paget Toynbee (London, 1912), i, 384; Pierre Le Tourneur, *Œuvres diverses du docteur Young* (1769–70), Discours préliminaire; F. Sarcey, *Quarante ans de théâtre* (1900), i, 185.

3. A. de Tocqueville, *L'Ancien Régime*, new edn (Oxford, 1904), 216; P. Martino, Préface, *Racine et Shakespeare* in Stendhal, *Œuvres complètes*, ed. P. Martino and V. del Litto (Geneva, 1970), xxxvii, p. cviii; C.-A. Sainte-Beuve, *Nouvelle correspondance* (1880), 123.

4. J. Michelet, *Histoire de France*, nouvelle édn (n. d.), i, p. xii; Swart, *Sense of Decadence*, 132–33; Pick, *Faces of Degeneration*, 56–7; R. Mortier, *L'Originalité: une nouvelle catégorie esthétique au siècle des lumières* (Geneva, 1982), 11.

5. Voltaire, 'Génie' (*Questions sur l'Encyclopédie*) in *Œuvres complètes*, xix, 244.

6. [P.-A. de La Place], 'Discours sur le théâtre anglais' in *Le Théatre anglais* (1745–9), i, pp. xi–xiii.

7. M. G. Cushing, *Pierre Le Tourneur* (New York, 1909), 215. See also C. B. West, 'La Théorie de la traduction au XVIIIe siècle': *Revue de la Littérature Comparée*, xii (1935), 330–55.

8. Cushing, *Pierre Le Tourneur*, 216n.

9. R. G. Saisselin, *Taste in Eighteenth-century France* (Syracuse N.Y., 1965), 11–12, 76, 90–3; N. Wagner 'Réflexions sur le chapitre "Du Génie" des

Essais de l'abbé Trublet': *Annales de Bretagne et des Pays de l'Ouest*, lxxxiii (1976), 771–77; J.-F. Marmontel, *Eléments de la littérature* in *Œuvres complètes* (1819–20), iv, 13–4, 565; 'Génie' (*Dictionnaire philosophique*) in ibid., xix, 245–46; C. Todd, *Voltaire's Disciple: Jean-François de La Harpe* (1972); R. de Chateaubriand, *Essai sur la littérature anglaise* in *Œuvres complètes* (1828), xxi, 44.

10. Rivarol, 'De l'Universalité de la langue française', 92; Chateaubriand, *Essai*, 44; Voltaire, 'Goût' (*l'Encyclopédie*) in *Œuvres complètes*, xix, 282; G. de Staël, *De l'Allemagne*, nouvelle édn (1958), ii, 216.

11. Voltaire, *Lettres philosophiques*, 18e Lettre; van Tiegham, *La Découverte de Shakespeare*, 61–2.

12. Desgranges, *Geoffroy*, 62, 69; C. Rollin, *De la Manière d'enseigner et d'étudier les Belles Lettres* (1754), cited in Saisselin, *Taste*, 52; West, 'La Théorie de traduction'; Voltaire, 'Goût'. See also Marmontel, *Œuvres complètes*, iv, 4–5, and J.-J. Rousseau, *Emile*, livre 4e.

13. Grimm and Meister, *Correspondance Littéraire*, xi, 215.

14. Gérard de Nerval, *Œuvres complètes*, ed. J. Guillaume and C. Pichois (1989), i, 945.

15. Théophile Gautier, *Histoire du Romantisme*, nouvelle édn (1929), 174–75, 178.

16. Eugène Delacroix, *Journal*, ed. A. Joubin (1932), i, 290; ii, 29, 103–4, 257.

17. F. Guizot, *Shakespeare and his Times*, Eng. trans. (London,1852), esp. 114–15, 142. For a discussion of Hegel's theory of tragedy see M. Gellrich, *Tragedy as Theory* (Princeton NJ, 1988).

18. P. Chasles, *Etudes sur William Shakespeare, Marie Stuart, et l'Arétin* (1851), 88, 193–94; A. Levin (ed.), *The Legacy of Philarète Chasles* (Chapel Hill NC, 1957), i, 85, 89.

19. Delacroix, *Journal*, ii, 324, 387; iii, 441.

20. *Action Française*, 11 juin 1917. Cited in M. Grivelet, 'La Critique française devant Shakespeare': *Etudes Anglaises*, xiii (av.–juin 1960).

21. Maria van Rysselberghe, *Les Cahiers de la petite dame* (*Cahiers André Gide*, iv, 1973), 43.

22. René Doumic, 'Revue dramatique': *Revue des Deux Mondes*, 15 juin 1914.

23. L. S. Auger, *Discours sur le Romantisme* (1824), 9–10.

24. A. Mézières, *Shakespeare: ses œuvres et ses critiques*, 2e édn (1865), 443.

25. T. R. Lounsbury, *Shakespeare and Voltaire* (New York, 1902), 185–86; de Staël, *De l'Allemagne*, ii, 251; Delacroix, *Journal*, ii, 42–3; iii, 23, 441; Chateaubriand, *Essai*, 66; Voltaire, *Jules César*, Préface (*Le Théâtre de Pierre Corneille*) in Besterman (ed.), *Voltaire on Shakespeare*, 95.

26. De Staël, *De l'Allemagne*, ii, 250–51; E. Montégut, *Essai sur la littérature anglaise* (1883), 199–207.

27. Denis Diderot, *Discours sur la poésie dramatique* in *Œuvres complètes*, ed. R. Abirachel (1970), iii, 442.

28. J. H. Davis, *Tragic Theory and the Eighteenth-century French Critics* (Chapel Hill NC, 1967); J.-J. Jusserand, *Shakespeare in France*; H. C. Lancaster, *French Tragedy in the Reign of Louis XVI and the Early Years of the French Revolution* (Baltimore, 1953); G. Lanson, *Esquisse d'une histoire de la tragédie française* (New York, 1920); J. Lough, *Paris Theatre Audiences in the Seventeenth and Eighteenth Centuries* (London 1957); J. D. Lyons, *Kingdom of Disorder: the Theory of Tragedy in Classical France* (Lafayette Ind., 1999); Todd, *Voltaire's Disciple*.

29. Diderot, *Discours*, 444.

30. Stendhal, *Racine et Shakespeare* in *Œuvres complètes*, xxxvii, 44.

31. P. Bourget, *Etudes et portraits* (1906), i, 313, 315–16.

32. A. Duval, *De la Littérature dramatique* (1833), 24.

33. Du Deffand, *Lettres*, i, 515; L. S. Mercier, *Du Théâtre: ou nouvel essai sur l'art dramatique* (Amsterdam, 1773), p. ix; de Staël, *De la Littérature*, nouvelle édn (Geneva, 1959), ii, 356.

34. Voltaire, 'Goût'; 'Art dramatique' (*Dictionnaire philosophique*) in *Œuvres complètes*, xvii, 405.

35. R. de Chateaubriand, 'De l'Angleterre et les Anglais' in *Œuvres complètes*, xxi, 21; *Essai*, 69–70.

36. Stendhal, *Racine et Shakespeare*, 144n.

37. Ballantyne, *Voltaire's Visit*, 280–81; Voltaire, 'Art dramatique', 397, 405.

38. Villemain, 'The Life and Genius of Shakespeare', 222–25. See also P. Lami, *Observations sur la tragédie Romantique* (1824), 15.

39. Paul Verlaine, 'Racine et Shakespeare' in *Œuvres en prose complètes*, ed. J. Borel (1972), 704–5.

40. Marmontel, *Œuvres complètes*, iv, 5, 13–4.

41. See E. Estève, *Byron et le Romantisme français* (1907).

42. J. Moreau, *La Psychologie morbide dans ses rapports avec la philosophie de l'histoire* (1859), esp. 216–19, 490–93. See also M. Gold, 'The Early Psychiatrists on Degeneracy and Genius': *Psychoanalysis and the Psychoanalytical Review*, xlvii (1960–61), 37–55; F. Gros, *Création et Folie: une histoire du jugement psychiatrique en France* (1997); I. Downbiggin, 'Degeneration and Hereditarianism in French Mental Medicine 1840–1890' in W. F. Bunyan, Roy Porter and Michael Shepherd (eds), *The Anatomy of Madness* (London, 1985), 189–207.

43. See also Hippolyte Taine, *Histoire de la littérature anglaise*, 11e édn (1903), ii, 159–259.

44. Gros, *Création et folie*, 71.

45. Bourget, *Etudes et portraits*, i, 364.

46. Montégut, *Essai*, 163–90.

47. C.-A. Sainte-Beuve, *Causeries du lundi*, 3e édn (n. d.), xv, 356ff; *Qu'est ce qu'un classique?* (1850).

48. De Staël, *De l'Allemagne*, ii, 316.

49. Gustave Flaubert, *Correspondance*, ed. J. Bruneau (1973–98), i, 396–97; ii, 204; iii, 353. Keats's theory of the 'negative capability' of Shakespeare is similar, but not related. Keats was virtually unknown in France at this time. Shakespeare's invisibility in his own creation became widely accepted in French critical circles, and featured as a leading theme in Paul Stapfer's *Shakespeare et l'antiquité* (1879–82). However, Sainte-Beuve's eclipse was not permanent. In the twentieth century some notable critics, including Caroline Spurgeon and René Girard, read in Shakespeare's texts clear evidence of his personality and beliefs.

50. Alfred de Vigny, *Œuvres complètes*, ed. F. and A. Jarry (1986), i, 212.

51. Mézières, *Shakespeare*, 51–2, 104, 460.

52. J. Barbey d'Aurevilly, Préface (1865) to *La Vieille maîtresse*, in *Œuvres romanesques complètes*, ed. J. Petit (1966), i, 1306.

Notes to Chapter 3: Stranger within the Gates

1. Michelet, *Histoire de France*, ix, Introduction.

2. G.-P. Brugière, baron de Barante, *Mélanges historiques et littéraires* (1835), iii, 258–9; Chasles, *Etudes*, 175–95, 231–2.

3. Mézières, *Shakespeare*, 217, 230, 269, 461–63, 484, 498–99, 504–6.

4. Bourget, *Etudes et portraits*, i, 313

5. England, 'Garrick's Stratford Jubilee'.

6. Grimm and Meister, *Correspondance Littéraire*, xi, 299.

7. Ballantyne, *Voltaire's Visit*, 320.

8. De Staël, *De la Littérature*, i, 193; *de l'Allemagne*, ii, 136.

9. Villemain, 'The Life and Genius of Shakespeare'.

10. Henri de Montherlant, *Essais* (1963), 1355.

11. Michèle Willems, *La Genèse du mythe shakespearien* (1979).

12. Villemain, 'The Life and Genius of Shakespeare'.

13. Bourget, *Etudes et portraits*, i, 361–62.

14. C. Cristin, *Aux Origines de l'histoire littéraire* (Grenoble, 1973); C. Moisan, *Qu'est ce que l'histoire littéraire?* (1987).

15. Abbé du Bos, *Réflexions critiques sur la poésie et la peinture* (1719). Cited in Wagner, 'Réflexions'.

16. Mercier, *Du Théâtre*, 206.

17. De Staël, *De l'Allemagne*, ii, 136.

18. Cited in Moisan, *Qu'est ce que l'histoire littéraire?*, 67.

19. Louis Ricconobi, *A General History of the Stage*, Eng. trans., 2nd edn (London, 1754), 171. See also de La Place, 'Discours sur le théâtre anglais'.

20. J.-J. Rousseau, 'Lettre à d'Alembert' in *Du Contract Social* etc., (1962).

21. Abbé Delille, *L'Imagination* (1788). Cited in Jusserand, *Shakespeare in France*, 324n.

22. Villemain, 'The Life and Genius of Shakespeare'.

23. Bourget, *Etudes et portraits*, i, 361.

24. Saisselin, *Taste*, 92.

25. Delacroix, *Journal*, iii, 275.

26. Voltaire, 'Discours prononcé à l'Académie Française en 1746' in *Œuvres complètes*, xiii, 208.

27. F. Brunetière, *L'Evolution des genres dans l'histoire de la littérature*, 5e édn (1910), pp. xii, 262.

28. G. Lanson, *Méthode de l'histoire littéraire*. Cited in Moisan, *Qu'est ce que l'histoire littéraire?*, 22. See also Cristin, *Aux Origines*; A. Compagnon, *La Troisième République des Lettres* (1983).

29. Taine, *Histoire de la littérature anglaise*, i, Introduction; ii, 3–7, 19, 52.

30. Ibid., iv, 442.

31. Ibid., i, 281.

32. Montégut, *Essais*, 289; Gide, *Journal 1889–1939*, 191; H. Peyre, *Shelley et la France* (Cairo, 1935), 413.

33. F. C. Roe, *Taine et l'Angleterre* (1923), pp. vii–viii.

34. P. Reboul, *Le Mythe anglais dans la littérature française sous la Restauration* (Lille, 1962), 271.

35. Levin (ed.), *The Legacy of Philarète Chasles*, i, 7.

36. M. Elkington, *Les Relations de société entre l'Angleterre et la France sous la Restauration 1814–1830* (1929), 35.

37. Reboul, *Le Mythe anglais*, 278.

38. Ibid., 91–7, 203–6.

39. Montégut, *Essais*, 6.

40. Taine, *Histoire de la littérature anglaise*, ii, 19.

41. Ibid., iv, 311, 343.

42. For critical reactions see Roe, *Taine et l'Angleterre*, 166–72.

43. Sainte-Beuve, *Causeries*, 9 and 16 mars, 1857. Sainte-Beuve is here discussing Taine's earlier work.

44. Brunetière, *L'Evolution des genres*, 22, 259, 261.

45. L. Cazamian, *L'Angleterre moderne*, nouvelle édn (1922), 12–13, 16, 142, 172, 297; *L'Evolution psychologique et la littérature en Angleterre* (1920), 21, 97.

46. Ibid., 20.
47. Taine, *Histoire de la littérature anglaise*, iii, 275.
48. Ibid., iii, 353.
49. P. Bourget, *Sensations d'Italie* (1891), 329–30.
50. Cazamian, *L'Angleterre moderne*, 2.
51. For a general discussion see R. C. Grogin, *The Bergsonian Controversy in France 1900–1911* (Calgary, 1988).
52. Bourget, *Etudes et portraits*, i, 301–4.
53. G. Pellissier, 'Le Drame shakespearien sur la scène française': *Revue d'Art Dramatique*, i (15 fev. 1886), 204–21.
54. H. Girard, *Emile Deschamps 1791–1871* (1921), 157–58.
55. E. Faguet, *La Tragédie française au XVIe siècle* (1894), 2, 20–1.
56. Jusserand, *Shakespeare in France*, 84, 96, 465–67.
57. Anatole France, *De la Vie littéraire*, 3e édn (1889), 288–89.
58. Gide, *Journal 1889–1939*, 812–13.
59. G. Larroumet, *Etudes d'histoire et de critique* (1892), 126.
60. Rousseau, 'Lettre à d'Alembert', 199. This claim is verified by the statistics in Lough, *Paris Theatre Audiences*, and by the evidence in K. L. Wood, 'The French Theatre in the Eighteenth Century According to Some Contemporary English Travellers': *Revue de Littérature Comparée*, xii (1932), 601–18.
61. A. de Musset, 'Une Soirée perdue' in *Poésies nouvelles*.
62. For Bernhardt's repertoire see Louis Vermeil, *The Fabulous Life of Sarah Bernhardt*, new edn (Westport Ct, 1972). Proust described Bernhardt ('La Berma') as Phèdre in *A l'Ombre des jeunes filles en fleurs* and in *Le Côté de Guermantes*. For audiences before the Revolution see Lough, *Paris Theatre Audiences*. For audiences in the nineteenth century see Sarcey, *Quarante ans de théâtre*, i, 179, 250, 269, 320–1. See also René Doumic, 'Shakespeare et la critique française': *Revue des Deux Mondes*, 15 oct. 1904; E. Legouis and L. Cazamian, *Histoire de la littérature anglaise* (1924), 381–82. The persistent Baroque strain in French classical culture is discussed by P. France, *Politeness and its Discontents* (Cambridge, 1992), 11–26.
63. J. Benda, *La Trahison des clercs*, 45e édn (1937), 79. Renan held that as a result of constant intermixing, races had been obliterated by nations, and that civilisation had superseded race as the main force of modern history. For a discussion of Renan and other French theorists of race see T. Todorov, *On Human Diversity: Nationalism, Racism, and Exoticism in French Thought*, Eng. trans. (Cambridge Mass., 1993), esp. ch. 2.
64. L. Gillet, *Shakespeare*, 10e édn (1931), 8, 27.
65. Ibid., 28.
66. J. Jackson, *France: The Dark Years* (Oxford, 2001), 511–12; M. Atack,

Literature and the French Resistance (Manchester, 1989), 36–41, 84–86. For collaborationist ideology see P. Ory, *Les Collaborateurs* (1976) and *La France Allemande* (1977). Louis Aragon's wartime fiction is overtly anti-German. See for example *Servitude et grandeur des Français* (1945).

67. J.-L. Barrault, *A Propos de Shakespeare et du théâtre* (1949), 10.

68. J.-P. Sartre, *Qu'est ce que la littérature?*, nouvelle édn (1985), 50, 81, 88, 90, 91, 184. In 'La Nationalisation de la littérature' (*Situations*, ii, 1948), Sartre argued that a writer's relationship with 'l'esprit objectif de l'époque' was never apparent to the writer himself, but could be perceived by the Taines and Michelets of subsequent generations. See also Sartre's *L'Existentialisme est un humanisme* (1946).

69. R. Barthes, 'Histoire ou littérature?' in *Sur Racine* (1963). Barthes' own critical language was anthropological and psychoanalytical.

70. Todorov, for example, is especially critical of Levi-Strauss. See *On Human Diversity*, ch. 1.

Notes to Chapter 4: A Story without an Ending

1. M. Horn-Monval (ed.), *Traductions et adaptations du théâtre étranger* (CNRS, 1963), v.

2. R. Zuber, *Les 'Belles Infidèles' et la formation du goût classique* (1968), 19–28.

3. R. Schwab, *The Oriental Renaissance: Europe's Recovery of India and the East 1680–1880*, Eng. trans. (New York, 1984); R. Irwin, *The Arabian Nights: A Companion* (1994).

4. Grieder, *Anglomania in France*, 73.

5. *Les Orientales* (1829), Préface.

6. G. Steiner, *After Babel: Aspects of Language and Translation* (Oxford, 1975), 73–8.

7. Marmontel, *Eléments de la littérature*, 198–99.

8. Voltaire, *Lettres philosophiques*, 19e Lettre.

9. Cited in West, 'La Théorie de traduction'.

10. J. Barbey d'Aurevilly, *Du Dandyisme et de George Brummel*, nouvelle édn (1989), 126–27.

11. Rivarol, 'De l'Universalité de la langue française'.

12. De Staël, *De la Littérature*, ii, 227.

13. Yves Bonnefoy, *Entretiens sur la poésie* (Neuchâtel, 1981), 95.

14. Chasles, *Etudes*, 331, 342.

15. W. Shakespeare, *Œuvres dramatiques*, trad. Georges Duval (1908–9), i, Préface.

16. Andre Gide, 'Avant-propos' in *Œuvres complètes de Shakespeare*, ed.

H. Fluchère, nouvelle édn (1959); *Divers* (1931), 191–94; 'Préface' to *Hamlet* (1944) in *Théâtre complet*, ed. R. Heyd (1947–9), vii, 201.

17. Bonnefoy, *Entretiens*, 99. Gide, too, found this word a problem. He rendered the phrase as *liquifiés de terreur*. Bonnefoy's *Hamlet* is discussed in R. Heylen, *Translation, Poetics and the Stage* (London, 1993).

18. Cited, from Bérault-Bercastel's 'Préface' to his trans. of Quevedo's *Le Voyage récréatif*, in West, 'La Théorie de traduction'.

19. Marmontel, *Eléments de la littérature*, 195.

20. Cited in Hazard, *La Crise*, 60.

21. Zuber, *Les 'Belles Infidèles'*, 78, 89, 194–5, 289–94, 337–80; Olivier Patru, 'La Vie de Monsieur d'Ablancourt' repr. in ibid., 424–33; E. Cary, *Les Grands traducteurs français* (Geneva, 1963), 15–24, 30–7.

22. Ibid., 30–7.

23. West, 'La Théorie de traduction'.

24. Voltaire, *Le Théâtre de Pierre Corneille*, Préface, in Besterman (ed.), *Voltaire on Shakespeare*, 94.

25. West, 'La Théorie de traduction'.

26. Voltaire, *Le Théâtre de Pierre Corneille*, Préface, in Besterman (ed.), *Voltaire on Shakespeare*, 95; 'Epopée' and 'Rime' (*Dictionnaire philosophique*) in *Œuvres complètes*, xviii.

27. *Le Pour et Contre*, ii (1733), no. 29.

28. F.-T. de Baculard Arnauld, *Le Comte de Comminges* (1764), Discours préliminaire. Cited in A. Lacroix, *Histoire de l'influence de Shakespeare sur le théâtre français* (Brussels, 1856), 194–95.

29. Levin (ed.), *The Legacy of Philarète Chasles*, i, 11.

30. [De La Place], *Le Théâtre anglais*, i, pp. iv–cxiii. The translation is discussed in H. E. Brooks, 'Eighteenth-century French Translations and Adaptations of Shakespeare' (unpublished dissertation, Northwestern University, Evanston, Illinois, 1960).

31. J.-B. Le Blanc, *Lettres d'un Français* (1745); P.-J. Fiquet du Bocage, *Lettres sur le théâtre anglais* (1752). Both cited in A. Genuist, *Le Théâtre de Shakespeare dans l'œuvre de Pierre Le Tourneur* (1971), 27, 35.

32. Voltaire, *Appel à toutes les nations*.

33. Pierre Le Tourneur, *Préface du Shakespeare traduit de l'Anglais*, ed. J. Gury (Geneva, 1990). Gury's Introduction provides a full scholarly and critical apparatus.

34. Ibid. See also J. Gury, 'Les Bretons et la shakespearomanie': *Annales de Bretagne et des Pays du Nord*, lxxxiii (1976), 703–14; J. Gury, 'Shakespeare à la cour de Versailles sous le règne de Louis XVI': *Revue de la Littérature Comparée*, jan.–mars 1975, 103–14.

35. Le Tourneur, *Préface*, 57.
36. Cushing, *Pierre Le Tourneur*, 273.
37. Du Deffand, *Lettres*, iii, 192, 206.
38. Grimm and Meister, *Correspondance Littéraire*, xi, 215.
39. Genuist, *Le Théâtre de Shakespeare*, 185–86, 203.
40. Cushing, *Pierre Le Tourneur*, 212–3, 215.
41. W. Shakspeare [sic], *Œuvres complètes traduites de l'anglais par Le Tourneur*, nouvelle édition revue et corrigée par F. Guizot (1821), x, 358. In his *Guizot pendant la Restauration* (1923), C. Pouthas claimed that the revision was the work of Guizot's wife, Pauline de Meulan. This seems from other evidence to be inaccurate, but she certainly assisted.
42. Cited in M. Gilman, *Othello in French* (1925), 82–3.
43. Chasles, *Etudes*, 332–40.
44. J. Mounet Sully, *Souvenirs d'un tragédien* (1917), 138.
45. J. B. Fort, 'François-Victor Hugo, traducteur de Shakespeare': *Etudes Anglaises*, xiii, no. 2 (av.–juin 1960); B. Leuilliot, 'L'Histoire réelle telle qu'en Shakespeare' in A. R. W. James (ed.), *Victor Hugo et la Grande Bretagne* (Liverpool, 1986).
46. Hugo, *William Shakespeare*, 168, 348–49.

Notes to Chapter 5: Desdemona's Handkerchief

1. George Sand, *Œuvres complètes* (1877), iv, 112–18.
2. *Le Grand Robert* locates the first use in 1784, in a text by Restif de La Bretonne.
3. Grimm and Meister, *Correspondance Littéraire*, xi, 380–81.
4. Cited in F. Baldensperger, *Esquisse d'une histoire de Shakespeare en France* in *Etudes d'histoire littéraire*, ii (1910), 179.
5. J.-F. Ducis, *Œuvres complètes* (Brussels, 1827), ii, 5.
6. S. Chevalley, 'Ducis, Shakespeare, et les Comédiens-Français': *Revue d'Histoire du Théâtre*, xvi (1964), 327–50; E. Partridge, *The French Romantics' Knowledge of English Literature 1820–1848* (1924), 54, 207.
7. J.-F. Ducis, *Lettres*, ed. P. Albert (1879), 8.
8. Ducis, *Œuvres complètes*, v, 12.
9. Ibid., ii, 5, 122; iii, 8; vi, 187, 193, 217–20. When Ducis wrote his *Roméo et Juliette* he knew nothing more of Shakespeare's play than the four-page summary given by La Place.
10. La Harpe and Julien-Louis Geoffroy were especially hostile. See Desgranges, *Geoffroy*, 146, 327–30; Jusserand, *Shakespeare in France*, 432n; H. F. Collins, *Talma: Biography of an Actor* (London, 1964), 158.

11. Barante, *Mélanges*, iii, 268.

12. De Nerval, *Œuvres complètes*, i, 353; Sainte-Beuve, *Causeries*, vi (1852), 46.

13. Marmontel, 'Imitation' in *Eléments de la littérature*.

14. Pierre Lami, *Observations sur la tragédie Romantique* (1824), 10.

15. C. G. Etienne and B. Martainville, *Histoire du théâtre français* (1802), iii, 26–28.

16. Victor duc de Broglie, 'Shakespeare's *Othello* and Dramatic Art in France', Eng. trans. in Guizot, *Shakespeare and his Times*, 294–95.

17. E. Deschamps, *Œuvres complètes* (1872–4), ii, 283–85; A. de Vigny, *Œuvres complètes*, ed. F. Germain and A. Jarry (1986), i, 412. See also Partridge, *The French Romantics' Knowledge*, 137, 203.

18. De Nerval, *Œuvres complètes*, i, 886.

19. Sarcey, *Quarante ans de théâtre*, iii, 349. See also Partridge, *The French Romantics' Knowledge*, 211; de Nerval, *Œuvres complètes*, i, 878.

20. De Vigny, *Œuvres complètes*, i, 400–4.

21. Ibid., i, 398, 421n.

22. A. Sesseley, *L'Influence de Shakespeare sur Alfred de Vigny* (Berne, 1928), 44.

23. De Vigny, *Œuvres complètes*, i, 409.

24. A. Jarry, 'De Vigny traducteur de Shakespeare' in de Vigny, *Œuvres complètes*, i, 1347–80.

25. Gilman, *Othello in French*, 111, 158, 168; de Vigny, *Œuvres complètes*, i, 408–9.

26. De Vigny also translated *The Merchant of Venice*, but this text ('recomposé et réduit') was never performed in his lifetime. See A. de Vigny, *Correspondance*, ed. M. Ambrière (1989), i, 364.

27. B. V. Daniels, 'Shakespeare à la Romantique: *le More de Venise* d'Alfred de Vigny': *Revue d'Histoire du Théâtre*, ii (1975), 125–35; F. Bassan, *Alfred de Vigny et la Comédie-Française* (Tübingen & Paris, 1984), 21–37; S. Haig, 'Vigny and Othello': *Yale French Studies*, xxxiii (1964), 53–64; Gilman, *Othello in French*, 94–109.

28. For the text, see Deschamps, *Œuvres complètes*, v. The translation is discussed in H. Girard, *Emile Deschamps* (1921), 142–56.

29. Deschamps, *Œuvres complètes*, ii, 283–85.

30. Text in ibid., v.

31. Montégut, *Essais*, 200–1. Lacroix's text had been published in 1840. For critical reactions see Partridge, *The French Romantics' Knowledge*, 306–7.

32. Dumas, *Mémoires*, i, 420.

33. Hippolyte Lucas, writing in *Le Siècle*. Cited in Partridge, *The French Romantics' Knowledge*, 255. Meurice's collaborator was Auguste Vacquerie.

34. A. Dumas, *Etude sur Hamlet et sur William Shakespeare* (1867), 12.

35. E.g., Armand de Pontmartin and Théophile Gautier. See *Revue des Deux Mondes*, 1 jan. 1848; T. Gautier, *Histoire de l'art dramatique en France depuis vingt-cinq ans* (1858–59), iv, 331–32.
36. Ibid., iv, 332.
37. A. Dumas and P. Meurice, *Hamlet Prince de Danemark* (1886), 139. Louis Ménard, who published his own verse translation in 1886, also argued along these lines. See P. Benchetritt, 'Hamlet at the Comédie-Française 1769–1896': *Shakespeare Survey*, ix (1956), 59–67.
38. J. Jacquot, 'Mourir! Dormir! ... Rêver peut-être?': *Revue d'Histoire du Théâtre*, xvi (1964), 407–37.
39. Stéphane Mallarmé, *Œuvres complètes*, ed. H. Mondor and G. Jean-Aubry (1945), 299–302, 349–51.
40. J. Lemaître, *Impressions du théâtre*, 16e édn (n. d.), i, 135.
41. Sarcey, *Quarante ans de théâtre*, iii, 356–57.
42. J. Bainville, *Une Saison chez Thespis* (1929), 240–8. Doumic's favourable judgement was a last-ditch effort to keep alive the classical tradition of translation. See his 'Revue dramatique'.
43. Vermeil, *Fabulous Life*, 184–5, 179; R. Davril 'Les Pionniers': *Etudes Anglaises*, xiii (av.–juin 1960), 162–71.
44. W. Shakespeare, *La Tragique histoire d'Hamlet*, trans. Marcel Schwob and Eugène Morand, nouvelle édn (1986), 27.
45. H. de Régnier, *Figures et caractères*, 6e édn (n. d.), 240.
46. Ibid., 242. For Berhardt's performance see E. Salman (ed.), *Bernhardt and the Theatre of her Time* (Westport Ct, 1984); E. Robbins, 'On Seeing Mme Bernhardt's Hamlet': *North American Review*, (Dec. 1900), 908–919.

Notes to Chapter 6: His Hour upon the Stage

1. Lemaître, *Impressions*, i, 127; iii, 52–8.
2. *L'Illustration Théâtrale*, 17 déc. 1904.
3. Baldensperger, *Esquisse d'une histoire*, 215.
4. Cited in Grivelet, 'La Critique française'.
5. Ibid.
6. De Montherlant, *Essais*, 260.
7. Gaston Baty, *Rideau baissé* (1948), 118.
8. Georges Pitoëff, *Notre théâtre*, ed. J. de Rigault (1949), 23–4.
9. Jacques Copeau, 'Un Essai de rénovation dramatique': *Nouvelle Revue Française*, 1913. Cited in J. Jacquot, *Shakespeare en France: mises en scène d'hier et d'aujourd'hui* (1964), 51.
10. Baty, *Rideau baissé*, 219.

11. Gaston Baty, 'Le Visage de Shakespeare' in ibid., 126–67. The only previous staging of the first quarto text had been an amateur production directed by William Poel at St George's Hall, London, in 1881.

12. André Antoine, *Mes Souvenirs sur le théâtre Antoine et sur l'Odéon* (1928), 244. For a discussion in English of Antoine's directorial career see J. Chothia, *André Antoine* (Cambridge, 1991).

13. Antoine, *Mes Souvenirs*, 244. For the Shakespeare-Bühne used by Ernst von Possart in Munich, see Williams, *Shakespeare on the German Stage*, 185–90.

14. *L'Illustration Théâtrale*, 17 déc. 1904.

15. Ibid., 18 oct. 1913. This number contains the text of the translation.

16. Grivelet, 'La Critique dramatique française'.

17. Jacques Copeau, *Souvenirs du Vieux Colombier* (1931), 73.

18. Jacques Copeau, *Journal 1901–1948*, ed. C. Sicard (1991), i, 716.

19. Jacquot, *Shakespeare en France*, 52; Copeau, *Souvenirs*, 56; *Journal*, ii, 191.

20. Bainville, *Une Saison chez Thespis*, 240–9.

21. Pitoëff, *Notre théâtre*, 8.

22. F. Anders, *Jacques Copeau et le Cartel des Quatre* (1959), 126.

23. J. Claude, *André Gide et le théâtre* (1992), i, 14, 262; Gide, *Journal 1889–1939*, 1020; Maria van Rysselberghe, *Les Cahiers de la Petite Dame 1929–1937* (*Cahiers André Gide*, v, 1974), 43–4.

24. André Gide, *Journal 1926–1950*, ed. M. Sagaert (1997) 1033–34.

25. André Gide and Dorothy Bussy, *Correspondance*, ed. J. Lamber, i (*Cahiers André Gide*, ix, 1979), 360.

26. Gide, *Journal 1889–1939*, 681.

27. Gide, *Théâtre complet*, iii, 223.

28. Gide, *Journal 1889–1939*, 891, 980–1; *Journal 1926–1950*, 721.

29. Ibid., 1026. Gide was vilified by Louis Aragon for not having involved himself with the Resistance.

30. Gide, *Journal 1889–1939*, 298.

31. Ibid., 874.

32. Gide, *Divers*, 285n; *Prétextes*, 15e édn (1926), 24–30.

33. Gide, *Journal 1926–1950*, 840.

34. Gide, *Journal 1889–1939*, 874.

35. André Gide, *Incidences* (1924), 211; *Journal 1889–1939*, 1187.

36. Copeau, *Journal*, ii, 314.

37. Cited in Claude, *André Gide et le théâtre*, i, 207.

38. Ibid., i, 116; Gide and Bussy, *Correspondance*, i, 359; van Rysselberghe, *Les Cahiers de la Petite Dame*, 137.

39. Gide, *Divers*, 178.

40. Gide, *Journal 1889–1939*, 733–34.

41. Gide and Bussy, *Correspondance*, i, 356.

42. André Gide and Dorothy Bussy, *Correspondance*, iii (*Cahiers André Gide*, xi, 1982), 595.

43. Gide, *Divers*, 177–78; Gide and Bussy, *Correspondance*, iii, 219.

44. Gide, *Divers*, 195.

45. Gide and Bussy, *Correspondance*, iii, 223, 225, 226, 229, 240; Gide, *Journal 1926–1950*, 827–28.

46. Claude, *André Gide et le théâtre*, i, 208–11.

47. Gide, *Divers*, 189; J. Claude, 'Gide, traducteur de *Hamlet*' in P. Pollard (ed.), *André Gide et l'Angleterre* (Birkbeck College, London, 1986).

48. Gide, *Journal 1926–1950*, 844.

49. For critical reactions, see Claude, *André Gide et le théâtre*, i, 212–13.

50. Ibid., i, 213; C. Pons, 'Les Traductions de *Hamlet* par des écrivains français': *Etudes Anglaises*, xiii (av.–juin 1960); P. Sollers, 'Shakespeare en directe': *Le Monde des Livres*, 10 déc. 1995.

Notes to Chapter 7: The Trumpets of Fortinbras

1. Albert Camus, *Le Mythe de Sisyphe*, nouvelle édn (1969), 18.

2. Marmontel, *Œuvres complètes*, v, 199–227.

3. Barrault, *A Propos de Shakespeare*, 60, 62.

4. Georges Magnane in *Franc Tireur*. Cited in J. Chatenet, *Shakespeare sur la scène française depuis 1940* (1962), 88.

5. Rivarol, 'De l'Universalité de la langue française'.

6. F. Espinasse, *The Life of Ernest Renan* (London, 1895), 175.

7. Diderot, *Discours sur la poésie dramatique*, 480–81.

8. Lanson, *Esquisse*, 140.

9. Jean Giraudoux, 'Bellac et la tragédie', Eng. trans. in L. Abel (ed.), *Moderns on Tragedy* (Greenwich Conn., 1967), 31–40. See also J. Truchet, *La Tragédie classique en France* (1975), 183.

10. Albert Camus, 'Conférence … sur l'avenir de la tragédie' in *Théâtre, Récits, Nouvelles* (1962), 1701–11.

11. Barthes, *Sur Racine*, 6–8.

12. Truchet, *La Tragédie classique*, 8, 87.

13. See G. Venet, *Temps et vision tragique: Shakespeare et ses contemporains* (1985); S. Iwasaki, *The Sword and the Word: Shakespeare's Tragic Sense of Time* (Tokyo, 1973).

14. Giraudoux, 'Bellac et la tragédie'.

15. Camus, 'Conférence'.

16. 'Discours à l'Académie Française', cited in Barrault, *A Propos de Shakespeare*, 56.

17. J.-C. Berton, *Shakespeare et Claudel: le temps et l'espace au théâtre* (1958), 27, 219–20. Significantly, the later French Catholic critic René Girard made the redemptive theme of *The Winter's Tale* central to his reading of Shakespeare. See *A Theatre of Envy*, new edn (Leominster, 2000), 334–42.

18. Steiner, among others, makes this point. See *The Death of Tragedy*, 343.

19. The most notable instances are Barbey d'Aurevilly, Huysmans, Péguy, and Barrès.

20. R.-P. Colin, *Schopenhauer en France* (Lyon, 1979), 106, 129, 142.

21. See *Ecce Homo*, trans. Walter Kaufman (New York, 1968).

22. Miguel de Unamuno, *The Tragic Sense of Life in Men and Nations*, trans. A. Kerrigan (1972), 117–18.

23. Louis Aragon, *Traité du style* (1928), esp. 83–5.

24. Camus, *Le Mythe de Sisyphe*, 162–66. This reading seems best adapted to Camus' own claim that the essay is a critique of existentialism.

25. Camus, 'Conférence'.

26. Diderot, *Discours sur la poésie dramatique*.

27. P. Bourget, *Essais de la psychologie contemporaine*, nouvelle édn (1920), i, pp. xxv–xxvi; H. Taine, *Derniers essais de critique et d'histoire*, 3e édn (1903), 345.

28. Sartre, *Qu'est ce que la littérature?*, 256–69, 371.

29. *Opéra*, mai 1945. Cited in Grivelet, 'La Critique dramatique française'.

30. Barrault, *A Propos de Shakespeare*, 20, 23.

31. *Paris-Presse*, 7 jan. 1950. Cited in Jacquot, *Shakespeare en France*, 94.

32. S. Added, *Le Théâtre dans les années Vichy* (1992), 257.

33. See G. Larroumet, *Etudes d'histoire et de critique* (1892), 134.

34. Ernest Renan, 'Les Sciences naturelles et les sciences historiques' in *Dialogues et fragments philosophiques* (1876). See also *Feuilles détachées* (1892).

35. H. Bergson, *L'Evolution créatrice* in *Œuvres*, ed. A. Robinet (1959), 701–2.

36. Unamuno, *The Tragic Sense of Life*, 137, 278.

37. Y. Conry, *L'Introduction du darwinisme en France* (1974), esp. 398–423.

38. P. Valéry, 'The Spiritual Crisis': *Athenaeum*, 11 April 1919, 182–84; 'The Intellectual Crisis': ibid., 2 May 1919, 279–80.

39. Todorov, *On Human Diversity*, 326–8.

40. Bergson, *L'Evolution créatrice*, 542–3, 569–84, 691–727.

41. For the changing fortunes of Bergson in France see Grogin, *The Bergsonian Controversy*.

42. F. Nietzsche, *The Birth of Tragedy*, trans. F. Golffing (New York, 1956), sec. 9, 15. For a discussion of Nietzsche's Hellenism see A. Stephen, 'Socrates or

Chorus-person? The problem of Individuality in Nietzsche's Hellenism' in G. W. Clark (ed.), *Rediscovering Hellenism* (Cambridge, 1989).

43. Nietzsche, *The Birth of Tragedy*, sec. 2, 3. See also *Twilight of the Idols*, sec. 24; *Daybreak*, sec. 240; *Ecce Homo; The Gay Science*, sec. 107. All in Oscar Levy (ed.), *The Complete Works of Friedrich Nietzsche* (1909–13).

44. Valéry, 'The Spiritual Crisis'.

45. Barrault, *A Propos de Shakespeare*, 20, 23.

46. Louis Aragon, *Le Crève-cœur et les Yeux d'Elsa* (London, 1944), 59, 77.

47. Pascal, *Pensées*, 139 [110].

48. Baudelaire, 'La Beauté' in *Les Fleurs du Mal*.

49. H. Bergson, *Essai sur les données immédiates de la conscience* in *Œuvres*, 67–151.

50. Pascal, *Pensées*, 129 [440].

51. Venet, *Temps et vision tragique*, 326.

Notes to Chapter 8: Waiting for Shakespeare

1. Cited in P. Blanchard, 'Le Théâtre contemporain et les Elizabéthains': *Etudes anglaises*, xiii (av.–juin 1960), 145–58.

2. Lough, *Paris Theatre Audiences*, 171–72, gives details for the houses of the Comédie-Française.

3. Antoine, *Mes Souvenirs*, 89.

4. H. Gaidoz, 'Le Roi Léar à Paris en 1783': *Revue Germanique*, vi (1910), 422–26.

5. F. Bassan and S. Chevalley, *Alexandre Dumas père et la Comédie-Française* (1972), 169.

6. Robbins, 'On Seeing Mme Bernhardt's Hamlet'.

7. Daniels, 'Shakespeare à la Romantique'.

8. Jacquot, 'Mourir! Dormir! …'.

9. Bainville, *Une Saison chez Thespis*, 249; Doumic, 'Revue dramatique'.

10. Lemaître, *Impressions*, i, 113–24.

11. *L'Eclair*, 27 fév. 1918. Cited in Grivelet, 'La Critique dramatique française'. See also Colette, *Œuvres*, ed. C. Pichois (1986), ii, 1596–97.

12. Firmin Gémier, *Le Théâtre*, ed. P. Gsell (1925), 14–23, 55, 69–73, 75–6, 137, 215.

13. Baty, *Rideau baissé*, 7, 118, 126.

14. Chatenet, *Shakespeare sur la scène française*, 50–2; J. Jacquot, 'Gaston Baty et les Elizabéthains': *Etudes Anglaises*, xiii (av.–juin 1960), 205–15.

15. J. Jacquot, 'Vers un théâtre du peuple: Shakespeare en France après Copeau et le Cartel des Quatre': ibid., 219–43. See also Chatenet,

Shakespeare sur la scène française; J.-L. Barrault, *Nouvelles réflexions sur le théâtre* (1959), 267–71, 274–76.

16. Letter to d'Argental in *Œuvres complètes*, xlvi, 473.

17. Gaidoz, 'Le Roi Léar à Paris'.

18. Daniels, 'Shakespeare à la Romantique'. See also B. V. Daniels, 'Sur les décors du *More de Venise*': *Bulletin de l'Association des Amis d'Alfred de Vigny*, vii (1976–7), 21–30.

19. Mézières, *Shakespeare*, 20.

20. Sarcey, *Quarante ans de théâtre*, iii, 359.

21. Bassan and Chevalley, *Alexandre Dumas père*, 175.

22. *Revue Hebdomadaire*, 1920. Cited in Grivelet, 'La Critique dramatique française'.

23. Ibid.; Jacquot, *Shakespeare en France*, 50.

24. Colette, *Œuvres*, ii, 936–37.

25. Claude, *André Gide et le théâtre*, i, 89–96; G. Painter, *Marcel Proust* (London, 1959–65), ii, 301; J. Depaulis, *Ida Rubinstein: une inconnue jadis célèbre* (1995), 233–41.

26. Charles Dullin, *Souvenirs et notes de travail d'un acteur* (1946), 142–43; Chatenet, *Shakespeare sur la scène française*, 49, 79; L. Gillet, 'Shakespeare à Paris': *Revue des Deux Mondes*, 15 mai 1932; Gémier, *Le Théâtre*, 56.

27. J.-L. Barrault, *Souvenirs pour demain* (1972), 205–6; C. Genty, *Histoire du Théâtre National de l'Odéon 1782–1982* (1982), 276–80.

28. Jacquot, *Shakespeare en France*, 42; Chothia, *André Antoine*, 136–54. Mention should also be made of Aurélian Lugné-Poë, who innovated by presenting *Mesure pour mesure* without scenery at the Cirque d'été in Paris in 1898.

29. Anders, *Jacques Copeau et le Cartel des Quatre*, 71.

30. J. Copeau, 'El Teatro llama a la poesia': *La Nación*, 1938. Cited in trans. in J. Rudkin and N. Paul (eds), *Copeau: Texts on Theatre* (London, 1990), 111–12.

31. Doumic, 'Revue dramatique'.

32. Pitoëff, *Notre théâtre*, 22.

33. Gillet, 'Shakespeare à Paris'.

34. Jean Vilar, *De la Tradition théâtrale* (1955), 42–3; Chatenet, *Shakespeare sur la scène française*, 78; Jacquot, 'Vers un théâtre populaire'; Marc Beigbeder, *Le Théâtre en France depuis la Libération* (1959), 193–216.

35. See, for example, Enzo Siciliano, *Pier Paolo Pasolini* (Milan, 1978), 325.

36. See Jacquot, 'Vers un théâtre populaire' for a discussion of Planchon's Shakespeare.

37. Pitoëff, *Notre théâtre*, 25–6.

38. Beigbeder, *Le Théâtre en France*, 205–6.

39. A. Artaud, 'Le Théâtre et son double' in *Œuvres complètes* (1964), iv.

40. Chatenet, *Shakespeare sur la scène française*, 41–2.

41. Vilar, *De la Tradition théâtrale*, 42–3, 102–4.

42. By the end of the century Gide's *Hamlet* and *Antoine et Cléopâtre* had not been revived following Barrault's productions in the 1940s. Copeau's *Macbeth* had been staged once, by the Comédie St. Etienne in 1952. Jouve's *Roméo* had had one revival, at Strasbourg in 1954. Maeterlink's *Macbeth* had never again been performed after its première at the Odéon in 1909. Bonnefoy's *Julius Caesar* and *Hamlet* had each been staged once, by Barrault, in 1960 at the Odéon, and by Chéreau, in 1988 at Avignon.

43. Edmond Jaloux, *Figures etrangères* (1925), 23.

44. Jacquot, *Shakespeare en France*, 50.

45. Jacquot, 'Vers un théâtre populaire'.

46. L. Champagne, *French Theatre Experiment since 1968* (Ann Arbor Mich., 1984), 87.

47. Ibid., 88–92; F. McGlynne, 'Postmodern and the Theatre' in H. J. Silverman (ed.), *Postmodernism: Philosophy and the Arts* (London & New York, 1990), 137–54; J. Gershman, 'Daniel Mesguich's *Shakespeare's Hamlet*': *The Drama Review*, xxv (1981).

48. J. Kristeva, 'Modern Theatre does not take (a) Place': *Substance*, 1977. Cited in McGlynne, 'Postmodern and the Theatre'.

49. Champagne, *French Theatre Experiment*, 24–49.

Notes to Chapter 9: The Metamorphosis of Envy

1. A. M. Rousseau, *L'Angleterre et Voltaire* (*Studies on Voltaire and the Eighteenth Century*, cxlv-cxlvii, Oxford, 1976), 677n; R. Blunt, *Mrs Montagu, Queen of the Blues* (Boston, 1923), i, 280; Ballantyne, *Voltaire's Visit*, 298–9; C. Phillips, *Joshua Reynolds* (1894), 179; P. Murray, 'The Source of Reynolds's "Triumph of Truth"': *Aberdeen University Review*, xxx (1944), 27–9.

2. Rousseau, *L'Angleterre et Voltaire*, 330, 352–53, 567; G. de Beer and A. M. Rousseau, *Voltaire's British Visitors* (*Studies on Voltaire and the Eighteenth Century*, xlix, Geneva, 1967), 147; J. Churton Collins, *Voltaire, Montesquieu, and Rousseau in England* (London, 1908), ch. 1; Ballantyne, *Voltaire's Visit*, passim; R. Babcock, *The Genesis of Shakespearean Idolatry* (Chapel Hill NC, 1931), 108–218; D. Nichol Smith, *Shakespearean Criticism 1623–1840*, new edn (London, 1968), 231. Blake's poem, usually anthologised under the title 'Scoffers', is from the Notebook Drafts.

3. J. Morley, *Voltaire*, new edn (London, 1886), 5.

4. Notes to *Don Juan*, Canto V.

5. *The Excursion*, Book IV.

6. Thomas Carlyle, *On Heroes, Hero-worship, and the Heroic in History*, new edn (London, 1901), 269, 271.

7. *Resignation*, Part II.

8. Blunt, *Mrs Montagu*, ii, 147. For Voltaire at Ferney, see de Beer and Rousseau, *Voltaire's British Visitors*.

9. Carlyle, *On Heroes*, 271.

10. Richard Neville, *The Gentleman's Magazine*, 1850. Cited in de Beer and Rousseau, *Voltaire's British Visitors*, 157. No such edition was, in fact, ever found.

11. A. Ralli, *A History of Shakespearean Criticism* (London, 1932), i, 465–66.

12. T. J. B. Spencer, 'The Tyranny of Shakespeare' in Peter Alexander (ed.), *Studies in Shakespeare* (Oxford, 1964), 149–70.

13. B. Vickers (ed.), *Shakespeare: The Critical heritage* (London, 1974–81), i, 250, 334; ii, 190–202.

14. Oliver Goldsmith, *An Enquiry into the Present State of Polite Learning in Europe* in *Collected Works*, ed. A. Friedman (Oxford, 1966), i, 326.

15. Rousseau, *L'Angleterre et Voltaire*, 505; David Hume, *A History of England* (London 1763), vi, 131.

16. Samuel Johnson, *Samuel Johnson on Shakespeare*, ed. H. R. Wouldhuysen (Harmondsworth, 1989), 121–46.

17. Smith (ed.), *Shakespearean Criticism*, 71.

18. Vickers (ed.), *Critical Heritage*, v, 452.

19. Hugh Blair, *Lectures on Rhetoric and Belles Lettres* (1784) in ibid., vi, 328, 331.

20. Carlyle, *On Heroes*, 365.

21. L. Strachey, *Landmarks in French Literature* (London, 1912), 91–3. See also M. Taylor, *Shakespeare Criticism in the Twentieth Century* (Oxford, 2001), 150–1.

22. Strachey, *Landmarks*, 91–3; Matthew Arnold, *Mixed Essays* (London, 1879), 193–4. See also L. Strachey, 'Shakespeare's Final Period' in *Books and Characters* (London, 1922).

23. G. H. Lewes, 'Shakespeare's Critics': *Edinburgh Review*, xc (1849), 39–77.

24. Cited in Willems, *La Genèse du mythe shakespearien*, 117.

25. There is an extensive literature on these adaptations. See especially A. C. Sprague, *Shakespeare and the Actors* (Cambridge Mass., 1945); F. E. Halliday, *The Cult of Shakespeare* (London, 1957); J. Bate, *Shakespearean Constitutions* (Oxford, 1989); Gary Taylor, *Reinventing*

Shakespeare (London, 1990); M. Dobson, *The Making of the National Poet* (Oxford, 1992).

26. Bogerhoff, *Le Théâtre anglais à Paris*, 56–7.

27. De Nerval, *Œuvres complètes*, i, 887, 893.

28. J. C. Eustace, *A Classical Tour Through Italy*, 7th edn (London, 1841), iii, 19.

29. J. E. C. Bodley, *France*, 2nd edn (1899), 174, 202.

30. Lounsbury, *Shakespeare and Voltaire*, 152.

31. E. Montagu, *An Essay on the Writings and Genius of Shakespeare*, 2nd edn (London, 1770), 2–4, 17, 79.

32. Vickers (ed.), *Critical Heritage*, vi, 477.

33. Smith (ed.), *Shakespearean Criticism*, 15.

34. Quotations from Rousseau, *L'Angleterre et Voltaire*, 458, 508, 591.

35. Lounsbury, *Shakespeare and Voltaire*, 400.

36. Grimm and Meister, *Correspondance Littéraire*, xi, 220–1; Blunt, *Mrs Montagu*, i, 329.

37. Matthew Arnold, 'The Function of Criticism at the Present Time' in *Essays in Criticism*, First Series, new edn (London, 1928), 9.

38. G. H. Lewes, 'Shakespeare in France': *Cornhill Magazine*, Jan. 1865, 33–51.

39. Morley, *Voltaire*, 1, 7, 41–2.

40. Clive Bell, *Civilisation* (London, 1928), 56, 144–6; *An Account of French Painting* (London, 1932), 74, 88, 102, 107, 118. See also J. Falkenheim, *Roger Fry and Formalist Art Criticism* (Ann Arbor Mich., 1980); F. Spalding, *Roger Fry: Art and Life* (London, 1980). On the unpopularity of French art in the nineteenth century see D. Mallet, *The Greatest Collector: Lord Hertford and the Founding of the Wallace Collection* (London, 1972), 54, 58, 70, 97.

41. E. Gosse, *Three French Moralists and The Spirit of Gallantry in France* (London, 1918), 72. See also L. Strachey, *Racine* (London, 1908); F. L. Lucas, *Studies French and English* (London, 1934).

42. P. Quennell, *Baudelaire and the Symbolists* (London, 1929), 101.

43. Peyre, *Shelley et la France*, 151n.

44. M. Morand, *Le Romantisme français en Angleterre* (1933), 222, 226–28, 277, 360; K. Hooker, *The Fortunes of Victor Hugo in England* (New York, 1938), 14, 52–4; L. Mitchell, *Bulwer Lytton: The Rise and Fall of a Victorian Man of Letters* (London, 2003), 161; Strachey, *Landmarks*, 213; Frances Trollope, *Paris and the Parisians in 1835* (London, 1836), ii, 37–8, 259, 275.

45. Hooker, *The Fortunes of Victor Hugo*, 98.

46. Trollope, *Paris*, i, 17–9, 325, 374–5.

47. Matthew Arnold, 'The French Play in London' in *English Literature and Irish Politics*, ed. R. H. Super (Ann Arbor Mich., 1973), 67.

48. Sarcey, *Quarante ans de théâtre*, i, 365–6, 368.

49. Hooker, *The Fortunes of Victor Hugo*, 226, 232–38, 258–61.

50. Strachey, *Landmarks*, 216.

51. Bodley, *France*, 49–50.

52. Harold Bloom, *The Anxiety of Influence* (New York, 1973). See also W. Jackson Bate, *The Burden of the Past and the English Poet* (London, 1971). René Girard's *A Theatre of Envy* explores mimetic desire as a prevailing psychological condition among Shakespeare's characters, but it is not concerned with the relationship between Shakespeare and other writers.

53. Sonnet LXI. See J. Bate, *Shakespeare and Ovid* (Oxford, 1993), 91.

54. *All For Love*, Preface.

55. 'Lines to Congreve'.

56. *Troilus and Cressida*, Preface.

57. *Lettres philosophiques*, 18e Lettre.

58. Morley, *Voltaire*, 133.

59. *A Defence of the Epilogue: or An Essay on the Dramatic Poetry of the Last Age* (London, 1672).

60. Arnold, 'The Function of Criticism', 18.

61. Cited in Sprague, *Shakespeare and the Actors*, 212.

62. Lewes, 'Shakespeare in France'.

63. A. C. Swinburne, 'General Introduction' to *The Oxford Edition of the Works of Shakespeare*, ed. W. J. Craig (London, 1911).

64. Spencer, 'The Tyranny of Shakespeare'.

65. M. Krieger, 'Shakespeare and the Critic's Idolatry of the Word' in G. B. Evans (ed.), *Shakespeare: Aspects of Influence* (Cambridge Mass., 1976), 193–210.

66. A. L. French, *Shakespeare and the Critics* (Cambridge, 1972).

67. T. Eagleton, 'Afterword' in G. Holderness (ed.), *The Shakespeare Myth* (Manchester, 1988), 204.

68. Taylor, *Reinventing Shakespeare*, 410–11.

69. Lanson, *Esquisse*, 123; G. Pellissier, *Etudes de la littérature contemporaine* (1898), 359.

70. F. C. Green, *Minuet: A Critical Study of French and English Ideas in the Eighteenth Century* (London, 1933), 467–70.

71. Voltaire, *Le Siècle de Louis XIV* in *Œuvres complètes*, xiv, 550, 552–53.

72. Ibid., 559–60.

73. Paul Valéry, *Œuvres*, ed. J. Hyter (1957), i, 519.

74. Theodore Besterman, 'Voltaire': *Travaux sur Voltaire et le dix-huitième siècle*, i (Geneva, 1955), 7–18.

Index